ADVANCES IN BUSINESS AND MANAGEMENT FORECASTING

Volume 2 • 1998

FORECASTING

ADVANCES IN BUSINESS AND MANAGEMENT FORECASTING

FORECASTING

Editors: **KENNETH D. LAWRENCE**
School of Management
New Jersey Institute of Technology

MICHAEL GEURTS
Marriott School of Management
Brigham Young University

JOHN B. GUERARD
Global Vantage Services

United Kingdom – North America – Japan
India – Malaysia – China

Emerald Group Publishing Limited
Howard House, Wagon Lane, Bingley BD16 1WA, UK

British Library Cataloguing in Publication Data
A catalogue record for this book is available from the British Library

ISBN: 978-0-76-230002-0
ISSN: 1477-4070 (Series)

Awarded in recognition of
Emerald's production
department's adherence to
quality systems and processes
when preparing scholarly
journals for print

INVESTOR IN PEOPLE

CONTENTS

PART III.   APPLICATIONS OF FORECASTING

LIST OF CONTRIBUTORS

Asokan Anadarajan	School of Management New Jersey Institute of Technology
Maria P. Boile	Department of Civil and Environmental Engineering Lafayette College
Eileen Bridges	Department of Marketing Kent State University
Gary C. Cornia	Marriott School of Management Brigham Young University
Katherine B. Ensor	Department of Statistics Rice University
Michael D. Geurts	Marriott School of Management Brigham Young University
Julie A. Hewitt	Department of Agricultural Economics and Economics Montana State University
Nikolas Heynen	Department of Geography Indiana University
Robert M. Hordon	Department of Geography Rutgers University
George M. Karlaftis	ADK Consulting Engineers
Matthew G. Karlaftis	School of Civil Engineering Purdue University
Gary Kleinman	School of Management New Jersey Institute of Technology

David C. Knudsen   Department of Geography
                            Indiana University

Kenneth D. Lawrence   School of Management
                            New Jersey Institute of Technology

Sheila M. Lawrence   School of Management
                            Rutgers University

Douglas A. MacDonald   Utah State Tax Commission

Charles Nanry   Institute of Management and Labor Relations
                            Rutgers University

Ray D. Nelson   Marriott School of Management
                            Brigham Young University

Michael Nieswiadomy   Department of Economics
                            University of North Texas

John A. Norton   Wirthlin-Reynolds, L.P.

Timothy D. Mount   Department of Agricultural, Resource and
                            Managerial Economics
                            Cornell University

Jason D. Papastavrou   School of Industrial Engineering
                            Purdue University

Lazar N. Spasovic   School of Management
                            Institute for Transportation
                            New Jersey Institute of Technology

Michael J. Swenson   Marriott School of Management
                            Brigham Young University

Weifeng Weng   Department of Agricultural, Resource and
                            Managerial Economics

David B. Whitlark   Marriott School of Management
                            Brigham Young University

Statement of Purpose

Advances in Business and Management Forecasting is a blind refereed serial publication published on an annual basis. The objective of this research annual is to present state-of-the-art studies in the application of forecasting methodologies to such areas as sales, marketing, and strategic decision making (an accurate, robust forecast is critical to effective decision making). It is the hope and direction of the research annual to become an applications- and practitioner-oriented publication.

The topics will normally include sales and marketing, forecasting, new product forecasting, judgmentally based forecasting, the application of surveys to forecasting, forecasting for strategic business decisions, improvements in forecasting accuracy, and sales response models. It is both the hope and direction of the editorial board to stimulate the interest of the practitioners of forecasting to methods and techniques that are relevant.

Editorial correspondence should be sent to:

Professor Kenneth D. Lawrence
School of Management
New Jersey Institute of Technology
Newark, NJ 07102

PART I

FORECASTING IN TRANSPORTATION

INFORMATION-BASED
ESTIMATION OF SPATIAL
INTERACTION:
THE CALIBRATION AND FORECASTING OF
COMMUTING IN THE STATE OF INDIANA

Daniel C. Knudsen and Nikolas Heynen

ABSTRACT

Information-theoretic methods allow construction of highly flexible models that replicate and predict interactions with a high degree of accuracy. Results of an analysis of commuting patterns in the state of Indiana reveal at least two things. First, that when properly specified, relatively simple models can explain large proportions of the variation in a data set. Second, the results highlight the importance of historical data in the analysis and prediction of events. Systems of interaction tend to contain considerable inertia, so that information on previous patterns of interaction tends to be a good predictor of future interaction, be it trade, commuting, or communications.

Advances in Business and Management Forecasting, Volume 2, pages 3–15.
Copyright © 1998 by JAI Press Inc.
All rights of reproduction in any form reserved.
ISBN: 0-7623-0002-7

I. INTRODUCTION

Traditionally, the analysis of transportation flows, such as commuting, has involved spatial interaction models (Wilson 1970). The use of this type of model reflects the importance of distance decay in the calculus of trip making. Despite the ability of interaction models to accurately estimate transportation flows, the models may be otherwise difficult to interpret (Cesario 1977; Knudsen and Fotheringham 1986).

Flowerdew and Aitkin (1982) argue that since spatial interaction models employ count data, errors in the models are Poisson distributed. Baxter (1982, 1984) explores the ties between Poisson regression and spatial interaction models derived from entropy maximization methods in some detail. Flowerdew and Lovett (1988) review and extend Poisson regression beyond the traditional four spatial interaction models. This research has helped to place spatial interaction models within a wider context and has enabled a more systematic consideration of model error structures, hypothesis testing, and model goodness-of-fit.

The purpose of this paper is to demonstrate the use of Poisson regression in the analysis of spatial interactions. We combine constrained minimum discrimination information (MDI) techniques (Haynes and Phillips 1982) for model building with Poisson regression (Flowerdew and Lovett 1988) for estimation of models of commuting. The methodology is then used to analyze commuting in the state of Indiana. We close with conclusions about the system of study and the utility of the approach.

II. THE MATHEMATICAL FRAMEWORK

To investigate commuting we construct an information-theoretic model minimizing information gain (Kullback and Leibler 1951; Kullback 1959; Berry and Schwind 1969; Thomas 1981) subject to suitable constraints that embody information about the problem. In business and planning applications the constraints may be explicitly treated as information bearing on enhanced possibilities of estimation. In scientific applications the constraints typically involve theoretically derived propositions (Haynes and Phillips 1982). Construction of a variety of models is possible by considering the general problem:

$$MIN\ I(P:Q) = \sum_i \sum_j p_{ij} \ln p_{ij}/q_{ij} \qquad (1)$$

subject to:

1. $\sum_i \sum_j p_{ij} f^r(x_{ij}^r) = x^r$; all r

2. $\sum_i \sum_j p_{ij} = 1$

3. $p_{ij} \geq 0$; all i and j

where q_{ij} is the prior probability of an event and p_{ij} is the posterior or observed probability. For our purposes p_{ij} is the frequency of an i to j commute defined as T_{ij}/T, where T_{ij} is volume of i to j commuting and T is total commuting, and q_{ij} is defined in ways that will be discussed later in the paper. Term $f^r(x_{ij}^r)$ represents some function of the observed values x_{ij} and x^r represents some exogenously specified limiting value.

Direct solution of (1) is possible using programming techniques, but it is more convenient to solve the dual of (1) which is the unconstrained geometric programming problem (Brockett, Charnes, and Cooper 1978; Knudsen 1985):

$$MAX \; F(\lambda^r) = \sum_i \sum_j q_{ij} \exp[\sum_r \lambda^r f^r(x_{ij}^r)] + \sum_r \lambda^r x^r + \lambda^0 \qquad (2)$$

where λ^r and λ^0 are unconstrained dual variables (Fiacco and McCormick 1968). However, this approach to the solution of (2) is not generally employed in practice. Rather, it is typically easier to exploit two other properties of (1) and (2).

First, when the constraints of the MDI primal are linear equalities as in (1), programs (1) and (2) lead directly to a model of quantities p_{ij} from the application of Lagrangian methods:

$$\ln p_{ij} = \ln q_{ij} - \lambda^0 - \sum_r \lambda^r f^r(x_{ij}^r) \qquad (3)$$

Second, quantities p_{ij}, λ^r, and λ^0 that result from solution of (1) or (2) are asymptotically maximum likelihood estimators (MLEs) under assumptions that the T_{ij}s are Poisson, multinomial, or product multinomial distributed (Fienberg 1981). Thus, it is typically easier to estimate model

(3) using maximum likelihood methods (Wilson 1970; Williams and Fotheringham 1984). Use of the maximum likelihood approach simplifies hypothesis testing and assessment of goodness-of-fit. The ratio of parameters to their standard errors are asymptotically normal and goodness-of-fit is measured as deviance which is asymptotically chi-square distributed with degrees of freedom equal to sample size minus the number of model parameters. Deviance, which is defined as the ratio of the likelihood of the model estimates to that of the observed values of the dependent variable in the model, is also equivalent to $2T$ times information gain (the minimand in (1)) where **P** is the matrix of observed frequencies and **Q** is the matrix of model predictions.

    The actual calibration of (3) can be undertaken in a variety of ways. For example, (3) belongs to the family of spatial interaction models (Williams and Fotheringham 1984; Knudsen 1985). Conversely, we could solve for quantities p_{ij} using the method of iterative proportional fitting (Ireland and Kullback 1968; Gokhale 1971; Bishop, Fienberg, and Holland 1975). Third, (3) is a generalized linear model (Baxter 1982, 1984; Flowerdew and Lovett 1988). This last approach seems uniquely appropriate since calibration of (3) in this manner allows easy identification of terms λ^r (these are not normally solved for in spatial interaction models, see Williams and Fotheringham 1984) and extension of the model to include interaction terms (McCullagh and Nelder 1983; Wonnacott and Wonnacott 1981).

III. METHODOLOGY

In what follows we formulate the model in three different ways. This is done by a different definition of the matrix **Q**. In the first instance we define terms q_{ij} as the inverse of intervening distances (e.g., $q_{ij} = 1/d_{ij}$ where d_{ij} is i to j distance). In the second instance we define q_{ij} as county i to j flow in 1980. In these first two cases the primal MDI program has the form:

$$MIN\ I(P{:}Q) = \sum_i \sum_j p_{ij} \ln p_{ij}/q_{ij} \tag{4}$$

subject to:

    1. $\sum_i p_{ij} = d_j$; all j

2. $\sum\limits_{j} p_{ij} = o_i;$ all i

3. $p_{ij} \geq 0;$ all i and j

where p_{ij} is the estimated frequency of an i to j commute in 1990 and q_{ij} is the prior expectation of that frequency (an inverse distance function, or the frequency of an i to j commute in 1980). The first constraint contains information on commuting trip designations, the second on commuting trip origins, and the third constraint is a nonnegativity constraint. Application of Lagrangian methods results in the model:

$$p_{ij} = q_{ij} \; \lambda^{(1)} \; \lambda^{(2)} \; \lambda^{(3)} \tag{5}$$

In the final model we include both information on 1980 commuting and county i to county j intervening distance. This last model is structured identically to model (4) above except that it includes an additional constraint:

4. $\sum\limits_{i} \sum\limits_{j} p_{ij} d_{ij} = k$ \hfill (6)

where d_{ij} is i to j commuting distance and k is mean commuting distance. In this instance, application of Lagrangian methods results in the model:

$$p_{ij} = q_{ij} \; \lambda^{(1)} \; \lambda^{(2)} \; \lambda^{(3)} \; \lambda^{(4)} \tag{7}$$

Given an assumption of Poisson distributed errors, models (5) and (7) can be formulated as Poisson regression models which then may be calibrated using commercially available generalized linear modeling software, for example GLIM (Fienberg 1981; McCullagh and Nelder 1983; Flowerdew and Lovett 1988). Consider the general form of a Poisson regression model:

$$\lambda_{ij} = n_{ij} \exp(\mathbf{Z}\beta) + e_{ij} \tag{8}$$

where λ_{ij} is a Poisson distributed dependent variable enumerated as a count, term n_{ij} is the "offset," Z is a set of covariates, β are the parameters of these covariates, and the e_{ij} are error terms. The similarity between (7) and (8) appears by noting that multiplication of (7) by total commuting trips T, observation that terms $\mathbf{Z}$ are categorical variables, addition of error terms e_{ij} yields the model used here:

$$t_{ij} = n_{ij}\exp(\beta) + e_{ij} \qquad (9)$$

Table 1 provides a copy of the GLIM program code for a simple Poisson regression of commuting flows along the lines of those used here. This listing bears some similarity to that provided by Lovett and Flowerdew (1989), except for the use of the OFFSET command.

In Poisson regression (as in other forms of linear modeling) parameters on categorical variables are determined only up to an additive constant because $(\mathbf{Z'Z})^{-1}$ is not of full rank. As a result, while the absolute values of parameters are meaningless, their relative values are not. Because of this, one category within each variable must be set to a predetermined value, usually zero. An additional common problem with Poisson regression is over-dispersion of the error terms (McCullagh and Nelder 1983; Davies and Guy 1987; Flowerdew and Lovett 1988). Davies and Guy (1987) prove that parameters of a model calibrated when over-dispersion is present remain unbiased, but that the corresponding standard errors are biased. Liaw and Bartells (1982; see also Baxter 1984; Davies and Guy 1987) suggest a correction to the standard errors involving multiplication of the original standard errors by the square root of the deviance (asymptotically Pearson chi-square) divided by the degrees of freedom. This quasi-likelihood estimation of the standard errors is equivalent to relaxing the unit mean/variance ratio assumption of the Poisson distribution (Davies and Guy 1987). There is, however, some

Table 1. GLIM Program Using Offsets

```
$echo off
$slength 8464  $factor origin 92 destine 92
$data int90 lag origin destin    $dinput 'infile'$
$calc newlag=%log(lag)
$offset newlag
$yvar int90 $error p
$fit $
$fit +origin
$display m
$fit +destin
$display me
$stop
```

discussion as to the appropriateness of this approach (compare Davies 1987; Davies and Guy 1987). Davies and Guy (1987) suggest the use of pseudo-likelihood estimates of the standard errors as being a more general approach to the over-dispersion problem. Pseudo-likelihood estimates of the model parameter's standard errors may be obtained by taking the square root of the diagonal elements of a matrix **C** where:

$$\mathbf{C} = \mathbf{H}^{-1} \mathbf{G} \mathbf{H}^{-1} \tag{10}$$

where **H** is the Fisherian information matrix and **G** is made up of elements:

$$g_{ij} = \sum_k x_{ik} x_{kj} e_k \tag{11}$$

where x_{ik} is element k of independent variable I, x_{kj} is element k independent variable j and e_k is element k of the residuals. There is no evidence of over-dispersion in this particular instance. The data contain a large number of small flows, hence there is reason to believe that the Poisson distribution is appropriate, and model goodness-of-fit is excellent, thus, poor model fit should not create over-dispersion problems (see Fowerdew and Aitkin 1982).

The data on 1990 commuting patterns for the paper are from the 1990 Census Transportation Planning Package, data on commuting patterns for 1980 are from the decennial census of that year. Intervening distances were determined using standard distance measurement techniques based on straight-line distances (for intercounty distances) and the area of counties (for intra-county distances).

IV. RESULTS OF THE ANALYSIS OF COMMUTING FLOWS

We began by first calibrating model (9) where **N** was defined as the matrix of county i to j distances. Deviance associated with the null model was 21,436,770 (Table 2). Introduction of the distances as an offset reduced this deviance to 13,055,641 accounting for 39% of null model deviance. The addition of the variables representing commuting trip origins in 1990 substantially improved the model. Deviance dropped to 9,654,154 accounting an additional 16% of null model deviance. Addition of commuting destination information totals for 1990 lead to another substantial improvement in the explanatory power of the model. Devi-

Table 2. Model Results

Distance Offset	Deviance
Null Model	21,436,770
Distance Offset Included	13,055641
Percent of Null Deviance Explained	39%
1990 Origin Totals Included	9,654,154
Percent of Null Deviance Explained	55%
1990 Destination Totals Included	6,514,416
Percent of Null Deviance Explained	70%
1980 Commuting Offset Model	*Deviance*
Null Model	21,436,770
1980 Commuting Offset Included	736,768
Percent of Null Deviance Explained	97%
1990 Origin Totals Included	583,631
Percent of Null Deviance Explained	97%
1990 Destination Totals Included	487,261
Percent of Null Deviance Explained	98%
1980 Commuting Offset Model	*Deviance*
Null Model	21,436,770
1980 Commuting Offset Included	736,768
Percent of Null Deviance Explained	97%
Commuting Distance Included	692,442
Percent of Null Deviance Explained	97%
1990 Origin Totals Included	546,495
Percent of Null Deviance Explained	97%
1990 Destination Totals Included	464,774
Percent of Null Deviance Explained	98%

ance dropped to 6,514,416 and this model accounted for 70% of the null model deviance. On the whole, however, the model incorporating distance as an offset is disappointing. Examination of the parameter associated with the model intercept indicates that considerable variation remains to be explained ($z = 75.6$). Typically models of this sort are able to account for over 90% of null model deviance.

Given the explanatory power of the origins and destinations of commuting in 1990 in this model, it is not surprising that the parameters associated with the origins and destinations were universally significant at conventional levels of significance ($\alpha = 0.05$). The parameters associated with commuting origins and destinations exhibit a pattern in which magnitude is a function of county population. Positive parameter values in the model are associated with the most populous counties in the state, while negative parameter values are associated with the least populous counties. This pattern of parameterization results from the definition of **N** as an inverse function of distance. Allen (Ft. Wayne), Elkhart (Elkhart), Lake (Gary and Hammond), and St. Joseph (South Bend) counties are each associated with large, positive, highly significant parameters, while Ohio County, the least populous Indiana county is associated with the most negative, highly significant origin, and destination parameters (Figure 1).

In the second model calibrated, **N** was defined as the matrix of county *i* to *j* commutes in 1980. Introduction of the 1980 commuting pattern as the offset reduced the deviance from 21,436,770 to 736,768 thus the 1980 pattern of commuting accounted for 97% of the null model deviance. Given the high degree of explanation provided by the 1980 commuting flows (and one might therefore infer the great degree of inertia in the commuting patterns within the state), the addition of information on commuting origins and destinations in 1990 only slightly improves the performance of the model. Inclusion of the information on 1990 commuting origins reduces deviance to 583,631, while inclusion of information on 1990 commuting destinations further reduces deviance to 487,261. The final model accounts for 98% of null model deviance.

The parameters in this model have a different interpretation than those in the previous model. Because **N** is defined in this model as 1980 commuting flow, parameters in this model reflect change in commuting flow between 1980 and 1990. La Grange County in northern Indiana became significantly more important as both an origin of and a destination for commuters, Scott County in southern Indiana became significantly more important as a commuting destination, and Warren County in western Indiana became significantly less important as a commuting destination.

In the third and final model calibrated, **N** was defined as the matrix of county *i* to *j* commutes in 1980. As before, introduction of the 1980 commuting pattern as the offset reduced the deviance from 21,436,770 to 736,768, accounting for 97% of the null model deviance. Inclusion of the intercounty and intra-county distances reduces deviance only slightly to 692,442. This indicates that, for commuting in Indiana, information on previous commuting patterns is preferable to information on commut-

Figure 1. The State of Indiana Including County Boundaries

ing distances alone (information on previous commuting patterns reduces null model deviance more than does information on commuting
distances), and that information on previous commuting patterns largely
contains within it the information on distances (given information on
previous commuting patterns, much of the information on commuting
distances is redundant). As was the case in the second model, inclusion
of information on the 1990 origins and destinations of commuting
provides only a slight reduction in deviance. Inclusion of these two
variables reduces deviance to 464,774 so that the final model accounts
for 98% of null model deviance. The parameters associated with commuting origins and destinations exhibit the same patterns as in the second
model.

V. CONCLUSIONS

The purpose of this paper has been to illustrate the power of information-theoretic methods for the prediction of commuting. Results of the
analysis of 1990 commuting patterns in the state of Indiana reveal at least
two things. First, that when properly specified relatively simple models
can explain large proportions of the variation in a data set. In this instance
the relatively simple model:

$$p_{ij} = q_{ij} + e_{ij} \qquad (12)$$

where p_{ij} is the probability of an i to j commute in 1990, q_{ij} is the
probability of an i to j commute in 1980, and e_{ij} is a Poisson distributed
error term accounted for 97% of the variation in commuting flows in
1990 in the state of Indiana. Second, the results highlight the importance
of historical data in the analysis and prediction of events. Systems of
interaction tend to contain considerable inertia, so that information on
previous patterns of interaction tends to be a good predictor of future
interaction, be it trade, commuting, or communications. Indeed Giddens
(1984) remarks that inertia is central to human action of virtually all
kinds.

Within the rather narrow confines of flow modeling, the information-
theoretic approach, coupled with maximum likelihood estimation permits the direct incorporation of either distance or historical information
into the model as an offset and hypothesis tests on variables not included
as offsets (that is, not included in the **N** matrix). Given multiple time
periods of historical data, the model could easily be extended to incor-

porate these (see Plane 1982). Conversely, if only a single time period is of interest, we can set $N = 1/n$ (where n is equal to the matrix dimensions) so that the method used here provides an entropic-like framework (Phillips 1981). The model can be extended in the same manner as any linear model for variables not included in the N matrix.

Lastly, it is worth reinforcing that constraints included in the original information-theoretic program (1) may include any relevant information that can be brought to bear to enhance the ability to predict outcomes. In business and public policy these may include not only marketing information, but strategic objectives, public policy goals, and various sorts of directives as well. Furthermore, the stipulation that these constraints be linear is only relevant if the resulting information-theoretic program is to be converted into a maximum likelihood problem for estimation of parameters. Information-theoretic programs involving nonlinear constraints can, of course, be solved using conventional geometric programming techniques.

REFERENCES

Baxter, M. 1982. "Similarities in Methods of Estimating Spatial Interaction Models." *Geographical Analysis* 14: 267–272.

Baxter, M. 1984. "A Note on the Estimation of a Nonlinear Migration Model Using GLIM." *Geographical Analysis* 16: 282–286.

Berry, B.J.L., and P.J. Schwind. 1969. "Information and Entropy in Migrant Flows." *Geographical Analysis* 1: 5–14.

Bishop, Y.M.M., S.E. Fienberg, and P.W. Holland. 1975. *Discrete Multivariate Analysis: Theory and Practice*. Cambridge, MA: MIT Press.

Brockett, P.L., A. Charnes, and W.W. Cooper. 1978. *M.D.I. Estimation via Unconstrained Convex Programming*. Austin: Center for Cybernetic Studies.

Ceasrio, F. 1977. "A New Interpretation of the 'Normalizing' or 'Balancing' Factors of Gravity-Type Spatial Models." *Socio-Economic Planning Sciences* 11: 131–136.

Davies, R.B. 1987. "Robustness in Modelling Dynamics of Choice." In Contemporary Developments in Quantitative Geography, edited by J. Hauer, H. Timmermans, and N. Wrigley. Dordrecht, Holland: D. Reidel.

Davies, R.B., and C.M. Guy. 1987. "The Statistical Modeling of Flow Data When the Poisson Assumption is Violated." *Geographical Analysis* 19: 300–314.

Fiacco, A.V., and G.P. McCormick. 1968. *Nonlinear Programming: Sequential Unconstrained Minimization Techniques*. New York: John Wiley and Sons.

Fienberg, S.E. 1981. *Analysis of Cross-Classified Categorical Data*. Cambridge: MIT Press.

Flowerdew, R., and M. Aitkin. 1982. "A Method of Fitting the Gravity Model Based on the Poisson Distribution." *Journal of Regional Science* 22: 191–202.

Flowerdew, R., and A. Lovett. 1988. "Fitting Constrained Poisson Regression Models to Interurban Migration Flows." *Geographical Analysis* 20: 297–307.

Giddens, A. 1984. *The Constitution of Society: Outline of the Theory of Structuration.* Cambridge: Polity Press.

Gokhale, D.V. 1971. "An Iterative Procedure for Analyzing Log-Linear Models." *Biometrics* 27: 681–687.

Haynes, K.E., and F.Y. Phillips. 1982. "Constrained Minimum Discrimination Information: A Unifying Tool for Modeling Spatial and Individual Choice Behavior." *Environment and Planning A* 14: 1341–1354.

Ireland, C.T., and S. Kullback. 1968. "Contingency Tables with Given Marginal Totals." *Biometrika* 55: 179–188.

Knudsen, D.C. 1985. "Exploring Flow System Change: U.S. Rail Freight Flows, 1972–1981." *Annals of the Association of American Geographers* 75: 539–551.

Knudsen, D.C., and A.S. Fotheringham. 1986. "Matrix Comparison, Goodness-of-Fit, and Spatial Interaction Modeling." *International Regional Science Review* 10: 127–147.

Kullback, S. 1959. *Information and Statistics.* New York: John Wiley and Sons.

Kullback, S., and R.A. Liebler. 1951. "On Information and Sufficiency." *Annals of Mathematical Statistics* 22: 78–86.

Liaw, K-L., and C.P.A. Bartels. 1982. "Estimation and Interpretation of a Nonlinear Migration Model." *Geographical Analysis* 14: 229–245.

Lovett, A., and R. Flowerdew. 1989. "Analysis of Count Data using Poisson Regression." *Professional Geographer* 41: 190–198.

McCullagh, P., and J.A. Nelder. 1983. *Generalized Linear Models.* London: Chapman and Hall.

Phillips, F.Y. 1981. *A Guide to MDI Statistics for Planning and Management Model Building.* Austin: Institute for Constructive Capitalism.

Plane, D. 1982. "An Information Theoretic Approach to the Estimation of Migration Flows." *Journal of Regional Science* 22: 441–456.

Thomas, R.W. 1981. *Information Statistics in Geography.* Norwich: Geo Abstracts.

Williams, P.A., and A.S. Fotheringham. 1984. *The Calibration of Spatial Interaction Models by Maximum Likelihood Estimation with Program SIMODEL.* Bloomington, IN: Indiana University, Department of Geography Geographic Monograph Series, Volume 7.

Wilson, A.G. 1970. *Entropy in Urban and Regional Modelling.* London: Pion Limited.

Wonnacott, H., and R.J. Wonnacott. 1981. *A Second Course in Regression.* New York: Wiley.

A COMBINED MODE CHOICE-TRAFFIC ASSIGNMENT MODEL FOR EVALUATING COMMUTER TRAVEL OPTIONS

Maria P. Boile and Lazar N. Spasovic

ABSTRACT

The paper presents the formulation and solution of a planning model that can be used in the travel demand forecasting process to analyze commuter travel on transportation networks. The model combines the mode choice and the traffic assignment steps of the traditional urban transportation planning process. The mode choice part utilizes demand functions that reflect travelers' preferences in selecting the travel mode. Within the traffic assignment, performance functions that reflect the level of service provided by the available transportation options are utilized. The model considers the interactions between the demand and performance functions to yield a well-defined equilibrium solution, namely modal and link flows on the network, as well as the resulting travel time costs. The unique feature of the model is the consideration of intermodal networks, a multi-modal transportation system in which travelers may use two or more travel modes during

Advances in Business and Management Forecasting, Volume 2, pages 17–37.
ISBN: 0-7623-0002-7

a single trip. The model was applied to a case study of an experimental intermodal network. Various operating and pricing policies designed to improve the efficiency and service quality of the transportation system are evaluated.

I. INTRODUCTION

The paper presents the formulation and solution of a planning model that can be used in the urban travel demand forecasting process to analyze commuter travel on transportation networks. The methods for forecasting urban travel demand differ from more common demand models which usually deal with estimating the demand for a particular service during a certain time period. The common models are usually in a form of a single equation that estimates the amount of travel as a function of socioeconomic characteristics (population and income) and the prices (fares) and service quality (frequency of departures, travel time) of modes that are available for travel. An example of this model is a model for intercity travel between a pair of cities in a corridor such as Boston to Washington DC, in the northeast United States, wherein the available modes are rail, bus, air, and auto.

The complexity of urban travel demand forecasting is reflected in a fact that there are many possible destinations which may satisfy a particular trip purpose, and that there are many routes available to travelers within each mode. Thus, in addition to determining the quantity of travel, that is, number of trips to be made from an origin, the travel demand forecasting process determines the likely destinations of these trips, the mode of travel, and the routes travelers are likely to take.

A set of well-established procedures is used by transportation planners to estimate travel demand in response to changes in land use, transportation system characteristics, and socioeconomic factors. The set of procedures, commonly referred to as the Urban Transportation Modeling System (UTMS), consists of four steps, namely trip generation, trip distribution, modal split, and route assignment. Trip generation is the estimation of trip ends, that is, the number of person-trips produced by, and attracted to each zone within the study area, typically as a function of land use or population. Trip distribution develops zonal trip interchanges by connecting trip ends at origins and destinations, usually as a function of the distance between zones. This is usually done by a gravity model (Voorhees 1955). Modal split allocates person-trips by mode of travel, typically as a function of the travel times, costs, and availability of the competing modes. Route assignment is the allocation of trips to various routes, typically as a function of the travel times of the competing routes.

The novel approach used in the model presented here is that it considers intermodal travel between an origin and destination pair. In general, an intermodal commuter network is defined as the integration of several passenger transportation systems (modes) to a single comprehensive system where travelers departing from their homes have several options available for their trip to work. They can use any mode available to them all the way from their origin to their destination, or they can begin their trip on one mode and then switch to another mode at selected transfer points along the way. In a typical auto-public transit intermodal network, an example of the later trip type is kiss-and-ride or park-and-ride. There is a clear benefit, in terms of reduced cost and improved service time and capacity, to society of having a well-integrated multimodal transportation system that provides for seamless transport of passengers from their origins to their destinations.

The model presented in this paper combines the mode choice and traffic assignment steps of the travel demand forecasting process. The mode-choice step utilizes demand functions that reflect travelers' preferences toward the available transportation modes. The modes in question are public rail transit and auto, and depending whether rail transit is accessible by walk or driving to the station, it can be divided to pure rail and intermodal (auto-to-rail).

The traffic assignment step utilizes performance functions that reflect the level of service provided by the links and or routes of the available modes. The performance functions reflect the fact that after certain design capacity the average travel time raises exponentially with volume. Assume that several travelers choose to drive and happen to select the same route. Their actions will increase travel time and may even result in high congestion on these routes. The route may now become unattractive in terms of increased disutility of travel. This can now be used by the traveling public to select some other less congested highway routes or modes of travel. One can assume that travelers will attempt to make their choices until they can no further improve their utility and/or reduce cost of using the mode. Also, travelers on the route facing congestion may decide to switch the mode of travel. Thus, the proposed model considers the interactions of the demand and performance functions to determine equilibrium link and path flows on a network, as well as the resulting time costs incurred by the travelers.

The scope of this paper is to present the formulation and solution of a model that can be used to forecast the travel patterns on an intermodal transportation system. The model can assist in finding ways to increase the attractiveness of public transit modes, improve transit operations, and alleviate highway congestion and its negative social, economic, and environmental effects.

The model considers limitations on parking and rail capacity. The model is formulated as a mathematical program with nonlinear objective function and linear constraints. Its solution is proved to satisfy well-defined equilibrium conditions.

The model is applied to the analysis of commuter travel on an experimental intermodal commuter network. Results of the analysis include the verification of the equilibrium conditions, prediction of traffic flow patterns and travel costs, and evaluation of various operating and pricing policies for improving the efficiency and service quality of the transportation system.

II. LITERATURE REVIEW

An extensive search revealed several papers dealing with mode choice and trip assignment in a bi-modal, auto and public transit, network (Abdulaal and LeBlank 1979; Dafermos 1982; Fisk and Nguyen 1981; Florian 1977; Florian and Nguyen 1974; Florian and Spiess 1983; LeBlanc and Farhangian 1981). Common to these papers is the assumption that travelers will select a mode of travel for the whole trip, that is, they consider only pure modes. A paper by Fernandez, DeCea, Florian, and Cabrera (1994) presents a formulation of the demand-supply equilibrium models that are used to analyze networks served by auto, metro, and combined (auto-to-metro) modes. Travelers from every origin can choose between two alternatives: (1) auto and metro for those origins where metro is accessible within walking distance, and (2) auto and combined mode for those origins without a close by metro station. This assumption limits the actual number of choices that travelers have, such as driving to a park-and-ride metro station, or being dropped off at a metro station along the way.

The model presented in this paper alleviates some of the deficiencies described above by considering intermodal travel in addition to travel by pure modes. It considers all the alternatives available to travelers for their trip to work, and balances demand and supply to determine well-defined equilibrium solutions.

III. MODEL FORMULATION

A. Problem Statement

The problem can be stated as follows: Given the trip-to-work travel demand between each origin and destination, the characteristics of an available intermodal network, the average travel time on the links of the network in form of volume-delay functions, the out-of pocket costs, a mode-choice demand function, and assuming that the travelers will attempt to minimize their individual travel costs, find the equilibrium modal shares for each mode between each origin-destination pair, and the link flows for the network.

B. Assumptions

The assumptions made in the modeling approach are that the total travel demand:

- for each origin and destination (O-D) pair is known, and
- is elastic, that is, sensitive to travel time/cost on alternative modes.

The travelers:

- have a range of mode and route choices available to them,
- have perfect information on travel times and costs on all routes,
- are identical in their behavior, and
- have modal preferences when selecting the mode.

C. Notation

The following notation is used in the model formulation:

Nodes, Links, and Modes

$$O = \text{origin}$$
$$D = \text{destination}$$
$$ij = \text{origin-destination pair}$$
$$l = \text{link}$$
$$z, r, t = \text{highway, rail, and transfer links, respectively}$$
$$m = \text{mode (auto or transit)}$$
$$A, T = \text{auto and transit modes, respectively}$$

$p =$ path

Sets

$$L =$$ set of all links
$$LH, LR, LCR, LT =$$ sets of all highway, rail, critical rail, and transfer links, respectively
$$P =$$ set of all paths
$$P_A, P_T, P_R, P_M =$$ set of all auto, transit, rail, and intermodal paths, respectively.

Parameters

$T^{ij} =$ total demand between origin i and destination j
$D_{ij} =$ demand function
$D_{ij}^{-1} =$ inverted demand function
$U_m^{ij} =$ utility of traveling from origin i to destination j via mode m
$GC_m^{ij} =$ minimum generalized cost of traveling from i to j via mode m
$GC_{pm}^{ij} =$ generalized cost of traveling on mode m path p from i to j
$\delta_{lpm}^{ij} =$ binary parameter, equals to 1 if link l is contained in mode m path p between i and j, and 0 otherwise
$\gamma =$ auto occupancy rate
$S_l =$ existing number of parking spaces at a rail station
$K =$ number of train seats per peak period
$\alpha, \beta =$ exogenously determined parameters of the mode choice model

Choice Variables

$x_l =$ flow on link l
$c(x_l) =$ cost of traveling on link l
$T_m^{ij} =$ travel volume between origin i and destination j on mode m.

D. General Approach

The general mathematical expression of this model is shown in equation (1). The model is formulated as a mathematical program with nonlinear objective function (z) and linear constraints.

$$\min z, \text{ s.t.: } a_i\mathbf{x} = b_i, \mathbf{x} \geq 0 \tag{1}$$

The equilibrium conditions for this problem are stated and the solution is proven to satisfy these conditions.

To find the problem solution, the Lagrangian (L) is formulated and its first derivatives with respect to the decision variables are calculated. This is formulated by multiplying the constraints with Lagrangian multipliers u_i, and introducing them in the objective function. Equation (1) then becomes equivalent to:

$$\min L = z + \sum_i u_i(b_i - a_i x), \, x \geq 0 \tag{2}$$

The multiplier u_i represents the shadow price for constraint i. Then, it is shown that, under certain conditions, the Karush-Kuhn-Tucker (K-K-T) conditions (Sheffi 1985) for the problem are necessary and sufficient for the optimal solution of the problem. The Karush-Kuhn-Tucker conditions can be expressed as:

$$\frac{\partial L}{\partial x} = \frac{\partial z}{\partial x} - \sum_i u_i a_i \begin{cases} = 0, \text{ if } x > 0 \\ \geq 0, \text{ if } x = 0 \end{cases} \tag{3}$$

By applying these conditions to equation (2), an optimal solution which is unique is obtained. It will be shown that it satisfies the equilibrium conditions.

E. Demand Function

In the demand side of the model, a binary logit model (Ben Akiva and Lerman 1985) is used to perform the mode choice between auto and transit. The auto mode (A) consists of auto paths (P_A), and the transit mode (T) consists of rail (P_R) and intermodal (P_M) paths. The model considers travelers' preferences between auto and transit and computes the number of trips for each mode. The model is of the form:

$$T_A^{ij} = T^{ij} \frac{\exp(U_A^{ij})}{\exp(U_A^{ij}) + \exp(U_T^{ij})} \tag{4}$$

The total demand for each origin-destination pair T^{ij} is fixed. The utilities of traveling between i and j via auto and transit are given as:

$$U_A^{ij} = -\beta * GC_A^{ij}, \text{ and}$$

$$U_T^{ij} = -\alpha - \beta * GC_T^{ij}$$

Substituting the expressions above in equation (4) the demand function (D_{ij}) becomes:

$$T_A^{ij} = T^{ij} \frac{\exp(-\beta * GC_A^{ij})}{\exp(-\beta * GC_A^{ij}) + \exp(-\alpha - \beta * GC_T^{ij})} \qquad (5)$$

This function generates the number of trips by mode as a function of the disutility (generalized cost) of that mode. The disutility depends on the values of service variables (in-vehicle travel time, out-of-vehicle time, and out-of-pocket costs) which are defined by the supply side of the model.

F. Performance Function

Several types of models of supply-side characteristics of transport systems have been developed (Morlok 1980). These models describe the performance of a transportation system as a function of traffic volumes. The supply side of the formulation presented in this paper considers the out-of-pocket costs, including parking fees, rail fares, highway tolls, and auto operating costs, and the travel time between each O-D pair. To capture the effects of highway congestion, appropriate time-volume functions are selected, which are modeled after the Bureau of Public Roads (1965) type congestion curves. These functions are of the general form:

$$t_l = t_{l0} * \left[1 + 0.15 \left(\frac{x_l}{c_l} \right)^4 \right] \qquad (6)$$

where:

t_l : the actual travel time on link l,
t_{l0}: the free flow travel time on link l,
x_l : the traffic volume on link l, and
c_l : the capacity of link l.

The free flow travel time is the time needed to traverse a link under normal (uncongested) conditions. Capacity relates to the physical capacity of a facility.

G. Equilibrium Conditions

An equilibrium solution must satisfy two conditions. The first condition, given by equation (7), states that, for each mode of travel, and an O-D pair, no traveler can reduce his or her travel cost by unilaterally changing routes.

$$GC^{ij}_{P_m} - GC^{ij}_m \begin{cases} = 0, \text{ if } f^{ij}_{P_m} > 0 \\ \geq 0, \text{ if } f^{ij}_{P_m} = 0 \end{cases} \quad \forall m, ij \tag{7}$$

According to this condition, a particular modal path between an O-D pair will be utilized only if the generalized cost on this path is equal to the minimum generalized cost for this mode and O-D pair.

The second condition, given by equation (8), states that at equilibrium no traveler has an incentive to unilaterally change modes.

$$GC^{ij}_T - GC^{ij}_A = -\frac{1}{\beta} \left(\ln \frac{T^{ij}_T}{T^{ij}_A} + \alpha \right) \quad \forall ij \tag{8}$$

H. Model Statement

The objective function minimizes the total individual user cost minus the integral of the inverse demand function (Sheffi 1985). Its mathematical expression is:

$$\text{Minimize } z(f,T) = \sum_{l \in L} \int_0^{x_l} c(\phi) d\phi - \sum_{ij} \int_0^{T^{ij}_m} D^{-1}_{ij}(\omega) d\omega \tag{9}$$

where D^{-1}_{ij}, derived from equation (4) (see Appendix) is:

$$D^{-1}_{ij} = GC^{ij}_T - GC^{ij}_A = -\frac{1}{\beta} \left(\ln \frac{T^{ij}_T}{T^{ij}_A} + \alpha \right) \tag{10}$$

Introducing equation (10) into equation (9) results in the following:

Minimize $z(f,T) =$

$$\sum_{l \in L} \int_0^{x_l} c[x_l(f)] dx_l - \sum_{ij} \int_0^{T^{ij}_T} -\frac{1}{\beta} \left(\ln \frac{T^{ij}_T}{T^{ij} - T^{ij}_T} + \alpha \right) dT^{ij}_T \tag{11}$$

In the first part of this expression the link cost functions are assumed separable (i.e., $\partial c(x_a)/\partial x_b = 0$ $\forall a \neq b$, and $dc(x_a)/dx_a > 0$ $\forall a$, where a, b are links of the network) and monotonicaly increasing functions of their argument. In the second part the demand function for each O-D pair (D_{ij}) is a monotonicaly decreasing function of its argument.

The demand conservation constraint divides the total demand for each O-D pair into auto and transit portions:

$$T^{ij} = T_A^{ij} + T_T^{ij} \qquad \forall \, ij \qquad (12)$$

The auto demand conservation constraint states that, for each O-D pair, the demand for auto is equal to the sum of flows on all auto paths available to travelers for this O-D pair:

$$T_A^{ij} = \sum_{P_A} f_{P_A}^{ij} \qquad \forall \, ij \qquad (13)$$

The transit demand conservation constraint states that, for each O-D pair, the demand for transit equals the sum of flows on all transit (rail and intermodal) paths available to travelers for this O-D pair:

$$T_T^{ij} = \sum_{P_T} f_{P_T}^{ij} = \sum_{P_R} f_{P_R}^{ij} + \sum_{P_M} f_{P_M}^{ij} \qquad \forall \, ij \qquad (14)$$

The link flow conservation constraint states that the total flow on a link is equal to the sum of flows on all paths containing the link. The auto occupancy rate (γ) converts person trips into vehicle trips. Thus, for highway and transfer links this constraint is:

$$x_l = \frac{1}{\gamma} \sum_{ij} \sum_{P_A} \delta_{lP_A}^{ij} * f_{P_A}^{ij} + \frac{1}{\gamma} \sum_{ij} \sum_{P_T} \delta_{lP_T}^{ij} * f_{P_T}^{ij} \quad \forall \, l \subseteq LH, LT \qquad (15)$$

The link flow conservation constraint for rail links is:

$$x_l = \sum_{ij} \sum_{P_T} \delta_{lP_T}^{ij} * f_{P_T}^{ij} \qquad \forall \, l \subseteq LR \qquad (16)$$

The parking capacity constraint ensures that the number of cars parked at a parking lot does not exceed the available number of parking spaces:

$$x_l \leq S_l \qquad \forall \, l \subseteq LT \qquad (17)$$

The rail capacity constraint ensures that the number of riders does not exceed the rail-line capacity:

$$x_l \leq K \qquad \forall \, l \subseteq LCR \qquad (18)$$

The last constraint of the formulation states that all path flows are nonnegative:

$$f^{ij}_{p_m} \geq 0 \qquad \forall p,m,ij \qquad (19)$$

I. Derivation of Equilibrium Conditions

To prove that a solution of the model satisfies the equilibrium conditions it is sufficient to show that the Karush-Kuhn-Tucker (KKT) conditions for the minimization program are identical to the equilibrium conditions (Sheffi 1985). For this purpose, the first derivatives of the Lagrangian (equation (2)) with respect to path flows and trip rates are estimated and introduced in the KKT conditions (equation (3)). The resulting expressions are shown to be identical to the equilibrium conditions in equations (7) and (8). To formulate the Lagrangian, the demand conservation constraints (equations (12–13–14)) are multiplied by Lagrangian multipliers (u^{ij}_m) and introduced in the objective function. In addition, the link flow conservation constraints (equations (15–16)) are directly introduced in the objective function. Equations (17–18) which model the capacity limitations on the network are omitted in the analysis of the equilibrium conditions. If during the analysis of a particular network these constraints become binding, the model will be precluded from reaching an equilibrium solution.

The Lagrangian is then as follows:

$$L(f, T, u) = \sum_l \int_0^{x_l} c[x_l(f)]dx_l - \sum_{ij} \int_0^{T^{ij}_T} -\frac{1}{\beta} \left(\ln \frac{T^{ij}_T}{T^{ij} - T^{ij}_T} + \alpha \right) dT^{ij}_T +$$

$$\sum_{ij} u^{ij} (T^{ij} - T^{ij}_A - T^{ij}_T) + \sum_{ij} u^{ij}_A (T^{ij}_A - \sum_{P_A} f^{ij}_{P_A}) + \sum_{ij} u^{ij}_T (T^{ij}_T - \sum_{P_T} f^{ij}_{P_T}) \qquad (20)$$

with $f^{ij}_{p_m} \geq 0 \quad \forall \, p,m,ij$

The first derivatives of the Lagrangian with respect to path flows $f^{ij}_{P_m}$, trip rates T^{ij}_m, and multipliers u^{ij}_m are derived, and used to state the optimality conditions for a stationary point.

The first derivative of the Lagrangian with respect to path flows is:

$$\frac{\partial L(f, T, u)}{\partial f^{ij}_{P_m}} = \frac{\partial z_1[x(f)]}{\partial f^{ij}_{P_m}} + \frac{\partial \sum\limits_{ij} u^{ij}_m (T^{ij}_m - \sum\limits_{P_m} f^{ij}_{P_m})}{\partial f^{ij}_{P_m}} =$$

$$\frac{\partial z_1(x)}{\partial x_l} \frac{\partial x_l}{\partial f^{ij}_{P_m}} + \frac{\partial \sum\limits_{ij} u^{ij}_m (T^{ij}_m - \sum\limits_{P_m} f^{ij}_{P_m})}{\partial f^{ij}_{P_m}} \qquad (21)$$

where:

$$z_1[x(f)] = \sum_l \int_0^{x_l} c[x(f)]dx_l \qquad (22)$$

Finding the first derivatives of equations (15) and (16) with respect to link flows resulted in:

$$\frac{\partial x_l}{\partial f^{ij}_{P_m}} = \frac{1}{\gamma} \delta^{ij}_{lp_m} \qquad \forall l \in LH, LT \qquad (23)$$

$$\frac{\partial x_l}{\partial f^{ij}_{P_m}} = \delta^{ij}_{lp_m} \qquad \forall l \in LR \qquad (24)$$

Replacing equations (23–24) in equation (21) for auto paths yields:

$$\sum_{l \in LH, LT} \frac{1}{\gamma} \delta^{ij}_{lp_A} \left[\frac{\partial z_1(x_l)}{\partial x_l} \right] + \sum_{l \in LR} \delta^{ij}_{lp_A} \left[\frac{\partial z_1(x_l)}{\partial x_l} \right] - u^{ij}_A =$$

$$\sum_{l \in LH, LT} \frac{1}{\gamma} \delta^{ij}_{lp_A} [c(x_l)] + \sum_{l \in LR} \delta^{ij}_{lp_A} [c(x_l)] - u^{ij}_A \qquad \forall p_A, ij \qquad (25)$$

Equation (21) for transit paths is written as:

$$\sum_{l \in LH,LT} \frac{1}{\gamma} \delta^{ij}_{lp_T} [c(x_l)] + \sum_{l \in LR} \delta^{ij}_{lp_T} [c(x_l)] - u^{ij}_T \qquad \forall p_T, ij \qquad (26)$$

The summations in equations (25) and (26) represent the average generalized cost on a mode m path p between an origin-destination pair ij, which is the sum of the costs on all links that compose the path, and is symbolized as $GC^{ij}_{p_m}$. Thus, equation (25) becomes:

$$GC^{ij}_{p_A} - u^{ij}_A \qquad \forall p_A, ij \qquad (27)$$

and equation (26) becomes:

$$GC^{ij}_{p_T} - u^{ij}_T \qquad \forall p_T, ij \qquad (28)$$

The derivative of the Lagrangian with respect to the auto trip rate T^{ij}_A is:

$$\frac{\partial L(f, T, u)}{\partial T^{ij}_A} = \frac{\partial \sum_{ij} u^{ij} (T^{ij} - T^{ij}_A - T^{ij}_T)}{\partial T^{ij}_A} + \frac{\partial \sum_{ij} u^{ij}_A (T^{ij}_A - \sum_{p_A} f^{ij}_{p_A})}{\partial T^{ij}_A} = -u^{ij} + u^{ij}_A$$

$$(29)$$

The derivative of the Lagrangian with respect to the transit trip rate T^{ij}_T is:

$$\frac{\partial L(f, T, u)}{\partial T^{ij}_T} = \frac{\partial z_2 (T)}{\partial T^{ij}_T} + \frac{\partial \sum_{ij} u^{ij} (T^{ij} - T^{ij}_A - T^{ij}_T)}{\partial T^{ij}_T} + \frac{\partial \sum_{ij} u^{ij}_T (T^{ij}_T - \sum_{p_T} f^{ij}_{p_T})}{\partial T^{ij}_T} =$$

$$\frac{\partial}{\partial T^{ij}_T} \left[-\sum_{ij} \int_0^{T^{ij}_T} D^{-1}_{ij} (T^{ij}_T) dT^{ij}_T + \sum_{ij} u^{ij} (T^{ij} - T^{ij}_A - T^{ij}_T) + \sum_{ij} u^{ij}_T (T^{ij}_T - \sum_{p_T} f^{ij}_{p_T}) \right] =$$

$$\frac{1}{\beta} \left(\ln \frac{T^{ij}_T}{T^{ij}_A} + \alpha_{TA} \right) - u^{ij} + u^{ij}_T \qquad (30)$$

The partial derivatives of the Lagrangian with respect to the Lagrangian multipliers are:

$$\frac{\partial L(f, T, u)}{\partial u^{ij}} = \frac{\partial \sum_{ij} u^{ij} (T^{ij} - T^{ij}_A - T^{ij}_T)}{\partial u^{ij}} = T^{ij} - T^{ij}_A - T^{ij}_T \qquad (31)$$

$$\frac{\partial L(f, T, u)}{\partial u^{ij}_A} = \frac{\partial \sum_{ij} u^{ij}_A (T^{ij}_A - \sum_{p_A} f^{ij}_{p_A})}{\partial u^{ij}_A} = T^{ij}_A - \sum_{p_A} f^{ij}_{p_A} \qquad (32)$$

$$\frac{\partial L(f, T, u)}{\partial u^{ij}_T} = \frac{\partial \sum_{ij} u^{ij}_T (T^{ij}_T - \sum_{p_T} f^{ij}_{p_T})}{\partial u^{ij}_T} = T^{ij}_T - \sum_{p_T} f^{ij}_{p_T} \qquad (33)$$

The Lagrangian multipliers u^{ij}_m represent the minimum average travel cost for mode m and for O-D pair ij (GC^{ij}_m). Substituting the first derivatives of the Lagrangian in the Karush-Kuhn-Tucker conditions (equation (3)) the following equations are obtained.

From equations (27–28):

$$GC^{ij}_{p_A} - GC^{ij}_A \begin{cases} = 0, \text{ if } f^{ij}_{p_A} > 0 \\ \geq 0, \text{ if } f^{ij}_{p_A} = 0 \end{cases} \qquad \forall p_A, ij \qquad (34)$$

$$GC^{ij}_{p_T} - GC^{ij}_T \begin{cases} = 0, \text{ if } f^{ij}_{p_T} > 0 \\ \geq 0, \text{ if } f^{ij}_{p_T} = 0 \end{cases} \qquad \forall p_T, ij \qquad (35)$$

From equation (29):

$$-u^{ij} + u^{ij}_A = 0, \text{ or } u^{ij} = u^{ij}_A \quad \forall ij \qquad (36)$$

Considering equation (36), equation (30) becomes:

$$u^{ij}_T - u^{ij}_A = GC^{ij}_T - GC^{ij}_A = -\frac{1}{\beta} (\ln \frac{T^{ij}_T}{T^{ij}_A} + \alpha_{TA}) \quad \forall ij \qquad (37)$$

From equations (31–33):

$$T^{ij} = T_A^{ij} + T_T^{ij} \qquad \forall ij \qquad (38)$$

$$T_A^{ij} = \sum_{p_A} f_{p_A}^{ij} \qquad \forall ij \qquad (39)$$

$$T_T^{ij} = \sum_{p_T} f_{p_T}^{ij} \qquad \forall ij \qquad (40)$$

Equations (34–35) state that if the generalized cost on mode m path p between i and j $(GC_{p_m}^{ij})$ is greater than the generalized cost on the lowest cost path for mode m between the same i and j (GC_m^{ij}), then, the corresponding flow on path p is zero. If the generalized costs are equalized, the flow on path p can be greater than or equal to zero. These conditions are identical to the first equilibrium condition for auto and transit modes stated in equation (7).

Equation (37) shows that the difference in the generalized cost of the two utilized modes is given from the inverted demand function. This is identical to the second equilibrium condition stated in equation (8).

Equations (38–40) are the demand conservation constraints for each O-D pair ij and for each mode m. The above analysis shows that the model solution satisfies the equilibrium conditions.

J. Convexity Analysis

To prove that the equivalent optimization program has a unique solution it is sufficient to show that the objective function is strictly convex, and that the feasible region defined by the constraints of the formulation is convex. Since the constraints of the formulation are linear equalities, the resulting feasible region is convex.

The first part of the objective function is a sum of the integrals of a monotonicaly increasing function. The integral of a monotonicaly increasing function is strictly convex and the sum of strictly convex functions is strictly convex. Thus, the first part of the objective function is strictly convex.

The second part of the objective function is a sum of the integrals of the inverse of a monotonicaly decreasing function (D_{ij}^{-1}) which is also a decreasing function. The integral of a decreasing function is strictly concave and the sum of strictly concave functions is strictly concave. The negative of a strictly concave function is strictly convex thus the second part of the objective function is strictly convex.

The objective function is strictly convex as the sum of two strictly convex functions. The strict convexity implies that the model has a unique solution in terms of O-D modal shares and link flows. This solution is given by the KKT conditions and it was shown to satisfy the equilibrium conditions.

IV. EXAMPLE

An experimental network of the simple intermodal commuter corridor, shown in Figure 1, has been developed to demonstrate the applicability of the model. Travelers in this corridor can access their destination via auto, rail, and intermodal auto-to-rail modes.

The network consists of one O-D pair, and four links, two highway (1,2) and two rail (3,4), forming three paths: auto path (P1), intermodal path (P2), and rail path (P3). The link-path matrix below indicates the path make-up. For example, rail path (P3) contains links 3 and 4.

$$\delta_{lp_m}^{O-D} = \begin{array}{ccc} P1 & P2 & P3 \\ \begin{vmatrix} 1 & 0 & 0 \\ 0 & 1 & 0 \\ 0 & 0 & 1 \\ 0 & 1 & 1 \end{vmatrix} & \begin{array}{c} 1 \\ 2 \\ 3 \\ 4 \end{array} \end{array}$$

A train station (T), connecting links 2, 3, and 4, serves as a transfer point for auto users to shift to rail. The highway links 1 and 2 have free-flow travel time of 10 and 3.6 minutes, respectively, and the rail links 3 and 4 have travel times of 5.8 and 6.7 minutes, respectively. The capacity of link 1 is 6,900 vehicles per hour, and the capacity of link 2 is 4,400 vehicles per hour. It is assumed that trains run every 7.5 minutes (i.e., there are eight departures per hour) and that the train seating capacity is 500 seats per train (four 125-seat cars), yielding the peak-hour

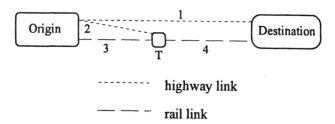

Figure 1. Intermodal Commuter Corridor

line seating capacity of 4,000 seats. The capacity of the parking lot at the rail station is 2,828 cars. The link travel times are estimated using the Bureau of Public Roads-type (U.S. Bureau of Roads 1965) congestion curves.

Travelers incur several out-of-pocket costs. Auto users incur highway tolls of $1.00 per trip, parking fees at the destination parking lot of $2.00 per trip, and an average auto operating cost of $0.25 per car-mile. Intermodal users incur a $1.00 parking fee at the rail station lot, an average operating cost of $0.25 per car-mile traveled, and a rail fare of $1.00 per trip. Rail users incur a $2.60 rail fare.

To determine a generalized cost of travel that considers both travel time and out-of-pocket costs, the travel time is multiplied by an average value of travel time which is assumed to be $20 per hour. The total travel demand in the corridor is 6,000 passengers per peak hour. The mode choice model coefficients are assumed to be $\alpha = 0.02$ and $\beta = 0.33$. In an actual application these parameters must be calibrated using the corridor specific data.

A. Results of the Analysis

The analysis had two objectives. First, it evaluated whether the MINOS solver (Murtagh and Sanders 1987) that was used to solve the problem indeed reached the equilibrium solution. Second, it demonstrated the use and the applicability of the model in analyzing various policies on an intermodal corridor.

Verification of the Equilibrium Conditions

The equilibrium solution is shown in Table 1.

The results satisfy the first equilibrium condition since the travel cost of $6.77 is the same on both transit, rail, and intermodal paths. The second equilibrium condition is satisfied if it can be shown that the numerical results satisfy equation (8).

From Table 1 the difference in generalized cost $GC_T^{ij} - GC_A^{ij}$ is calculated to be -1.837 ($6.771 - 8.608$). This is identical to the result obtained by introducing the resulting auto and transit modal shares from Table 1 $T_T^{ij} = 2,828 + 1,027 = 3,855$, $T_A^{ij} = 2,145$ in equation (4):

$$-\frac{1}{\beta}\left(\ln\frac{T_T^{ij}}{T_A^{ij}} + \alpha\right) = -\frac{1}{0.33}\left(\ln\frac{3855}{2145} + 0.02\right) = -1.837$$

This result indeed satisfies the second equilibrium condition.

Table 1. Corridor Analysis Results

Path	Travel Cost ($/passenger)	Path Flow (passengers/hr)
Auto Path (P1)	8.608	2,145
Intermodal Path (P2)	6.771	2,828
Rail Path (P3)	6.771	1,027

Pricing and Operating Policies

The model is used to predict the effects of various pricing and operating policies on the equilibrium traffic flow patterns and travel costs. The policies include both incentives to use transit (increasing parking availability at rail stations, decreasing rail fares, increasing rail frequency) and impediments in using private auto (increasing highway tolls, increasing downtown parking fees). Results of the analysis of five policies are shown in Table 2. They are: (1) baseline, which represents the existing situation, (2) decrease rail fare by 5%, (3) increase rail frequency by 50%, (4) increase highway tolls by 10%, and (5) increase parking fees at the downtown parking lot by 10%.

Currently, 35.8% of travelers use auto mode and 64.2% transit (47.1% intermodal and 17.1% pure rail). A decrease in rail fare by 5% translates

Table 2. Results of Various Policies

		A Baseline	B Decrease Rail Fare	C Increase Rail Frequency	D Increase Highway Tolls	E Increase Parking Fees
Path Flow	P1	2,145	2,055	1,821	2,101	2,056
(pass/hr)	P2	2,828		2,828	2,827	2,828
	P3	1,027	3,945	1,351	1,072	1,116
Path Cost	P1	8.61	8.605	8.60	8.71	8.81
($/pass)	P2	6.77	6.629	6.02	6.77	6.77
	P3	6.77	6.568	6.02	6.77	6.77
Added Seats		–	35	–		34
AddedSpaces		–	–	–	–	–
Mode	A	35.8%	34.3%	30.4%	35%	34.3%
Shares	I	47.1%	–	47.1%	47.1%	47.1%
	R	17.1%	65.7%	22.5%	17.9%	18.6%

Notes: A: Auto, R: Rail, I: Intermodal.

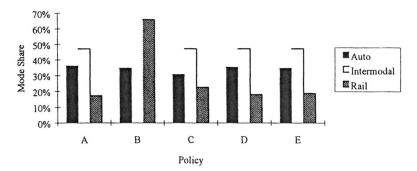

Figure 2. Modal Shares

to $0.95 rail fare for the intermodal trip, and $2.47 for the rail trip. The decreased rail fare resulted in 90 auto commuters and all intermodal commuters shifting to rail. This solution required a marginal increase in rail capacity.

Increasing rail frequency by 50% implies that trains depart every five minutes. The new rail line capacity is 6,000 seats per hour. Table 2 shows that the increased rail frequency resulted in 324 auto travelers shifting to rail.

Increasing highway tolls from $1.00 to $1.10 resulted in 0.8% decrease in auto travelers (from 35.8% to 35%), and a marginal decrease in intermodal passengers. The percentage of travelers using rail increased from 17.1 to 17.9%.

The last case considered a 10% increase in the parking fee at the downtown parking lot. As a result of this increase, the percentage of auto users decreased from 35.8% to 34.3%. The percentage of rail users increased from 17.1 to 18.6%. This solution required the rail capacity of 4,034 seats per hour.

Figure 2 shows the percentage of the travelers using auto, rail, and intermodal paths for each of the five policies, respectively. The figure shows that policy C yields the most promise in reducing auto commute, while smaller decrease in auto commute results from policies B, D, and E.

V. CONCLUSIONS

The paper presented the formulation and solution of an equilibrium travel demand forecasting model. The use of the model for the analysis of travel patterns and costs on an experimental intermodal commuter corridor was demonstrated. In addition, the model determined whether there is a sufficient rail seating and/or parking capacity available. Whenever the traffic flows exceeded the capacity limit, the model was able to estimate the number of additional train seats or parking spaces required to accommodate the equilibrium traffic volumes. The model was used to analyze several operating and pricing policies. The effects of each of the policies on travel patterns and travel costs were estimated. A comparative analysis identified the most promising policy in terms of increasing rail ridership and decreasing highway congestion. The model presents a promising approach in analyzing intermodal networks and it represents the improvement of the existing travel demand forecasting process.

ACKNOWLEDGMENT

This research, was partially supported by the Knight Foundation Grant from Lafayette College, and the "National Center for Transportation and Industrial Productivity" grant from the U.S. Department of Transportation, University Transportation Centers Program. This support is gratefully acknowledged, but implies no endorsement of the conclusions by these organizations.

APPENDIX

Derivation of the Inverted Demand Function

$$T_A^{ij} = T^{ij} \frac{\exp(U_A^{ij})}{\exp(U_A^{ij}) + \exp(U_T^{ij})} \text{ or}$$

$$\frac{T_A^{ij}}{T^{ij}} = \frac{1}{1 + \exp(U_T^{ij} - U_A^{ij})} \text{ or}$$

$$\exp(U_T^{ij} - U_A^{ij}) = \frac{T^{ij}}{T_A^{ij}} - 1 \text{ or}$$

$$\exp(U_T^{ij} - U_A^{ij}) = \frac{T^{ij} - T_A^{ij}}{T_A^{ij}} \text{ or}$$

$$U_T^{ij} - U_A^{ij} = \ln \frac{T_T^{ij}}{T_A^{ij}} \text{ or}$$

$$-\alpha - \beta * GC_T^{ij} + \beta * GC_A^{ij} \doteq \ln \frac{T_T^{ij}}{T_A^{ij}} \quad \text{or}$$

$$GC_T^{ij} - GC_A^{ij} = -\frac{1}{\beta} \left(\ln \frac{T_T^{ij}}{T_A^{ij}} + \alpha \right)$$

REFERENCES

Abdulaal, M., and L.J. LeBlanc. 1979. "Methods for Combining Modal Split and Equilibrium Assignment Models." *Transportation Science* 13: 292–314.

Ben Akiva, M., and S. Lerman. 1985. *Discrete Choice Modeling: Theory and Applications to Travel Demand.* Cambridge, MA: MIT Press.

Dafermos, S.C. 1982. "The General Multimodal Network Equilibrium Problem with Elastic Demand." *Networks* 12: 57–72.

Fernandez, E., J. DeCea, M. Florian, and E. Cabrera. 1994. "Network Equilibrium Models with Combined Modes." *Transportation Science* 28 (3): 182–192.

Fisk, C., and S. Nguyen. 1981. "Existence and Uniqueness Properties of an Asymmetric Two-Mode Equilibrium Model." *Transportation Science* 15: 318–328.

Florian, M. 1977. "Traffic Equilibrium Model of Travel by Car and Public Transit Modes. *Transportation Science* 11 (2): 166–179.

Florian, M., and S. Nguyen. 1974. "A Method for Computing Network Equilibrium with Elastic Demands." *Transportation Science* 8 (4): 321–332.

Florian, M., and H. Spiess. 1983. On Binary Mode Choice/Assignment Models." *Transportation Science* 17 (1): 32–47.

LeBlanc, L.J., and K. Farhangian. 1981. "Efficient Algorithms for Solving Elastic Demand Traffic Assignment Problems and Mode Split-Assignment Problems." *Transportation Science* 15 (4): 306–317.

Morlok, E.K. 1980. "Types of Transportation Supply Functions and their Applications." *Transportation Research* 14B: 9–27.

Murtagh, B.A., and M.A. Saunders. 1987. *MINOS 5.1 User's Guide.* Technical Report SOL83–20R, Stanford University, Stanford, CA.

Sheffi, Y. 1985. *Urban Transportation Networks: Equilibrium Analysis with Mathematical Programming Methods.* Englewood Cliffs, New Jersey: Prentice-Hall Inc.

U.S. Bureau of Public Roads, Department of Commerce. 1965. *The National System of Interstate and Defense Highways: Status of Improvements as of* Dec. 31, 1965, Washington, DC.

Voorhees, A. 1955. "A General Theory of Traffic Movement." *Proceedings of the Institute of Traffic Engineers*: 46–56.

THE USE OF NONLINEAR TIME SERIES IN AIRPORT FORECASTING

A CASE STUDY OF THE GREEK AIRPORT SYSTEM

Matthew G. Karlaftis, Jason D. Papastavrou, and George M. Karlaftis

ABSTRACT

The availability and timely operation of airports is a critical component of the infrastructure of countries whose economy is extensively tied to tourism. This is the case for Greece, where tourism constitutes one of the major sources of income. Greece's infrastructure development has centered extensively around the capital city of Athens, while tourism has grown almost exclusively in the islands. This discrepancy in the infrastructure investments and growth of tourism raises questions regarding the ability to predict the growth of airport traffic for both the large Hellinikon International Airport of Athens, and the much smaller airports located in the islands. The objective of this paper is to examine the difference in the nature of air-travel demand models for scheduled and chartered passenger traffic. The results of this analysis suggest that there is a distinct difference in the nature of

Advances in Business and Management Forecasting, Volume 2, pages 39–59.

forecasting models developed for airports with high and for airports with low scheduled passenger traffic. In airports with predominantly scheduled passenger traffic, causal models are the most appropriate, while for chartered traffic, time-series models provide the best fit.

I. INTRODUCTION

Airports are one of the most important components of the overall transportation system. Over the years, airports have become very large and expensive projects that provide the basis for a country's economic development. It is estimated that the passenger terminal of a modern international airport can be as expensive as $200 million (Odoni and de Neufville 1992). The same authors also estimated that a fully completed space in airport terminals is at least $2,000 per square meter.

Forecasting is at the core of the planning and design process of airports. Airport terminals, runways, freight storage facilities, parking lots, and even the roadway network to and from an airport are all based on the air-traffic demand forecasts. Forecasts of passenger volumes are directly translated to space requirements for the terminal buildings.

The forecasting process can be the most critical factor in the development of an airport (Howard 1974). Errors made in this phase of the process can be very costly and damaging to local economies. Underestimating demand can lead to increased congestion and delay, while overestimating demand could also create significant economic problems by planning for airports that will eventually be practically empty and underutilized for years (de Neufville 1976).

Therefore, errors in the forecasting process can cause significant problems to the economy of an airport's hinterland that depends on the successful operation of that airport. This is the case for Greece, where the entire national economy is closely tied to the revenues generated by the tourism industry. It should be noted that the Greek government does not keep official statistical data on the revenues generated by tourism. The ratio of private consumption in foreign currency to total private consumption is one of the few economic indicators that exist (Figure 1). This is certainly a severe underestimation of the importance of tourism to the Greek economy. It does not include, (i) the considerable consumption related to the trip in the tourists' own countries (i.e., payments to travel agents and hotels), and (ii) any of the indirect effects of tourism such as the investments in infrastructure and the decrease in unemployment.

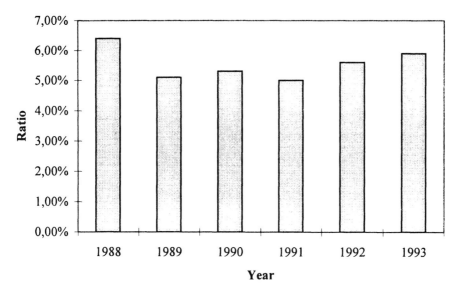

Figure 1. Ratio of Private Consumption in Foreign Currency to Total Private Consumption

Greece has one major international airport, the Hellinikon International Airport in Athens, that has been for years the main point of entry into the country for airline passengers from across the world. In the early eighties following Greece's entry into the European Union (then European Economic Community), Greece experienced a significant increase in the influx of tourists, who traveled with newly created charter airlines, that offered much lower fares. These charter airlines, in an effort to cut their operating expenses, decided to service directly the island destinations of the passengers. This shift caused a tremendous increase in passenger traffic at the considerably smaller island airports that were not designed and equipped to handle efficiently this new demand (for airport services). As a result of this "spread-out" type of demand, a modeling effort was undertaken to examine the effectiveness and validity of the available forecasting techniques, and examine their applicability to chartered airport traffic.

The objective of this paper is twofold. First, it traces the changes in air-travel demand patterns of passenger traffic for the Greek airport system. Second, it examines the differences in the predicting ability and forecasting accuracy of air-travel demand models developed for airports with a high percentage of scheduled passenger traffic, and for airports with a high percentage of charter passenger traffic. The remainder of his paper is organized as follows: The next section provides a brief overview of previous work on airport demand forecasting. In Section III the methodology utilized in this paper is presented. In Section IV forecasting models for both charter and scheduled traffic are developed for the major components of the Greek airport system. In Section V some important implementation issues are discussed, and finally, in Section VI the findings of this work are reviewed and summarized.

II. RELATED WORK

The goal of the review is to identify the work done for airport-specific rather than for corridor forecasting, similar to the work performed in the present paper. Corridor forecasting is concerned with the demand for air travel in a given travel route (corridor), say the New York–Athens (Greece) corridor. While this type of forecasting is certainly of great interest to airline companies, it is not as useful to airport planners who are mainly concerned with the aggregate passenger forecasts for a given airport (Whitford 1990). Knowledge of the aggregate passenger forecasts for an airport will provide planners with the necessary guidelines for the planning and design of the entire airport facilities. It is the goal of this paper to develop such aggregate airport-specific forecasts for the Greek airport system.

One of the first published efforts about airport-specific forecasting was by Jacobson (1970). The model predicted the *trips generated at an airport* (dependent variable) based only on the *average airfare per mile* for all routes in the United States, and the *total income per capita* for the airport catchment area. The model was calibrated with 18 years of data from the airports of Virginia. A rather similar model was developed by Haney (1975) to analyze airport specific demand for the St. Louis, Missouri airport. The model is a typical airport forecasting model in that the explanatory variables are socioeconomic in nature and refer to the metropolitan area served by the airport.

A different type of forecasting model was developed by Thomet and Sultan (1979) for the Riyadh International Airport in Saudi Arabia. The model used imports and exports of crude oil and petroleum products as the sole independent variable, to account for the fact that most travel to and from Saudi Arabia was related to the oil emporium.

Another interesting example of placing a special effort in the direction of identifying key growth factors unique to an area, is the case of Mexico City's airport traffic by Zuñiga, de Neufville, Kanafani, and Olivera (1978). Approximately 20% of the population and wealth of Mexico are concentrated in the capital, and the fast growth rates of these characteristics certainly influence the future airport traffic. The models that were developed for domestic traffic included as variables the population of Mexico City and the cost of transportation in constant pesos.

Mellman, Nelson, and Pino (1980) developed a model for Boston's Logan airport. Unlike many other airports where transit passengers are a significant portion of the airport's traffic, Logan's traffic is mostly Boston based. Explanatory variables in this case related air travel to the socioeconomic characteristics of the Boston region.

All the models cited established an analytical relationship between air-travel demand and a set of independent variables. These variables are usually socioeconomic measures, expressing the affinity for air travel in the geographical area where the airport is located. A common measure of effectiveness, used to evaluate the quality of statistical fit of the various models to the available data, is the R^2 (Draper and Smith 1981). The R^2 statistic can be described as the ratio of the explained variation over the total variation in the dependent variable. That is, R^2 denotes the variation in the dependent variable explained by the variation in the independent variable(s). Although a high R^2 does not necessarily imply a "good" model, a "good" model is expected to have a reasonably high R^2 (for the purposes of this research, and given the high quality of travel data available, a "good" R^2 was considered to be higher than 0.80). The R^2 statistic provides for a useful tool in evaluating how well the proposed model fits the available data, yet it does not give a clear indication on the forecasting ability of the model. To overcome this disadvantage of the R^2 statistic, the Mean Absolute Percent Error (MAPE) was used in the model evaluation phase of the research. The MAPE is the percent difference between projected and actual values of travel demand. The MAPE is a much better measure of the forecasting ability of a model, since it compares the actual values of the dependent variable with the projected values (of the dependent variable) resulting from the model. Low values of the MAPE indicate that there is low discrepancy between the projected (forecasted) and actual values of travel demand, and thus the model could be used for forecasting purposes with a high degree of confidence. A rule-of-thumb suggests that MAPE values below 5% indicate models that are "highly reliable," while MAPE values between

5 and 10% are "good" (Levenbach and Cleary 1985). In the following section the methodology used to develop the models for the Greek airport system is presented.

III. METHODOLOGY

The key issue in the development of successful airport forecasts is the ability to identify those factors that influence the change in the volume of passenger traffic at an airport. There are two major approaches in the development of forecasting models: *Simple time series* (STS) and *causal modeling*. STS methods are the most widely used methods for predicting air-travel demand, and assume that "history repeats itself," in that the underlying stochastic structure of the data does not change with time. The common characteristic, and weakness, of all time-series methods is that they ignore the determinants of demand such as fares, income, GNP, and do not attempt to *explain* the causes of change in demand. Causal modeling attempts to determine, from given data, causation or at least explanation when analyzing the relationship between certain data; that is, the relationship between two or more variables is used to predict one variable (the dependent) from the others (independent).

In the modeling effort for the Greek airport system, the initial approach was to develop causal models that link passenger traffic with a set of explanatory variables. Unfortunately, and due to the very high percentage of charter traffic present at the island airports, reasonable causality was impossible to establish. Thus, STS modeling, the alternative forecasting method, was utilized. STS modeling has been used extensively in the literature in those cases where causality could not be established, or where economic information on the airport's catchment area was not readily available (ICAO 1985). As an example, passenger forecasts for the Cornavin Airport in Geneva, Switzerland have been obtained using STS methods (ICAO 1985); SST methods were also used extensively in the forecasts for the fourth airport in the Chicago region (al Chalabi and Mumayiz 1991; al Chalabi 1993; Whitford 1990). Moreover, forecasts of air travel growth for the Airbus industries are often obtained by using STS methods (Lenormand 1989).

In performing regression analysis certain assumptions are made concerning the error term. The assumptions are that the error terms are independent, have zero mean, a constant variance, and follow a normal distribution. To ensure that the regression analysis is correct and valid, the examination of the residuals should confirm these assumptions. In order to assess the reliability of our models and test for violations from regression assumptions, each estimated model was evaluated in terms of its consistency with the underlying hypotheses, goodness of fit, presence of serial correlation and heteroscedasticity, empirical specification, and error normality.[1] If a regression model does not confirm these assumptions, then either corrective measures should be employed (as in the present analysis for the case of serial correlation), or an alternative model should be developed.

There are two basic approaches in evaluating the potential forecasting accuracy of a given model (Taneja 1978). In the first approach the entire data set is utilized in the calibration of the model, and the observed historical data is then compared to the forecast produced by the data, using criteria such as the R^2 statistic and the Mean Absolute Percent Error (MAPE). The second approach is to divide the data set into two parts. The first part is used to calibrate the model and produce forecasts that are then compared with the actual data from the second group. This type of evaluation process is known as post-fact (or ex post) forecasting, and its main advantage is that it makes it possible to check forecasts against actual values. Its main disadvantage is that it "wastes" a large part of the data set (approximately 1/3 of the data is used for the post-fact comparisons) which happens to be the most recent information on the dependent variable. Moreover, as Karlaftis, Zografos, Papastavrou, and Charnes (1996) showed in a post-fact analysis of the Miami and Frankfurt International Airports, this type of analysis is sensitive to the exact time periods used for the model calibration phase. Furthermore, the "best" models reached by the post-fact analysis method were very similar to the ones selected when the entire data set was used for the model calibration phase and the model selection was based on the R^2 and MAPE criteria.

In the case of the Greek airport system, most of the island airports have faced a high growth in passenger travel in recent years. As a result, it was decided to utilize the entire data set in the model calibration phase in order to capture the most recent trends in passenger travel. In this paper, once a demand model has been calibrated and evaluated, the model is used to provide in-sample predictions of air-travel demand in order to assess whether the model successfully tracks this demand. The approach used to evaluate the potential forecasting accuracy of the models is to compare the observed historical data to the forecast produced by the data using the R^2 statistic and the MAPE.

It should be again noted that due to the time-series data set available for this research, the issue of serial correlation (residual autocorrelation), which is common in regression models that utilize time-series data, was accounted for. Moreover, care was taken in the case of the causal models to avoid developing models with an excessive number of explanatory variables that would not only present multicollinearity problems, but also hinder the forecasting process (Karlaftis et al. 1996). In regression analysis, multicollinearity (or linear dependency) is present when a high degree of correlation exists among independent variables. This can occur when either a large number of independent variables is included in a model or different independent variables are used to measure similar phenomena. It should be noted that while collinearity does not affect the estimation of the dependent variable, it leads to inflated variances on the predicted value with a resulting lack of statistical significance, or incorrect signs or magnitude (Draper and Smith 1981). Since the interpretation of the coefficients is very important in most regression analyses, the problem of collinearity should be addressed in the variable selection process for the forecasting models.

IV. CASE STUDY

The Greek airport system comprises 35 airports that accept commercial flights. From these airports, approximately half are international; that is, open to direct flights from airports outside of Greece. The airports that were mostly affected by the increase in direct flights were the airports located in major resort areas. The airports that are considered in this case study are: Hellinikon, the major international airport of Athens, the airports of Zakynthos and Kerkyra (Corfu) islands (both located off the west coast of mainland Greece), the airports of Kos and Rhodes (both located off the east coast of mainland Greece), and the airport of Hania (on the island of Crete, at the south of Greece). The airports off the west (east) coast serve as destinations to passengers visiting the "west" ("east") islands, because tourists can either remain on those islands or take a small boat and visit the neighboring islands (a type of intermodal hub-and-spoke system). Similarly, passengers to the airport of Hania are visitors of Crete, the largest Greek island.

The origin of the tourists visiting Greece is important in attempting to identify the key factors affecting the dramatic increase in island airport traffic. From Figure 2 (OECD 1994), it is evident that approximately 90% of the tourists visiting Greece originate in Europe. To account for this, the explanatory variables that were selected for inclusion in the models were socioeconomic measures for Europe.

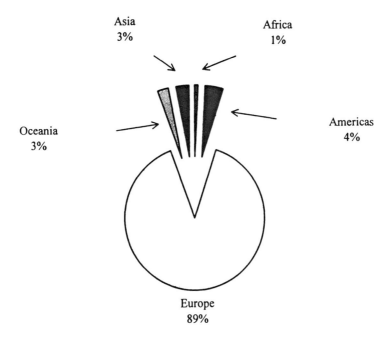

Figure 2.   Origin of Visitors to Greece

The sample period for this yearly analysis was the period 1979–1993 (with the exception of the Zakynthos and Hania international airports, where the periods were 1983–1993 and 1981–1993 respectively, due to the promotion of those airports to international status in those years). The dependent variable for the models was the international passenger traffic, and it was provided for the purposes of this research by the Greek Civil Aeronautics Board, which collects this data on an annual basis for all Greek airports. The independent variables that were considered for inclusion in the models were the Gross National Product (GNP) per capita for Europe, the Personal Consumption Expenditures (PCE) per capita for Europe, and the Disposable Income (DI) per capita for Europe,[2] all measured in constant 1985 dollars. It was hypothesized that the inclusion of these measures is more appropriate because it accounts for some of the determinants of the behavior of tourists visiting Greece. Furthermore, the yield was included as a measure of the price of travel; the information on this variable was obtained from ICAO (1991).

The abovementioned explanatory variables were chosen for inclusion in the model because they are widely considered as some of the "best" descriptors of the ability (and desire) for tourists to travel. The development of air travel is also affected by a large number of external economic factors, government policies and regulations (such as travel advisories and strikes of the air-traffic controllers), physical phenomena (Greece has faced a large decrease in the number of international tourists in the years when earthquakes occurred), technological developments, and the operating economics of the air-transportation industry (ICAO 1985). Unfortunately, these occurrences cannot be forecasted, and as a result the models have to be built on measures that are not only diligently observed in the past, but also for which forecasts exist (Kanafani 1981). In the preparation and application of the forecasts these uncertainties have to be recognized; nevertheless, a forecaster's task is to use the data sources available, and apply methods that minimize the range of uncertainty (ICAO 1991).

A. Scheduled Passenger Traffic

The *only* Greek airport with a significant amount of scheduled international passengers is the Athens international airport. In *all* of the island airports the charter passenger traffic accounts for more than 95% of the entire international traffic. Therefore, since scheduled traffic is not significant in the island airports, the models calibrated for scheduled traffic are developed only for the Athens airport, where scheduled passenger traffic has been highly variable through the years (Figure 3a). In developing the model different specifications and forms were examined, but overall, the double-log model presented below provided the best fit. The model that was calibrated for scheduled traffic at this airport is:

$$\log Y_t = 13.996 - 0.531 \log Y_{t-1}$$
$${\scriptstyle (3.42)} {\scriptstyle (-2.128)}$$

$$- 0.394 \log(Yield) + 1.184 \log(PCE) \qquad (1)$$
$${\scriptstyle (-1.867)} {\scriptstyle (2.988)}$$

where Y_t is the passenger traffic in year t, Y_{t-1} is the passenger traffic in the previous year, *Yield* is an aggregate proxy used for fare prices, and *PCE* is the personal consumption expenditures per capita for Europe. The coefficients for *Yield* and per capita *PCE* have the expected signs and are significantly different from 0 at the 90 and 95% level of signifi-

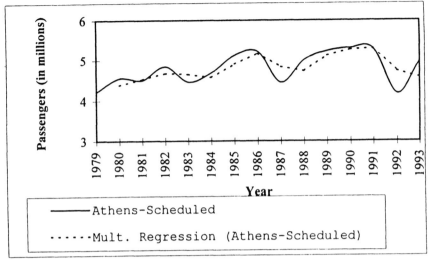

a. Scheduled International Traffic

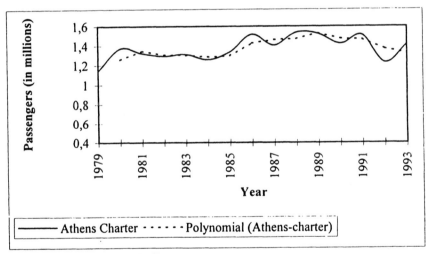

b. Charter International Traffic

Figure 3. Athens International Airport Passenger Traffic

cance equivalently. Consistent with part of the current literature on demand models, demand for air travel is price inelastic (Raphael and Starry 1995). It should be noted that due to differences in the way the yield (or fare) variable is estimated, a wide range (–0.2 to –4.0) in the price elasticities derived is observed (Kanafani 1981). A 1% increase in

Table 1. Performance of the Forecasting Models

Airport	R^2	MAPE
Athens - scheduled	0.83	7.3%
Athens - charter	0.90	6.31%
Zakynthos	0.993	3.53%
Corfu	0.91	5.62%
Kos	0.86	5.13%
Rhodes	0.88	4.96%
Hania	0.95	4.88%

the price of travel reduces the quantity of international passengers by .394%, all else held constant (yield elasticity is rather low at −0.4, yet within reasonable limits [Kanafani and Behbehani 1978]). The international passenger traffic is also income elastic. During the period of the analysis, a 1% increase in per capita *PCE* increases the passenger traffic at the airport by 1.184%. The negative coefficient of the lagged dependent variable can be interpreted as a kind of cyclic behavior of scheduled international airport passenger traffic in Athens; that is, periods of higher than average traffic are followed by periods of lower than average traffic. Statistically, the model fits the data rather well, with an R^2 of 0.83, and MAPE of 7.3% (Table 1).

In the calibration of this model the presence of autocorrelation was identified by the use of the DW-*h* statistic, which is the alternative to the popular DW-*d* statistic (Durbin and Watson 1950, 1951) when the dependent variable is used in its lagged form as an independent variable (Greene 1991). The residuals of this model follow a second order autoregressive process.[3] The multiple regression model is also presented in Figure 3a.

B. Charter Traffic

Modeling the charter traffic for the Athens and the island airports proved a cumbersome process, since there is no a priori consideration of appropriate explanatory variables, and hence a straightforward causality cannot be established. Charter traffic for the Greek islands is affected by a large number of factors that cannot be readily quantified and used in the building of forecasting models (Kanafani 1981); for example, occasional low airfares, low hotel rates, advertising campaigns in foreign countries by the Greek tourist bureau, promotion of alternate destinations, and the availability (or not) of alternate destinations. Initially, for the charter traffic in Athens, the attempt was to establish a causal model with explanatory variables. After repeated attempts with a large number of different modeling formulations and combinations of variables, the model that resulted from this process was:

$$Y_t = -1184043 - 0.091Y_{t-1} - 13179(Yield)$$
$$(-0.086) \qquad (-0.06) \qquad (-0.493)$$

$$+473.15(PCE) - 54239D \qquad (2)$$
$$(1.21) \qquad (-1.57)$$

The very low t-statistics for most of the variables and the very low R^2 (0.32) for the model, indicate that this model is clearly *not* appropriate for the forecasting process that would be based on it. When causality cannot be clearly established[4] and air-travel forecasts are nevertheless required, alternate forecasting methods should be examined. The alternate type of methodology is that of using STS models. In developing STS models the overall trend and fluctuation of demand are examined, and different model specifications are utilized, to lead up to the model that best describes the data available. This search for the case of charter passenger traffic for Athens ended in the calibration of a STS polynomial type model. This is a third degree polynomial model with respect to time, and its advantage over alternate STS specifications is that it has the ability to model the *high fluctuation* in charter passenger traffic that was observed in Athens. The model is specified as:

$$Y_t = 72516 - 110600D + 21623D^2 - 1008.1D^3 \qquad (3)$$
$$(7.61) \qquad (-2.839) \qquad (3.91) \qquad (-4.463)$$

In this model D takes the value of 0 for 1979, 1 for 1980, and so forth up to 14 for 1983. The model fits the data well (Table 1), and is presented in Figure 3b, together with the actual data.

The modeling effort for the various island airports encountered the same problems as the modeling of charter traffic for Athens. Namely, the inability to establish a clear causal relationship between the changes in traffic and different explanatory variables. Moreover, these models have to account for the explosive growth of charter traffic. For the Zakynthos airport (Figure 4), the best model is the "power" model (ICAO 1985), that performed the best in modeling the explosive growth and the low variability in demand. The model is given by the following equation:

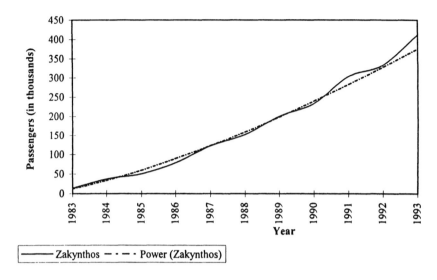

Figure 4. Zakynthos International Airport Passenger Traffic

$$Y_t = 12657 \ X^{1.4144} \tag{4}$$
$$\text{(7.818)}$$

Where X is the year for which the forecasts are done. The R^2 of the model, 0.993, indicates a very good fit of the data (Table 1), while the MAPE of 3.53% indicates a very reliable forecasting model.

For the Hania international airport, the charter traffic demonstrated the same essential characteristics as the traffic at the Zakynthos airport; that is, explosive growth and a low variability in demand. In this airport the use of the exponential curve was preferred, because of the very high rate of increase at that airport for the years after 1988. The model formulation for this airport is (Figure 5 for the model and Table 1 for the R^2 and MAPE):

$$Y_t = 12247e^{0.29t} \tag{5}$$
$$\text{(5.92)}$$

Initially there was an attempt to establish causal models for the Zakynthos and Hania airports. Again, the t-statistics for the variables and the R^2 were too low, indicating (1) statistically *not* significant relationships between the passenger travel demand and the explanatory variables, and (2) that models provided an inadequate fit to the data. Subsequently, different types of STS models were fit, such as autoregressive and polynomial (with time as the explanatory variable). Unfortu-

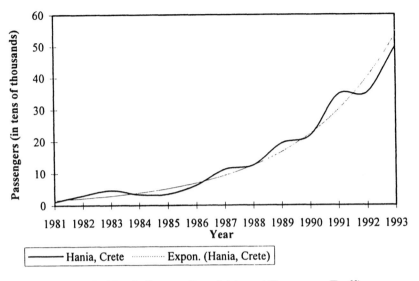

Figure 5. Hania International Airport Passenger Traffic

nately, the parameters were again statistically *not* significant and the R^2 was too low (.30 to .40). In the last step, growth curves were fit to the available data (such as linear, exponential, power, parabolic, Gompertz as described by ICAO [1985]), and based on the R^2 and the MAPE, the growth curve that provided the best fit was chosen.

Finally, in the next three airports, the Corfu, Kos, and Rhodes international airports, the charter international traffic demonstrated high rates of increase (yet lower than that of the Zakynthos and Hania international airports) and with a passenger variability that could not be ignored (yet lower than the variability of passenger traffic at the Athens airport). The difficulties in establishing causal relationships continued. The models that performed the best for these three airports are the autoregressive models with a time-trend term.[5] These models are presented in Table 2, with the *t*-statistics for the parameters in parentheses, Figures 6, 7, and 8 depict the models, and Table 1 presents the measures of fit for these models.

All the simple time-series models that were calibrated for the airports provide very good fit to the data, are able to model both the fluctuation in passenger traffic and the rather high growth rates, and are fairly straightforward in the calibration process. It is essential, when developing these STS models, to fit the data with that model specification that can capture the unique passenger traffic characteristics of the airport.

Table 2. Autoregressive Models for the Corfu, Kos, and Rhodes Airports

	Corfu	Kos	Rhodes
Constant	367967	−64552	616700
Y_{t-1}	0.805 (3.1)	0.259 (2.13)	0.311 (3.01)
Y_{t-2}	−0.671 (−2.56)	−0.423 (−2.45)	−0.338 (−2.10)
D	58383 (3.17)	66378 (3.77)	76870 (4.23)

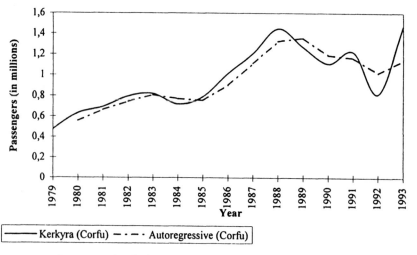

Figure 6. Corfu International Airport Passenger Traffic

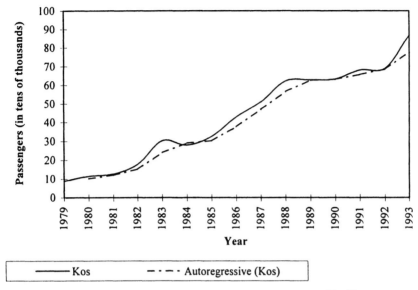

Figure 7. Kos International Airport Passenger Traffic

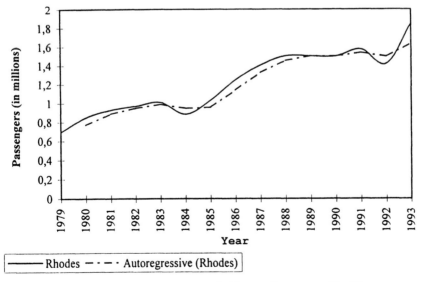

Figure 8. Rhodes International Airport Passenger Traffic

V. IMPLEMENTATION ISSUES

When planning and designing airport terminals there is a significant number of traffic characteristics that must be forecasted: total number of passengers for the design period, domestic, commuter, and international passenger ratios at peak hours, seasonal variations in demand, volumes of transfer and/or transit passengers for each type of traffic, and sometimes origin and destination of flights for immigration, customs, and health control purposes. The aggregate passenger forecasts, such as the ones presented in this paper, are used to determine the space requirements for new terminals or the expansion of existing facilities.

Forecasting is also very important for the economic development of airline fleets. Airline fleets have grown significantly in the last few decades, and orders for commercial transport aircraft have reached an all time high, with delivery rates now backed up into the mid-1990s for some aircraft types (ICAO 1991). Future fleet development has an important role in the design of terminals, since the aircraft size is critical to some geometric characteristics such as the main deck elevation and the lateral clearance at gates due to the aircraft wing span.

The basis for the development of new and expansion of already existing terminal facilities in the Greek airport system is based on these forecasts. The data necessary for these forecasts is readily available through the Greek Civil Aeronautics Board, and the analysis has attempted to establish causal relationships between passenger traffic and a set of explanatory variables. These explanatory variables are statistically adequate; that is, the data is collected by the Greek government in a consistent manner at equally spaced time intervals. Causal relationships were not established for charter passenger traffic, since both the rate of growth for this traffic is very high, and the very nature of this type of demand is not clearly understood. As a result, it is suggested that the charter passenger traffic forecasts are used cautiously, and for a short to medium forecasting horizon (five to 10 years).

It is also important to note that the analysis of time-series data should be done cautiously, to account for the presence of error term serial correlation. In the case of serial correlation, the conclusion that the parameter estimates are more precise than they actually are, could be reached.

It is evident that until actual values of the future air-travel demand are known, a model's accuracy cannot be precisely ascertained. Nevertheless, it is important to ensure the statistical validity of the forecasting models that will be used in practice, so that a rational basis for the selection of the appropriate model exists.

VI. CONCLUSIONS

The goal of this paper was to examine and analyze the differences between the forecasting process for chartered and scheduled international passenger traffic, and to develop air-travel demand models that are applicable to the Greek airport system.

Two major types of models were examined: the simple time-series and the causal models. Both types of models provided a good fit to the data. Only the scheduled airport passenger traffic was modeled with the causal models. The time-series models were primarily used for the modeling of the charter airport traffic, due to the inability to establish causality between the set of explanatory variables and the passenger traffic.

The results of the calibration of traffic demand models for all the airports appear to be very good. In fact, given the nature of the database and the rather uncertain and variable conditions that exist in the various airports, the results are surprisingly good. All the models appear to be statistically significant and to exhibit good fit with historic trends. It is interesting that model structures and, to a certain degree, parameter values are quite similar in signs and magnitudes.

Further work on charter passenger traffic is certainly warranted, given the inability to formulate causal relationships between explanatory variables and changes in traffic. This inability could lead to estimates that seriously over- or underestimate future airport traffic, with severe planning consequences. Forecasts are generally uncertain, yet the establishment of causal relationships gives a more rational and scientific basis for model development, and makes airport planners more secure in planning and designing for airports based on the available forecasts. Nevertheless, use of the current STS models in short-term forecasting is feasible. The good statistical results obtained by using these models show rather low standard error values and permit forecasting with confidence.

Again, careful work should be done in the direction of chartered traffic, to identify the factors that affect passenger demand. This will become increasingly important as the passenger volumes approach the airports' capacity, and the rates of increase continue to grow but at a decreasing pace.

The analyses reinforced the well-documented belief that forecasts are generally uncertain. The case study results reported in this paper dem-

58 KARLAFTIS, PAPASTAVROU, and KARLAFTIS

onstrate the difficulty in developing a universal air-travel demand model. It is important to recognize the limitations of qualitative forecasting models and to combine them with expert judgment taking into consideration external factors that are difficult to be quantified. As a consequence, it is desirable to plan airport facilities in a flexible way so as to overcome possible inaccuracies in forecasting.

NOTES

1. Draper and Smith (1981) suggest a variety of residuals plots to check for consistency with the underlying assumptions. Normal probability plots check nonnormal errors, time plots of residuals identify problems of heteroscedasticity, standardized residuals checks for outliers, and plots of residuals against predicted values provide insights on the appropriateness of the empirical specification.
2. These measures (and their forecasts) are available from the Organization of Economic Development and Cooperation (OECD) on an annual basis.
3. The model calibration was done with the SAS software. The PROC AUTOREG and PROC ARIMA were used, and the unconditional least squares estimation option was specified.
4. "Causality cannot be clearly established" implies that statistically it is not feasible to build models that attempt to explain changes in charter traffic based on any explanatory variables.
5. The autoregressive terms capture the variability in traffic, and the time trend term captures the increase in traffic.

REFERENCES

al Chalabi, S. 1993. "Aviation Demand Forecasting—Traditional and New Approaches (The application of ground transport methodologies to enplanement forecasting)." Submitted to the Transportation Research Board in July.
al Chalabi, S., and S. Mumayiz. 1991. "Allocation of Enplanement Forecasts to Alternative Airports." Working paper no. 10 of the Illinois-Indiana Regional Airport study.
Draper, N., and H. Smith. 1981. *Applied Regression Analysis.* New York: John Wiley and Sons.
de Neufville, R. 1976. *Airport Systems Planning: A Critical Look at the Methods and Experience.* Cambridge, MA: MIT Press.
Durbin, J., and G.S. Watson. 1950. "Testing for Serial Correlation in Least Squares Regression I." *Biometrica* 37: 409–428.
Durbin, J., and G.S. Watson. 1951. "Testing for Serial Correlation in Least Squares Regression II." *Biometrica* 38: 159–178.
Greene, W.H. 1991. *Econometric Analysis.* New York: Macmillan Publishing Company.
Haney, D.G. 1975. "Review of Aviation Forecasting Methodology." US DOT, Report DOT-40176-6.
Howard, G.P. 1974. *Airport Economic Planning.* Cambridge, MA: MIT Press.

International Civil Aviation Organization. 1985. "Manual on Air Traffic Forecasting." Doc. 8991-AT/722/2, Montreal, Canada.

International Civil Aviation Organization. 1991. "Airport Economics." Doc. 8991-AT/722/2, Montreal, Canada.

Jacobson, I.D. 1970. "Demand Modeling of Passenger Air Travel." NASA Report CR-157469.

Kanafani, A. 1981. *Transportation Demand Analysis*. New York: John Wiley and Sons.

Kanafani, A., and R. Behbehani. 1978. "Demand Analysis for International Air Travel." *Transportation Research Record* 732: 5–15.

Karlaftis, M.G., K.G. Zografos, J.D. Papastavrou, and J.C. Charnes. 1996. "Methodological Framework for Air-Travel Demand Forecasting." ASCE *Journal of Transportation Engineering* 122 (2): forthcoming.

Lenormand, D. 1989. "European Aircraft Manufacturers' Forecasting Methodology." *Transportation Research Circular* 348: 35–41.

Levenbach, H., and J.P. Cleary. 1985, *The Beginning Forecaster.* Belmont, CA: Lifetime Learning Publications.

Mellman, R., M. Nelson, and J. Pino. 1980. "Forecasts of Passenger Traffic and Air Cargo Activity at Logan International Airport." *Transportation Research Record* 768: 31–37.

Odoni, A.R., and R. de Neufville. 1992. "Passenger Terminal Design." *Transportation Research* 26A: 27–35.

Organization for Economic Cooperation and Development. 1994. *System of National Accounts 1992.* Washington, DC: OECD Publications.

Raphael, D.E., and C. Starry. 1995. "The Future of Business Air Travel." Transportation Research Record, No. 1506, 1–7.

SAS Institute Inc. 1988. *SAS/ETS User's Guide, version 6.* Cary, NC: SAS Institute Inc.

Taneja, N.K. 1978. *Airline Traffic Forecasting.* Lexington, MA: Lexington Books.

Thomet, M.A., and S.M. Sultan. 1979. "Traffic Forecasting for the New Riyadh International Airport." ICAO Manual on Air Traffic Forecasting, Montreal, Canada.

Whitford, R.K. 1990. "Sketch Planning-Forecasting Future Requirements for Airports in the Chicago Region." Working paper for the Indiana Department of Transportation, Division of Aeronautics.

Zuñiga, S., R. de Neufville, A. Kanafani, and R. Olivera. 1978. "Forecasting Airport Traffic: Mexico City as a Case Study." *Transportation Research Record* 732: 24–39.

PART II

FORECASTING DEMAND FOR WATER AND ENERGY

WATER DEMAND ESTIMATES IN TEXAS

Michael Nieswiadomy

ABSTRACT

This paper presents estimates of water demand in Texas using a cross-section of utilities surveyed by the Texas Natural Resources Conservation Commission (TNRCC) in 1993. Since many cities are using increasing block rates, it is useful to determine if consumers respond to marginal or average prices. Shin's (1985) price perception model is used to test consumers' responsiveness. The models use a log-log specification and rainfall, temperature, population, per capita income, and water and sewage prices to explain summer (June–August) water use. They are estimated separately for two types of price structures: uniform and increasing. Consumers appear to react to average prices rather than marginal prices. Consumers also appear to respond more to price signals when faced with an increasing block rate schedule, as shown by the larger (in absolute value) price elasticity of demand for cities using increasing block rates (–0.31) versus cities using uniform rates (–0.17).

Advances in Business and Management Forecasting, Volume 2, pages 63–76.
ISBN: 0-7623-0002-7

I. INTRODUCTION

Texas has experienced rapid population growth in recent years. Population grew 19.4% in the 1980–1990 period and 8.2% for the 1990–1994
period compared to the U.S. rates of 9.8% and 4.7%, respectively.
Furthermore, the Texas economy is rapidly evolving into a commercial
and industrial-based economy. By the year 2005 municipal and industrial
use is forecasted to exceed agricultural use. If these trends continue,
demand will exceed supply in 2030. These changing conditions have
forced water officials to cope with ever-growing urban demands.

Whereas expansion of water supplies could be relied on to solve these
problems in the past, very few opportunities for expansion exist today.
Thus, state planners are now focusing on water conservation efforts
which are projected to reduce municipal demand by 18% below the level
it is expected to reach in 2050 without conservation. As is the case across
the United States, many Texas water suppliers are considering raising
water rates and adopting increasing block rate structures as part of their
overall conservation plans. Water planners are keenly interested in having
accurate and current water demand estimates, particularly price elasticity
estimates (Mercer and Morgan 1985; Moncur 1987).

This paper presents estimates of water demand equations for a cross-
section of Texas cities from the summer of 1993. In Section II a review
of the water demand estimation literature is given. In Section III the data
and the methodology are described. In Section IV the water demand
estimates are presented and discussed. Section V presents the conclusions.

II. ISSUES IN WATER DEMAND ESTIMATION

Water demand estimation presents many interesting problems. Researchers have debated several issues such as the proper functional form
to use, the variables to include, and the appropriate methodology to use.
These issues are difficult to resolve because water is not sold under a
simple pricing scheme. Typically water utilities choose among three
types of pricing schemes (uniform, decreasing, or increasing block rates),
as well as a variety of fixed fees for water and sewer, or some combination
of these, to influence water use. These complicated price structures pose
several theoretical and econometric problems. First among these is the
potential awareness of consumers. Do customers understand the complexity of the rate structure and react to the fixed and variable fees or do

they simply react to some kind of average price? The second issue involves the appropriate methods to test various competing econometric models.

Opinions concerning the appropriate methodology for estimating water demand differ significantly. Early water studies ignored the presence of block rates by simply using an ex post calculated average price (Gottlieb 1963; Young 1973; Foster and Beattie 1979). Taylor (1975), studying electricity demand, suggested that under the blocking rate-pricing scheme the explanatory variables should include marginal and average prices. Subsequently, Nordin (1976) demonstrated that Taylor's specification should be modified to include a difference variable to account for the effects of infra-marginal rates and fixed fees. Difference is defined as the total bill minus what the bill would have been if all units had been purchased at the marginal price.

The introduction of the Nordin difference variable has had limited success (Billings and Agthe 1980; Howe 1982; Jones and Morris 1984),[1] although the need for the difference variable appears theoretically sound. However, the measure(s) of price to which consumers respond is perhaps more of an empirical question yet to be conclusively answered (Foster and Beattie 1981; Opaluch 1982; Shin 1985; Chicoine and Ramamurthy 1986). Failing to find a statistically significant difference coefficient (of the proper magnitude) could imply that consumers do not react to relatively low current water prices in the precise fashion predicted by the Nordin model (Terza and Welch 1982; Terza 1986).

One problem, which must be addressed by all researchers using data with block rate pricing, is simultaneity. Clearly the price of water both determines, and is determined by, consumption. Hence, OLS estimation of any of the above models will yield biased and inconsistent estimates. Many different types of data sets have been used to study this simultaneity problem, ranging from household data to aggregate data, and many different techniques have been used. The simultaneity bias is more likely to be found in micro data sets than in aggregate cross-section data sets. This is due to the variety of rates used across cities. Even if all cities use block rates, some cities will have lower overall prices. Thus, it is harder to find a situation where consumption is higher in cities that have higher rates. It is much easier to find a situation where individual consumers (all facing the same rate structure) who use more water pay a higher marginal price. Instrumental variable (IV) techniques have been used by some to address the simultaneity problem: in electricity demand, Wilder and Willenborg (1975), McFadden, Puig, and Kirschner (1977), and

Henson (1984); and in water demand estimation, Jones and Morris (1984), Deller, Chicoine, and Ramamurthy (1986), and Agthe, Billings, Dobra, and Raffiee (1986).[2] Schefter and David (1985) noted the problems involved in using aggregate rather than micro data. They hypothesize that some of the controversy in the water demand estimation literature is directly attributable to the use of aggregate data. Many of the earlier studies relied on *decreasing* block rate data because it was the most frequently used structure (Danielson 1979; Hanke and de Mare 1982; Jones and Morris 1984; Chicoine, Deller, and Ramamurthy 1986).[3] Several more recent studies have examined data sets using both increasing and decreasing block rates (Nieswiadomy and Molina 1989, 1991; Stevens, Miller, and Willis 1992; Hewitt and Hanemann 1995). This paper compares the two-stage least squares (2SLS) and OLS methods in estimating water demand using a data set for both *uniform* and *increasing* block rates.[4]

III. DATA AND METHODOLOGY

The water-use data come from a survey conducted by the TNRCC and the University of North Texas of all public water suppliers serving over 100 persons in Texas. The survey polled water utility managers about the importance of water conservation, their conservation plans, and reasons for implementing these plans. The survey also gathered data on water-use patterns, water rates, and cost effectiveness of water conservation programs (for a review of the survey results see Nieswiadomy and Stuewe 1996). It should be noted that Texas has very diverse climatic conditions. In the summer months rainfall varies significantly. Rainfall varies from the desert southwest, which receives eight inches, to far east Texas, which receives 52 inches of rain annually.

Eighty-three utilities provided complete water use and rate information. The summary statistics for these data are shown in Table 1. Forty-nine % of the responding utilities used a uniform block pricing structure, 41% used increasing block rates, and 10% percent used decreasing block rates. Decreasing block rates have become very unpopular in Texas as well as in many other western states.

The per capita average daily summer use for the months of June, July, and August was obtained from the survey, as well as the number of customers served by the utility. The water and sewer rate structure information was also provided in the survey. The rate information was standardized into three blocks: 0–7,500; 7,501–22,500; over 22,500 gallons. Several cities based their sewer rates throughout the year on the use in the winter months of December through February. This implies that the sewer rate in the summer months has no variable component, that is, it is a fixed fee. Additionally, this data set was augmented by gathering demographic data and weather data for each city. Per capita income data for the cities were obtained from the 1990 U.S. Census for Texas. The data for the average rainfall for the months of June, July, and August of 1993 and the average temperature for these months were obtained from the National Oceanic and Atmospheric Administration.

Several different models have been used in the literature. Three of these models are examined in this study.[5] One type of model uses the marginal price as the price variable. The second type of model uses the average price as the price variable. The third model used in this study is Shin's (1985) price perception model, which tests whether consumers react to average or marginal prices. All three models were estimated for two subgroups of cities, those using increasing block, and uniform rate structures, and for the whole data set. Because of the paucity of cities using decreasing rate structures, these cities are not separately econometrically analyzed in this paper.

Table 1. Summary of Water Use, Prices, and Demographic Data

Variable	Mean	Standard Deviation	Minimum	Maximum
Average Summer Monthly Use per Capita per Day (gallons)	209.75	62.51	96.00	378.40
Increasing Block	199.33	64.71	96.00	378.40
Uniform Block	219.35	62.57	99.10	347.30
Decreasing Block	204.84	35.14	156.50	260.00
Avg. Price of Water ($/1,000 gals.)	2.08	0.87	0.71	4.74
Avg. Price of Sewage	1.28	1.04	0.00	3.87
Avg. Price of Water and Sewage	3.36	1.44	0.83	7.25
Increasing Block	2.85	1.30	1.17	5.53
Uniform Block	3.73	1.47	0.83	6.54
Decreasing Block	3.70	1.09	2.18	5.48
Marginal Water Price	1.93	0.81	0.42	4.50
Marginal Sewage Price	0.79	0.97	0.00	3.58
Marginal Price of Water and Sewage	2.72	1.37	0.71	7.08
Temperature average (degrees Fahrenheit) June–August 1993	83.26	1.74	75.97	88.57
Rainfall average (inches per month) June–August 1993	2.65	1.42	0.75	6.31
Population	75,058.74	228,942.24	2,537.00	1,680,994.0
Annual per capita income ($)	12,738.84	4,667.09	4,717.00	34,664.00

Because a standard log–log model is estimated for the marginal and average price models, it does not need to be described. However, because the Shin (1985) model is not well known, it will be presented briefly here for the benefit of the reader. The basic concept underlying the Shin (1985) price perception model is that it is costly for consumers to determine the actual rate schedule. There are several reasons that make this process costly. First, it is difficult to determine one's water (say, vis-à-vis electricity) use during the month because water meters are generally more difficult to read. This makes it difficult for the consumer to know when she has switched from one block to another. A second difficulty faced by water consumers is the inclusion of a sewage charge in their water bill which may or may not be shown separately. The consumer may also confuse the sanitation (solid waste) charge with the sewage charge. Also, many sewage charges are determined by winter usage, but consumers may be unaware of this rule.

If the expected marginal benefit of learning the true nature of the rate schedule is less than the expected marginal cost, it is likely that the consumer will react to some proxy marginal price, such as an ex post calculated average price, from a recent bill, as Shin (1985) notes. However, if the expected marginal benefits are greater than the expected marginal costs, the consumer will investigate the problem more carefully and will probably react to the true rate schedule. If the consumer stops searching for information when expected marginal benefit equals expected marginal cost, perceived price (P^*) may lie between marginal and average price since some part of the difference variable may be embedded in the perceived price. P^* is a function of the marginal price, average price, and a price perception parameter, k, as follows:

$$P^* = MP(AP/MP)^k \tag{1}$$

The price perception parameter, k, shown in equation (1), is expected to be nonnegative. If the consumer only responds to MP, then $k = 0$. If the consumer only responds to AP, then $k = 1$. If the perceived price is between AP and MP, then $0 < k < 1$. However if k is greater than one or less than zero, it has different interpretations under different block structures. In a *decreasing* block rate scheme, $k > 1$ implies that $P^* > AP > MP$, and $k < 0$ implies that $P^* < MP < AP$. However, in an *increasing* block rate scheme (with a relatively small fixed charge), $k > 1$ implies that $P^* < AP < MP$, and $k < 0$ implies that $P^* > MP > AP$ (see Nieswiadomy and Molina 1991 for further discussion and diagrams).

The model in this paper is specified in equation (2). It should be noted that another variable (often called the difference variable or rate structure premium) is sometimes used in the marginal price model, as described by Nordin (1976), to account for the effect of fixed fees and infra-marginal prices. Theoretically it should be equal in magnitude and opposite in sign of the income effect. It does not enter Shin's (1985) model directly, because it affects the consumer's perception of price rather than entering the analysis through an income effect.

$$\ln Q = \beta_0 + \beta_1 \ln Marpws + \beta_1 k \ln(Avgpws/Marpws) + \beta_2 \ln Perinc$$

$$+ \beta_3 \ln Rain + \beta_4 \ln Temp + \beta_5 \ln Pop \qquad (2)$$

where Q is the average summer monthly water use (in thousands of gallons) per capita per day in the city,[6] *Marpws* is the combined marginal price of water and sewage, *Avgpws/Margpws* is the ratio of average price of water and sewage to the marginal price, *Perinc* is the per capita income of the city, *Rain* is the average monthly rainfall for June–August 1993, *Temp* is the average monthly temperature for June–August 1993, and *Pop* is the number of customers served by the utility. Note that the marginal price (*Marpws*) model is specified similarly as the Shin model (equation (2)), with the exception that the *Avgpws/Margpws* variable is not included. The average price model is specified similarly as the marginal price model, with the exception that the average price (*Avgpws*) variable is substituted for *Margpws*.

One econometric issue of model specification that must be considered is the potential endogeneity of several variables. The potential endogeneity of the price variables (depending on which model is used) will be tested with a Hausman (1978) statistic. The Hausman test utilizes the result that the OLS estimator will be consistent and asymptotically efficient under the null hypothesis that the price variables are exogenous, but will be inconsistent under the alternative hypothesis. The instrumental variable estimators will be consistent under both the null and alternative hypotheses, but will not be asymptotically efficient under the null hypothesis. The test statistic is $m = \mathbf{b}' (V_{iv} - V_{ols})^{-1} \mathbf{b}$, where $\mathbf{b} = b_{iv} - b_{ols}$, and V_{iv} and V_{ols} are variance-covariance estimates under instrumental variable and OLS techniques, respectively. This statistic has an asymptotic chi-square distribution with degrees of freedom equal to the number of explanatory variables.

IV. RESULTS

The estimates are presented in Tables 2–4 for cities using increasing block rates, uniform block rates, and the overall data set. The models were estimated with both OLS and 2SLS techniques for each of the three types of models. However, the Hausman test statistics were insignificant for all rate structures for all models, implying that endogeneity is not a problem. The insignificant Hausman test statistics probably are due to the cross-sectional nature of the data. As noted above, the endogeneity problem is more likely to show up in data sets on individual customers facing the same rate structures. Thus, the OLS estimates are efficient and are the appropriate ones to use for the analysis in this paper.

Another specification issue was also addressed. The use of the Shin (1985) model for testing the reactions of consumers to marginal and average prices implicitly relies on the assumption that a log-log model

Table 2. Water Demand Estimates: Increasing Block Rate Structures

Variable	OLS Estimates			2SLS Estimates		
	Average	*Marginal*	*Shin*	*Average*	*Marginal*	*Shin*
Constant	−22.25	−31.72	−19.97	−26.63	−31.41	−32.07
	(−1.48)	(−2.00)	(−1.29)	(−1.88)	(−2.18)	(−1.96)
Lnmarpws		−0.17	−0.29		−0.20	−0.20
		(−1.55)	(−2.48)		(−1.75)	(−1.49)
Lnapmp			−0.41			0.02
			(−2.38)			(0.09)
Lnavgpws	−0.31			−0.19		
	(−2.82)			(−1.57)		
Lnperinc	0.23	0.20	0.22	0.20	0.21	0.21
	(1.89)	(1.51)	(1.80)	(1.76)	(1.71)	(1.68)
Lnrain	−0.25	−0.23	−0.23	−0.22	−0.25	−0.24
	(−2.75)	(−2.19)	(−2.36)	(−2.44)	(−2.47)	(−2.44)
Lntemp	5.83	7.99	5.33	6.85	7.91	8.06
	(1.69)	(2.20)	(1.50)	(2.10)	(2.40)	(2.16)
Lnpop	0.004	0.000	0.004	0.001	0.000	0.000
	(0.11)	(0.00)	(0.12)	(0.05)	(0.02)	(0.01)
N	34	34	34	34	34	34
R^2	0.48	0.39	0.49	0.46	0.39	0.37
Hausman test				4.49	1.58	4.78
Shin's k			1.44			−0.12
$H_0{:}k = 0$			1.44			−0.12
			(5.40)			(−0.08)
$H_0{:}k = 1$			0.44			−1.12
			(1.65)			(−0.75)

Table 3. Water Demand Estimates: Uniform Block Rate Structures

	OLS Estimates			2SLS Estimates		
Variable	Average	Marginal	Shin	Average	Marginal	Shin
Constant	12.25	11.63	12.22	11.63	11.63	11.67
	(1.43)	(1.34)	(1.40)	(1.43)	(1.43)	(1.43)
Lnmarpws		−0.15	−0.18		−0.15	−0.15
		(−1.95)	(−2.12)		(−1.73)	(−1.53)
Lnapmp			−0.20			−0.017
			(−0.86)			(−0.05)
Lnavgpws	−0.18			−0.16		
	(−2.16)			(−1.70)		
Lnperinc	0.29	0.28	0.29	0.28	0.28	0.28
	(2.33)	(2.24)	(2.30)	(2.44)	(2.41)	(2.40)
Lnrain	−0.37	−0.38	−0.36	−0.37	−0.38	−0.38
	(−4.82)	(−4.94)	(−2.30)	(−5.22)	(−5.34)	(−4.98)
Lntemp	−2.13	−1.99	−2.12	−1.98	−1.99	−1.99
	(−1.09)	(1.01)	(−1.07)	(−1.07)	(−1.07)	(−1.07)
Lnpop	0.033	0.032	0.033	0.032	0.032	0.032
	(1.38)	(1.32)	(1.36)	(1.44)	(1.42)	(1.42)
N	41	41	41	41	41	41
R^2	0.52	0.51	0.52	0.52	0.51	0.51
Hausman test				0.21	0.000	0.55
Shin's k			1.11			0.11
$H_0{:}k = 0$			1.11			0.11
			(7.68)			(0.05)
$H_0{:}k = 1$			0.44			−0.89
			(0.77)			(−0.42)

(as opposed to say a linear model) is appropriate. Thus, the demand equations (using marginal price or average price) were estimated using a Box-Cox transformation (see Kmenta 1986, pp. 518–519 for a discussion of the Box-Cox test). In all cases, the likelihood ratio tests rejected the null hypothesis of linearity, but failed to reject the null hypothesis of log-log. Thus, it appears that a log-log model is a reasonably appropriate form to use for this Texas data set.

The hypothesis tests concerning Shin's (1985) price perception parameter, k, are shown at the bottom of each column in Tables 2–4. First it should be noted that for uniform price structures, there is only one marginal price. Average price only differs from marginal price due to the existence of the fixed fee. In Table 3 customers appear to react to average prices when faced with a uniform block structure. But since the rate structure is flat this is not an extremely interesting result. In Table 2,

Table 4. Water Demand Estimates: All Rate Structures

	OLS Estimates			2SLS Estimates		
Variable	Average	Marginal	Shin	Average	Marginal	Shin
Constant	5.02	3.07	4.98	4.25	4.43	3.35
	(0.84)	(0.50)	(0.84)	(0.72)	(0.73)	(0.49)
Lnmarpws		-0.13	-0.20		-0.18	-0.14
		(-2.19)	(-3.33)		(-2.57)	(-1.56)
Lnapmp			-0.37			0.29
			(-2.90)			(0.95)
Lnavgpws	-0.21			-0.17		
	(-3.37)			(-2.27)		
Lnperinc	0.27	0.25	0.26	0.26	0.26	0.26
	(3.17)	(2.88)	(3.15)	(3.17)	(3.10)	(2.74)
Lnrain	-0.33	-0.33	-0.31	-0.33	-0.35	-0.37
	(-5.99)	(-5.62)	(-5.48)	(-6.01)	(-5.94)	(-5.37)
Lntemp	-0.44	0.01	-0.41	-0.26	-0.32	-0.09
	(-0.32)	(0.01)	(-0.31)	(-0.19)	(-0.23)	(-0.06)
Lnpop	0.025	0.024	0.022	0.024	0.026	0.03
	(1.39)	(1.29)	(1.27)	(1.38)	(1.45)	(1.40)
N	83	83	83	83	83	83
R^2	0.42	0.37	0.43	0.42	0.37	0.22
Hausman test				0.49	1.86	0.55
Shin's k			1.84			-2.08
$H_0:k = 0$			1.84			-2.08
			(3.42)			(-0.31)
$H_0:k = 1$			0.84			-3.08
			(1.57)			(-0.45)

where customers are faced with increasing block prices, this becomes a more interesting question. However, the customers definitely do not react to marginal prices since k is significantly greater than zero (t-value of 5.4). However, k is also moderately significantly greater than one ($t = 1.65$, p value $= 0.09$). Thus, we can conclude that customers may be reacting to average prices, but the evidence is weak. They certainly are not reacting to marginal prices, at least for this data set. In Table 4, where all cities are considered, a similar comment regarding price awareness holds. Customers are not reacting to marginal price, and there is weak evidence that they are reacting to average price.

Due to the lack of significance of the Hausman statistic, the OLS estimates in Table 2 provide the appropriate estimates of water demand under the marginal, average, and Shin models. The estimated coefficients are generally similar for all three models except for the price variables. The average price model yields an estimate of −0.31 for the price elasticity of demand, while the marginal price model yields an estimate of -0.17 for the price elasticity of demand. The average price model's price elasticity (-0.31) estimate is quite similar to Griffin and Chang's (1989) estimated summer elasticities which ranged from -0.24 to -0.38 and which were higher than in the winter months.

Once again, due to the lack of significance of the Hausman statistic, the OLS estimates in Table 3 provide the appropriate estimates of water demand under the marginal, average and Shin models. The estimated coefficients are generally similar for all three models including the price variables. The average price model yields an estimate of -0.18 for the price elasticity of demand, while the marginal price model yields an estimate of -0.15 for the price elasticity of demand. The average price model's price elasticity (-0.18) estimate is smaller than Griffin and Chang's (1989) estimated summer elasticities which ranged from -0.24 to -0.38. However, Griffin and Chang (1989) did not estimate their models for different block structures. Thus, it is interesting to note that the price elasticities are larger (in absolute value) when customers are faced with increasing block rates. In fact, this is the reason that many utilities have commenced adopting block rates. They want their customers to be more aware of prices and to conserve water.

The non-price variables generally have the expected signs. Income clearly has a positive effect on water use and its coefficient is highly significant. Rich suburban consumers consume more water in the summer, ceteris paribus. The coefficient on rainfall is also always significant and is negatively related to water use. The temperature variable has a strong positive effect for those cities facing increasing block rates, but has no significant effect for the uniform block rate cities. The population variable is not significant for the increasing block rate cities. However, population has weakly positive effect for uniform block rate cities. This seems to indicate that per capita use is higher in the larger cities. Perhaps there is "social pressure" to keep one's lawn as green as one's neighbor or perhaps lawns are more important to consumers in a crowded urban environment.

V. CONCLUSIONS

Water availability will continue to be of paramount importance in growing urban environments. Thus, water planners need to carefully model the water demands of customers. No longer will it be a needs-based approach, which assumes that each customer consumes/needs a fixed amount of water. Research has shown that customers will respond to higher prices. This study has shown that the price, income, and rainfall are all important explanatory variables. The estimate price elasticity appears to be higher in cities that use increasing block rates (−0.31) versus cities that use uniform rates (−0.17). This seems to indicate that consumers respond more to price signals when faced with an increasing block rate schedule. Thus, increasing block rate schedules will continue to be used to encourage water conservation. On the other hand, decreasing block structures are so seldom used in Texas that their impact cannot be estimated.

The puzzle of consumer price perception cannot be solved in one study. This study seems to indicate that consumers react more to average price than marginal price. This finding is somewhat surprising given that the elasticity of demand is greater (in absolute value) for cities that use increasing block rates, which rely on higher *marginal* prices to discourage use. Furthermore, it should be noted that the price elasticities are rather small in comparison to other consumer goods. However, as the price of water continues to rise, the price elasticity will most likely rise.

NOTES

1.   The difference variable coefficient usually has not been significant or, if significant, it has been much larger in absolute value than the income coefficient. In the case of increasing block rates, Schefter (1987) has shown that one reason for the lack of success of the Nordin model may be that marginal price is a faulty transmitter of marginal willingness to pay if the customer is at or near a block boundary. However, this data set uses aggregate data for each city, not individual customer data.

2.   Martin and colleagues (1984) perform an interesting analysis of an increasing block rate micro data set for Tucson, Arizona but do not statistically estimate a demand equation. See Hall (1996) for a review of the water demand literature.

3.   It is common for declining block rate schedules to include a limited amount of water at zero marginal price with a monthly minimum charge. Technically, these schedules have an increasing part (at a discontinuous point). However, this is a relatively minor problem.

4.   Many earlier studies focused on the difference in the signals sent to customers under increasing versus decreasing block rates. However, very few Texas cities now use decreasing rates. Increasing block rates have become very common and are used almost as often as uniform rates.

5.   This methodology section utilizes heavily the discussion of the Shin (1985) model from Nieswiadomy and Molina (1991) and Nieswiadomy (1992).

6.   The average household had 3.3 persons.

REFERENCES

Agthe, D.E., B.R. Billings, J.L. Dobra, and R. Kambizz. 1986. "A Simultaneous Equation Model for Block Rates." *Water Resources Research* (January): 1–4.

Billings, R.B., and D.E. Agthe. 1980. "Price Elasticities for Water: A Case of Increasing Block Rates." *Land Economics* (February): 73–84.

Chicoine, D.L., and G. Ramamurthy. 1986. "Evidence on the Specification of Price in the Study of Domestic Water Demand." *Land Economics* (February): 26–32.

Chicoine, D.L., S.C. Deller, and G. Ramamurthy. 1986. "Water Demand Estimation Under Block Rate Pricing: A Simultaneous Equation Approach." *Water Resources Research* (June): 859–863.

Danielson, L.E. 1979. "An Analysis of Residential Demand for Water Using Micro Time–Series Data." *Water Resources Research* (August): 763–767.

Deller, S.C., D.L. Chicoine, and G. Ramamurthy. 1986. "Instrumental Variables Approach to Rural Water Service Demand." *Southern Economic Journal* (October): 333–46.

Foster, H.S., Jr., and B. Beattie. 1979. "Urban Residential Demand for Water in the United States." *Land Economics* (February): 43–58.

Foster, H.S., Jr., and B. Beattie. 1981. "Urban Residential Demand for Water in the United States: Reply." *Land Economics* (May): 257–265.

Gottlieb, M. 1963. "Urban Domestic Demand for Water: A Kansas Case Study." *Land Economics* (May): 204–210.

Griffin, R.C., and C. Chang. 1989. "Community Water Demand in Texas." Texas Water Resources Institute Report, April.

Hall, D. 1996. *Advances in the Economics of Environmental Resources: Marginal Cost Rate Design and Wholesale Water Markets*. Greenwich CT: JAI Press, Inc.

Hanke, S., and L. de Mare. 1982. "Residential Water Demand: A Pooled, Time Series, Cross Section Study of Malmo, Sweden." *Water Resources Bulletin* (August): 621–625.

Hausman, J.A. 1978. "Specification Tests in Econometrics." *Econometrica* (November): 1251–1271.

Henson, S. 1984. "Electricity Demand Estimates Under Increasing Block Rates." *Southern Economic Journal* (July): 147–156.

Hewitt, J.A., and W.M. Hanemann. 1995. "A Discrete/Continuous Choice Approach to Residential Water Demand under Block Rate Pricing." *Land Economics* (May): 173–192.

Howe, C.W. 1982. "Impact of Price on Residential Water Demand: Some New Insights." *Water Resources Research* (August): 713–716.

Jones, C.V., and J.R. Morris. 1984. "Instrumental Price Estimates and Residential Water Demand." *Water Resources Research* (February): 197–202.

Kmenta, J. 1986. *Elements of Econometrics*. New York: Macmillan Publishing Company.

Martin, W.E. et al. 1984. *Saving Water in a Desert City*. Washington DC: Resources for the Future.

McFadden, D., C. Puig, and D. Kirschner. 1977. "Determinants of the Long-Run Demand for Electricity." Proceedings of the American Statistical Association, Business and Economic Section, Part I, August, 109–113.

Mercer, L.J., and D.W. Morgan. 1985. "Conservation Using a Rate of Return Decision Rule: Some Examples from California Municipal Water Departments." *Water Resources Research* 21 (7): 927–933.

Moncur, J. 1987. "Urban Water Pricing and Drought Management." *Water Resources Research* 23 (3): 393–398.

Nieswiadomy, M.L., and D.J. Molina. 1989. "Comparing Residential Water Demand Estimates under Decreasing and Increasing Block Rates Using Household Data." *Land Economics* 65 (3): 280–289.

Nieswiandomy, M.L., and D.J. Molina. 1991. "A Note on Price Perception in Water Demand Models." *Land Economics* 67 (3): 352–59.

Nieswiadomy, M.L. 1992. Estimating Urban Residential Water Demand: Effects of Pricing Structure, Conservation, and Education, *Water Resources Research* 28 (3): 609–615.

Nieswiadomy, M.L., and C. Stuewe. 1996. "Evaluation of Water Conservation Programs of Texas Public Water Suppliers." Proceedings of Conserv96: Responsible Water Stewardship, American Water Works Association, January 4–6.

Nordin, J.A. 1976. "A Proposed Modification on Taylor's Demand Analysis: Comment." *The Bell Journal of Economics* (Autumn): 719–721.

Opaluch, J.J. 1982. "Urban Residential Demand for Water in the United States: Further Discussion." *Land Economics* (May): 224–227.

Schefter, J.E. 1987. "Increasing Block Rate Tariffs as Faulty Transmitters of Marginal Willingness to Pay." *Land Economics* (February): 21–33.

Schefter, J.E., and E.L. David. 1985. "Estimating Residential Water Demand under Multi-Part Tariffs Using Aggregate Data." *Land Economics* (August): 272–280.

Shin, J-S. 1985. "Perception of Price When Information is Costly: Evidence from Residential Electricity Demand." *Review of Economic and Statistics* (November): 591–598.

Stevens, T.H., J. Miller, and C. Willis. 1992. "Effect of Price Structure on Residential Water Demand." *Water Resources Research* (August): 681–685.

Taylor, L.D. 1975. "The Demand for Electricity: A Survey." *The Bell Journal of Economics* (Spring): 74–110.

Terza, J.V., and W.P. Welch. 1982. "Estimating Demand Under Block Rates: Electricity and Water." *Land Economics* 58 (2): 181–188.

Terza, J.V. 1986. "Determinants of Household Electricity Demand: A Two-Stage Probit Approach." *Southern Economic Journal* (April): 1131–1139.

U.S. Weather Bureau. 1993. *Climatological Data, Texas.* Asheville, NC: National Oceanic and Atmospheric Administration.

Wilder, R.P., and J.R. Willenborg. 1975. "Residential Demand for Electricity: A Consumer Panel Approach." *Southern Economic Journal* (October): 212–217.

Young, R.A. 1973. "Price Elasticity of Demand for Municipal Water: Case Study of Tucson, Arizona." *Water Resources Research* (December): 1068–1072.

DEMAND AND REVENUE
ELASTICITIES AND INCREASING
BLOCK RATE PRICING OF
RESIDENTIAL WATER SERVICES

Julie A. Hewitt

ABSTRACT

Employing an increasing block rate is a means for a utility to provide its customers
with an incentive to conserve. Water utilities have been slow to adopt increasing
block (IB) rates, in part because of difficulties inherent in estimating and predicting
consumption and utility revenue under IB rates—difficulties not present under
simpler rate structures. A discrete/continuous choice model of household demand
for water under IB rates that addresses such difficulties is presented and estimated.
This model is then used in micro simulation to predict consumption and revenue—
and associated elasticities—under a continuum of rate changes. These predictions
allow utility management to better choose rates which meet their goals with respect
to conservation and revenue. The methodology employed is based on data a water
utility will generally have access to, and does not require a water utility to be
currently using IB rates to forecast household behavior under IB rates.

Advances in Business and Management Forecasting, Volume 2, pages 77–100.
Copyright © 1998 by JAI Press Inc.
All rights of reproduction in any form reserved.
ISBN: 0-7623-0002-7

Economists have long argued that markets are institutions which efficiently transmit, through price, information about the relative scarcity of commodities: excess demand causes prices to rise while excess supply causes prices to fall. However, commodities such as water are sold at prices that are determined administratively. As administrative prices do not necessarily respond to forces for change, like market prices must, periods of excess demand or excess supply may occur. Water utility managers are nonetheless expected to cope with periods of excess supply or demand.

Water utility managers have two types of tools with which to deal with excess demand, in particular.[1] Engineering solutions enable people to use less water to accomplish the same ends, but when offered by a utility to its customers, tend to result in costly programs if they are to be effective. Price incentives can both reduce demand for the ends for which water is a means, as well as induce private undertaking of engineering solutions. Determining the optimal combination of reliance on these two tools depends critically on determining how responsive consumers are to price. This chapter is about the efficacy of price incentives, specifically when price households face is an increasing block rate. Increasing block rates involve a higher marginal price (volume charge) for consumption beyond a threshold than the pre-threshold marginal price.[2]

The narrow focus on increasing block (IB) rates is due to the fact that IB rates introduce some interesting problems for econometric estimation of demand and prediction. Briefly, one difficulty in estimating the demand function is that marginal price and quantity demanded are co-determined. Dealing with this difficulty will also be important for purposes of predicting consumption due to a rate change.

Although there is little attempt in the empirical analysis that follows to control for the effects of engineering solutions (e.g., noting whether households have standard, low-flush, or composting toilets), this is not meant to deny the importance of doing so. The analysis that follows uses only information that a utility can gather *without* resorting to an expensive household survey or audit program. The data employed are billing data, supplemented by tax assessment data.[3] A utility that undertakes the collection of survey data will be rewarded with a model that explains more of the variation in consumption than the example that follows, and forecast accuracy will also improve. A utility's choice in the tradeoff between accuracy and expense will depend on the utility's situation. Furthermore, the model below is amenable to improvements that other authors of this volume have proposed.

The paper begins with a brief discussion of the demand model appropriate for households facing IB rates (the two-error discrete/continuous choice model), followed by a description of the data and estimation. A methodology for prediction is outlined and then employed in the section on elasticities—measurements of behavioral changes that are likely to be of great interest to utility decision makers. The final section discusses how this model may be employed by water utilities not currently employing block rate pricing.

I. A MODEL OF DEMAND UNDER INCREASING BLOCK RATE PRICING

The academic literature on residential water demand began to focus in the 1970s on block rates and the appropriate specification of demand when households face a price schedule. When a block rate is in effect the household chooses both its consumption amount, and given the rate schedule, the price it pays for the marginal unit. Many authors recognized the difficulties in econometric estimation implied by the co-determination of price and quantity. One type of solution involved basing quantity on average price, to reflect the fact that some households pay a higher price for some units than others, with average price sometimes decomposed into marginal price and a *difference* variable (see Billings and Agthe 1980; Foster and Beattie 1981; Opaluch 1982). A second solution was to employ a simultaneous equations approach to estimation (see Houston 1982; Jones and Morris 1984; Nieswiadomy and Molina 1988, 1989). Still, the estimation of both types of models often resulted in an upward sloping demand curve. An explanation for their counterintuitive results is that these models are reduced form models, estimating conditional demands, or quantity demanded, conditional upon locating in the kth block and paying the kth marginal price. Thus, econometric estimation of these models identified the positive relationship between price and quantity that is implied by an IB rate, rather than the structure of demand.

By treating demand as a combination of discrete and continuous choices, Hewitt and Hanemann (1995) were able to demonstrate the expected negative relationship between price and quantity demanded. Their model does so by explicitly incorporating the intimate relationship between price and quantity that is the block rate price schedule, so that the relationship between price and quantity that is the demand curve can be teased from the data.[4] The discrete choice is the choice of block in which to consume (and hence marginal price to pay), while the continuous choice is the choice of the level of consumption, conditional of course, upon the marginal price associated with the discrete choice.

The discrete/continuous (D/C) choice approach leads to a more complex and resource-intensive estimation procedure than standard demand estimation; this is the cost of removing the bias of other estimation methods. By explaining only continuous demand conditional on consuming in a particular block, the reduced form models don't explain the discrete block choice, but take the observed choice as fixed. The reduced form models do not then allow for rate changes to induce a household to switch blocks, although surely such a household reaction is possible. Thus, an added benefit to using the D/C choice approach is that it leads to more accurate prediction, ceteris paribus, relative to the reduced form models, because the discrete choice is modeled.

When IB rates are in effect, households face a piecewise linear budget constraint. Their behavior is modeled *as if* they divide the multiply priced budget set into a number of singly priced and individually convex budget subsets. The household then determines the continuous choice or utility maximizing point within each convex budget subset, that is, conditional on being restricted to that budget subset. Next, a comparison is made of the (indirect) utility associated with each of the conditional continuous choices. The budget subset associated with the *maximum maximorum* of these utility levels constitutes the discrete choice of the household, and the continuous choice is the conditional continuous choice of that subset. The discrete and continuous choices are thus intimately connected—the continuous choice is necessarily located in the discrete choice budget subset.

To formalize the heuristic description of household behavior, let x be a good which is priced according to a block rate structure. Suppose also that this rate is a two-block, increasing rate. Let p_k be the marginal price of consumption in the kth block; let x_1 denote the boundary point between the two blocks; let y denote income. Denote the Marshallian demand which is the solution to utility maximization subject to a standard linear budget constraint with a single price, p, as $x^*(p,y)$. The description of household behavior above implies that the budget constraint is linearized; such linearization produces budget constraints with different apparent (or virtual) incomes. Denote virtual income for the kth block by $y + d_k$, where d_k is the *difference* between linearized income and actual income, y. Note that *difference* will include the negative of the fixed charge (*FC*), should the rate structure contain one. Thus, d_1 is exactly $-FC$, while $d_2 = FC + (p_2 - p_1)x_1$. A theorem due to Hausman (1979) greatly simplifies the statement of demand in a D/C choice framework. Hausman's theorem essentially states that when the block rate is increasing (hence the budget set is convex though piecewise linear), if $x^*(p_k, y + d_k)$ is in the interior of the kth block, then this solution is not only a statement of the conditional continuous choice, but also the *maximum maximorum*. Thus, the full demand expression for x is:

$$x = \begin{cases} x^*(p_1, y + d_1) & \text{if } x^*(p_1, y + d_1) < x_1 \\ x_1 & \text{if } x_1 \leq x^*(p_1, y + d_1) \text{ and } x^*(p_2, y + d_2) \leq x_1 \\ x^*(p_2, y + d_2) & \text{if } x_1 \leq x^*(p_2, y + d_2). \end{cases} \quad (1)$$

The left-hand portion of each line of (1) is the conditional continuous choice, while the right-hand portion describes the condition in which the particular discrete choice is made.[5] This expression is deterministic; the inclusion of error terms transforms this expression into an econometric model.

The rationale usually proffered for including an error term in an otherwise deterministic regression model is to pick up the influence of omitted and unobservable variables as well as other misspecification in the model. An adaptation of this rationale will also justify the stochastic model used here. Characterizing "the" dependent variable (consumption) as having two decision components suggests that there is likely to be an error component in the modeling of each. In the standard demand context, although there may be several sources of error, they cannot be separately identified. The structure of the demand expression in the block rate case allows the identification of separate error terms.

Neither discrete nor continuous choices are directly observable in actual consumption data. The discrete choice can only be indirectly inferred ex post from the observed continuous choice.[6] Even if consumption could be directly observed without error, unless the functional form and independent variables are known to the econometrician without error, econometric expression of the conditional continuous choice introduces specification error in some fashion. Furthermore, it is not likely that consumption is measured without error, due to meter error and rounding of consumption amounts. In fact, because of these errors, the intimate connection between the discrete and continuous choices can no longer be assumed to hold. That is, a particular household might choose an unconditional consumption level very near but above the upper limit of the first block, implying a discrete choice of block two. However, due to meter error, their consumption level might appear to be just below the upper limit of the first block, and hence imply a discrete choice of the first block. Though the error associated with the continuous choice may not be great, the discrete choice is now incorrectly characterized according to the ex post observed continuous choice.

Furthermore, there are sources of errors that the household has limited control over. These sources of error are part of the error term attached to the continuous choice expression—called the perception error—and include leaks as well as the aforementioned meter error and rounding error.[7] The perception error thus separates planned consumption from actual consumption.[8] Planned consumption, which drives the discrete choice, contains an error term whose sole explanation is that the econometrician cannot perfectly describe household heterogeneity. Thus, planned consumption is known to the household, but unobserved and imperfectly modeled by the econometrician. The error term associated with the discrete choice is thus referred to as the heterogeneity error term. Planned consumption drives the discrete choice: if planned consumption is in the range of the first block, then the first block is the discrete choice. Actual consumption, defined as planned consumption times a multiplicative (plus an additive) error term, is the conditional continuous choice expression.

Let the heterogeneity error term be denoted by ε, and the perception error term by η. The demand expression that results from utility maximization subject to a piecewise linear budget constraint, including multiplicative error terms as described above, is:

$$x = \begin{cases} x^* (p_1, y + d_1)\varepsilon\eta & \text{if } \varepsilon < x_1/x^* (p_1, y + d_1) \\ x_1 \eta & \text{if } x_1/x^* (p_1, y + d_1) \leq \varepsilon \leq x_1/x^* (p_2, y + d_2) \\ x^* (p_2, y + d_2)\varepsilon\eta & \text{if } x_1/x^* (p_2, y + d_2) < \varepsilon \end{cases} \quad (2)$$

The right-hand side of each line of (2) expresses the discrete choice, based on planned consumption and heterogeneity error, which here is the product, $x^*(\cdot)\varepsilon$. This error also appears in the continuous choice expressions on the left-hand side, because the continuous choice is expressed by planned consumption times the perception error, when planned consumption is in the interior of a block. When planned consumption at p_1 and $y + d_1$ falls outside block one and planned consumption at p_2 and $y + d_2$ falls outside block two, then the utility maximizing planned consumption is exactly at the kink point, x_1. However, a nonzero perception error can still cause actual consumption to differ from the planned consumption at x_1.

A heuristic expression of the likelihood function of an observation of demand in (2) is as follows:

$$Pr(x) = f_{\epsilon\eta}(x/\bar{x}^1) \, F_{\epsilon}(x_1/\bar{x}^1) + f_{\eta}(x/x_1) \, [F_{\epsilon}(x_1/\bar{x}^2) - F_{\epsilon}(x_1/\bar{x}^1)]$$

$$+ f_{\epsilon\eta}(x/\bar{x}^2) \, [1 - F_{\epsilon}(x_1/\bar{x}^2)]. \tag{3}$$

The inclusion of the perception error term, η, severs the intimate relationship between the discrete and continuous choices; the econometric implication is that there is no sample separation. That is, every observation must be treated as if it was the result of each of the three discrete choices, in concert with a perception error large or small enough to support the observed consumption value. As such, there is not a separate likelihood attributed to observed consumption less than, equal to, and greater than x_1. Thus does (3) represent the likelihood of each and every observation.

With the likelihood of an observation of quantity demanded using the D/C choice model expressed in (3), I turn now to the empirical application, including functional and distributional assumptions.

II. THE DATA AND ESTIMATION RESULTS

The functional and distributional assumptions made here to fully specify (3) are due to the skewed nature of the dependent variable in the data set used. It is assumed here that ϵ and η are independently lognormally distributed, and that they are multiplicative errors. Furthermore, it is assumed that household tastes and preferences are such that the Marshallian demand function is exponential, and may be expressed in a semilogarithmic transformation. The data are originally due to Nieswiadomy and Molina (1988, 1989), and are the same, with the exceptions noted below.

Generally, the differences in the data used in estimation were dictated by differences in the underlying economic models the data were used to estimate, and are not improvements to the Nieswiadomy and Molina (N&M) data set. Although the N&M data set is a pooled cross-section time series of monthly observations of 121 households in Denton, Texas, over 10 years, this study uses only 1,703 observations: those from the months of June, July, and August, from 1981 to 1985—the periods with two-block increasing block rates in effect. Table 1 shows summary statistics of the subset of the data used. As in N&M, a proxy for income is constructed from the value of the home for tax assessment purposes and, for this study, the monthly income is converted to a billing period equivalent, using the number of days in a billing period. As constructed, income is assumed to reflect real income and hence is not deflated.[9] Prices, and hence, the calculated *difference* variables were originally in nominal terms and are thus deflated. Lawn size is constructed as the lot size minus one-half the house size.[10] Finally, the number of bathrooms and days in the billing period were used as variables in this study though they proved insignificant in N&M.

The use of the variable number of days per billing period bears some explanation. In their studies, N&M convert the dependent variable, x, to a 30-day equivalent for consistency. The water utility does not do the same, however, when determining a household's bill. The longer the billing period, the higher the probability that a household consumes in the second block and pays the higher marginal price, ceteris paribus. The weather variable is exactly as constructed by N&M, and measures in inches the potential evapotranspiration for Bermuda grass less actual rainfall, with both potential evapotranspiration and actual rainfall based on observed daily weather for the days comprising each household's billing period.

Table 1. Descriptive Statistics for June to August Dataset

Variable Name	Units[a]	Means	Standard Deviations	Minimum	Maximum
x	1000 gals	14.966	12.435	0.1	212.8
y	$1000	1.156	0.485	0.137	2.967
lawn	1000 sq ft	9.887	3.383	4.61	25.96
weather	inches	0.464	0.149	-0.1004	0.6324
bathrooms	number	1.635	0.520	1	3
house size	100 sq ft	18.337	5.288	4.44	36.11
days	number	30.508	2.786	4	62
p_1	$/1000 gals	1.206	0.090	1.09	1.34
p_2	$/1000 gals	1.442	0.147	1.25	1.67
x_1	1000 gals	20.000	.0000	20	20
d_1	$1000	-0.03346	0.00740	-0.04611	-0.00667
d_2	$1000	-0.02873	0.00630	-0.03964	-0.00019

Note: [a]The variables x, y, weather, and days are all on a billing period rather than monthly or 30-day basis.

One final assumption is that sociodemographic variables enter the model so as to help explain why households facing the same prices and with similar incomes are observed to consume different quantities of water, though the same utility function is used to describe their behavior. The sociodemographic variables are arrayed in the matrix Z, and $\exp(Z\delta)$ enters the Marshallian demand as a constant of proportionality.

Taking the logarithm of x implies taking the logarithm of ε and η. If these terms are lognormally distributed, then their logarithms, $\varepsilon^* = \ln(\varepsilon)$ and $\eta^* = \ln(\eta)$, are normally distributed. The demand expression from which the likelihood function is constructed is:

$$\ln x = \begin{cases} Z\delta + \alpha p_1 + \mu(y + d_1) + \varepsilon^* + \eta^* & \text{if } \varepsilon^* < \ln x_1 - Z\delta - \alpha p_1 - \mu(y + d_1) \\ \ln x_1 + \eta^* & \text{if } \ln x_1 - Z\delta - \alpha p_1 - \mu(y + d_1) \le \varepsilon^* \le \ln x_1 - Z\delta - \alpha p_2 - \mu(y + d_2) \\ Z\delta + \alpha p_2 + \mu(y + d_2) + \varepsilon^* + \eta^* & \text{if } \ln x_1 - Z\delta - \alpha p_2 - \mu(y + d_2) < \varepsilon^*. \end{cases} \quad (4)$$

The parameters to be estimated are δ, α, μ, σ_{ε^*}, and σ_{η^*}.

The results of estimation are reported in Table 2. There are several things to note about these results. First, as MaCurdy, Green, and Paarsch (1990) have pointed out, the estimates meet the second order condition for utility maximization. The price coefficient is negative while the income coefficient is positive. Intuition, not economic theory per se, suggests that the signs of all the coefficients on the sociodemographic variables included in Z would be positive (weather reflects the lawn water

Table 2. Maximum Likelihood Estimates

Parameter	Estimate	Standard Error	Asymptotic t-Ratio
δ_1: *constant*	1.6790	0.3966	4.2300
δ_2: *lawn*	0.2214	0.0844	2.6240
δ_3: *weather*	1.5856	0.1741	9.1090
δ_4: *bathrooms*	0.1656	0.0663	2.4990
δ_5: *house size*	0.1611	0.1432	1.1250
δ_6: *days*	1.1456	0.2754	4.1600
α	−1.5079	0.2426	−6.2150
μ	0.0778	0.0838	0.9280
σ_{ε}^*	0.8705	0.0287	30.2840
σ_{η}^*	0.3941	0.0447	8.8080
Mean log-likelihood	−1.26457		

needs *not* met by rainfall). The final a priori expectation is that $\sigma_\varepsilon > \sigma_\eta$, which is to say that more of the unexplained variability of observed consumption is due to the econometrician's inability to perfectly characterize heterogeneous preferences than to random impercipience, whether on the part of the econometrician or the household.[11] Finally, with the exception of the coefficients on house size and income, the parameter estimates are asymptotically significantly different than zero. With the estimation of the unknown parameters of demand accomplished, prediction is possible, and the task I now turn toward.

III. PREDICTION

In the linear regression context the hypothesized model, $y = X\beta + \varepsilon$ is estimated to produce parameter estimates, $\hat{\beta}$. If $E(\varepsilon) = 0$, then $E(y) = X\beta$. Also, if $\hat{\beta} = (X'X)^{-1} X'y$ is the estimator of β, X is nonstochastic, and one defines $\hat{y} = X\hat{\beta}$ then $E(\hat{y}) = E(X\hat{\beta}) = X\beta$. Thus $E(y) = E(\hat{y})$, which leads Schmidt (1976, p. 10) to conclude that, for a particular X, $\hat{y} = X\hat{\beta}$ is both an estimator for $E(y) = X\beta$ and a predictor of y. Can one similarly define a combined estimator and predictor for the dependent variable in the two-error D/C choice model?

Although one can define a predictor for our dependent variable, x, it will not lead to as simple an analytical expression as $X\hat{\beta}$. From (2) one can easily evaluate $x^*(p_k, y + d_k)$ at the argument pairs $(p_1, y + d_1)$ and $(p_2, y + d_2)$ with the ML parameter estimates. However, these results are merely predictions of the conditional continuous choices, and do not predict unconditional demand, x, as the left-hand side of (2) expresses. This leaves unanswered the question of which conditional continuous choice to use as the predictor, or how to combine them. The answer to this question depends on the discrete choice conditions, which in turn, depend on the value of ε, which is unknown. Although ε is unknown, one can use the probabilities inherent in the discrete choice expressions as weights on the conditional continuous choices in calculating an unconditional choice. Furthermore, because $E(\eta)$ is greater than one, the conditional continuous choice values will underpredict consumption. Multiplying by $E(\eta)$ will correct this underprediction. The combination of these steps thus taken results in the predictor:

$$\hat{x} = \bar{x}^1 E(\varepsilon | 0 < \varepsilon \leq x_1/\bar{x}^1) E(\eta) + x_1 \Pr(x_1/\bar{x}^1 < \varepsilon \leq x_1/\bar{x}^2) E(\eta)$$

$$+ \bar{x}^2 E(\varepsilon | x_1/\bar{x}^2 < \varepsilon) E(\eta) \tag{5}$$

To determine whether the predictor, $\hat{x}$, is also an estimator of $E(x)$, one must look at the expectation of (2).[12] Taking the expectation of x, with respect to ε and η, where $f(\varepsilon, \eta)$ is the joint lognormal distribution yields:

$$E[x] = \exp[Z\delta + \alpha p_1 + \mu(y + d_1)] \times \int_0^\infty \int_0^{x_1/\bar{x}^1} \eta \varepsilon f(\varepsilon, \eta) d\varepsilon \, d\eta$$

$$+ x_1 \int_0^\infty \int_{x_1/\bar{x}^1}^{x_1/\bar{x}^2} \eta f(\varepsilon, \eta) d\varepsilon \, d\eta$$

$$+ \exp[Z\delta + \alpha p_2 + \mu(y + d_2)] \times \int_0^\infty \int_{x_1/\bar{x}^2}^\infty \eta \varepsilon f(\varepsilon, \eta) d\varepsilon \, d\eta \qquad (6)$$

The right-hand sides of (5) and (6) are equivalent, except for the use of the MLE of parameters in (5) and the true parameter values in (6). Using the MLE in lieu of the true unknown parameters leads to the equivalency of (5) and (6), of $\hat{x}$ and $E(x)$, of the predictor of x and the estimator of $E(x)$.

Before employing (5) and (6) one may note a surprising aspect of these expressions. Suppose the expectation in (6) is taken for a household possessing Z and y values representative of households firmly in the lower range of the first block. Suppose also that p_1 is left unchanged, but p_2 is increased (hence, d_2 decreases). Note, however, that p_2 and d_2 do not appear at all in the first line of (6); thus one concludes that this term does not change. Does this imply that this low-consumption household is left unaffected by the rate change? A bit surprisingly and counterintuitively, the answer is no.

Although there is intuitive appeal to concluding that a change in p_2 would have no impact on households previously choosing the first block, this ignores the impact that such a change will have on the discrete choice probabilities for kink point and block two consumption. Even for a low-consumption household, the probabilities of choosing the kink point or block two, although very low, are greater than zero. An increase in p_2 and subsequent decrease in d_2 causes the block two probability to decline and the kink point probability to increase. Consequently, $E[x]$ falls, even for the household which is not very likely to consume anywhere but the first block, although it would, prima facie, appear to be unaffected by this rate change. That $E[x]$ will fall in such a situation is to be expected; however, one would not expect that this decrease would be very great.[13] I now use the prediction method of this section and turn to the estimation of elasticities of interest to utility management.

IV. ELASTICITIES

I begin the discussion of elasticity calculations by noting that demand elasticity is defined as the logarithmic derivative of demand with respect to a determinant of demand, such as price or income. To differentiate the predictor of demand in (5), one must employ the product rule, for the discrete choice probabilities are also influenced by price, income, and other determinants of demand.[14] Thus, an elasticity expression calculated from (5) contains six additive terms: three with conditional continuous choice multiplied by the derivative of discrete choice probability, and three with conditional continuous choice derivative multiplied by the discrete choice probability.

Further inspection also reveals that the values in the elasticity expression are observation dependent, regardless of functional form, due to the observation dependence of the discrete choice probabilities. To make full use of the household data at hand, I numerically predict consumption before and after a rate change, household by household.[15] Elasticities are then calculated as the ratio of the percentage change in estimated consumption to the percentage change in price (or other variate).[16] As the relationship between quantity and bill amount (utility revenue) is not strictly linear under block rate pricing, the standard relationship between elasticity and the direction of change in revenue when price is increased no longer holds.[17] Calculating predicted consumption on a household-by-household basis (via micro-simulation) allows straightforward calculation of bill amounts and revenue the utility can expect to collect under a new rate structure. The level of revenue is of as much—if not greater—concern to municipal water utilities than consumption.

Micro-simulation elasticities, based on all 1,703 observations, are presented in Table 3 for a range of policy experiments, including changes in the rate structure and changes in other explanatory variables, for comparison. The first and third elasticity columns are based on 1% increases, while the second and fourth are based on 10% increases, though all elasticities are reported per percentage point change in the independent variable. The 10% elasticities are reported to demonstrate the nonlinear impact of changes of different magnitudes. The elasticities

Table 3. Elasticity Calculations

Variable Changed	Consumption Amounts		Revenue Streams	
	1% Increase	10% Increase	1% Increase	10% Increase
p_1, p_2 and fixed charge	−1.65980	−1.52079	0.34652	0.35642
p_1 and p_2	−1.65769	−1.51897	−0.27779	−0.26796
p_2	−0.88339	−0.74038	−0.32757	−0.27701
p_1	−0.77433	−0.77885	0.05177	0.02814
fixed charge	−0.00217	−0.00217	0.62430	0.62430
days	1.01047	1.05935	0.39346	0.41660
x_1	0.14733	0.14194	0.04389	0.04433
weather	0.65457	0.67616	0.25712	0.26748
bathrooms	0.24063	0.24362	0.09439	0.09583
lawn	0.19418	0.19616	0.07615	0.07709
house size	0.13122	0.13209	0.05145	0.05185
income	0.08219	0.08256	0.03242	0.03259

are arranged in three groups. The first grouping is of changes the water utility has control over (and taken as given by households), *and* with a negative impact on consumption. Only the block prices and fixed charge and their combinations fall into this category. The second grouping is of changes the water utility has control over, but with a positive impact on consumption. The third grouping is of changes not under the utility's control (and in the case of weather, not under households' control either).[18] Within each grouping, the changes are given in order of most impact to least, where impact is with respect to consumption.

There are several points of note in the table. First, the impact of a change in p_1 plus the impact of a change in p_2 equals (to the fourth decimal place) the impact of equivalent changes in both p_1 and p_2, as one would expect.[19] As the transformation from quantity to revenue is even more nonlinear, the sum of individual revenue impacts is slightly greater (affects the third decimal place) than the revenue impact when the changes are considered simultaneously. When price changes by 1%, the p_2 elasticity is of greater magnitude than the p_1 elasticity, but when price changes by 10%, this reverses. Next, note that when both p_1 and p_2 are increased by 1% with or without a fixed charge change, the quantity response is an elastic −1.66%, while when p_1 or p_2 alone are increased, the impact is inelastic.

Although increasing the fixed charge is akin to decreasing income, the elasticity with respect to the fixed charge is much smaller in absolute value than the income elasticity, because the fixed charge is small relative to income. As well as changing the marginal price for some units sold, increasing x_1 is akin to giving households in the second block a higher income through the *difference* variable. Increasing x_1 by 1% leads to a larger addition to income for most observations than does a 1% decrease in the fixed charge, explaining the larger magnitude of the x_1 elasticity. Increasing x_1 by 1% also leaves households in block one relatively unaffected,[20] so that this elasticity represents the impact on households at and above the kink point, and changes in discrete choice probabilities.

The largest impact on consumption outside of increasing both prices or both prices and the fixed charge is found when the number of days per billing period is increased. This elasticity is somewhat misleading, however, because the utility cannot increase the length of one billing period without reducing the length of another, unless they institute longer, less frequent billing. Such billing would be counter to the recent trend of more frequent billing. Of the explanatory variables not under the direct influence of the water utility, the largest impact is due to weather, not surprisingly. Summer water consumption contains a sizable outdoor usage component which is generally thought to be sensitive to weather.[21] Number of bathrooms and lawn size follow in importance.[22] A utility considering a program of rebates for installing water saving plumbing fixtures or landscaping may be particularly interested in these elasticities.

The differences in the consumption elasticities for 1% and 10% increases are generally not large. With the exception of changing x_1 or p_1, if the elasticity is negative (positive), a 10% change in the independent variable produces a smaller (larger) change per percentage point.

The revenue elasticities reported in Table 3 show some differences from the demand elasticities. Of first note is that p_2 must increase for revenue to fall, though this is not a sufficient condition for revenue to decrease. In the case of both p_1 and p_2 increasing, the lower revenue resulting from higher prices appears to confirm the result that is predicted under a single price. Note, however, that when only p_2 changes, revenue still falls though the demand elasticity in this case appears to be inelastic. This suggests that analysts might do well to place less faith in the magnitude of the demand elasticity as an indicator of demands which are elastic and inelastic, relying instead on whether quantity consumed and revenue change in the same (elastic) or opposite (inelastic) directions.[23] The revenue elasticities are generally smaller in magnitude than the demand elasticities, with one exception. That exception is when the fixed charge is changed. This is not surprising: one would expect that the fixed charge has little influence on consumption (and it does), and so there is little consumption response to offset the increase in revenue due to the larger fixed charge. Of note also is the fact that only when the fixed charge or p_1 is changed do the quantity demanded and revenue collected move in opposite directions. That p_1's effect is similar to the fixed charge is seen by noting that a higher p_1 is much like a higher fixed charge to households in the second block.

V. RATE CHANGES TO ACHIEVE CONSUMPTION AND REVENUE TARGETS

Of much more concern to water utility management than unitless elasticity values would be rate changes whose impacts on consumption and revenue achieve certain targets for these variables. A utility which uses a block rate price schedule has a much more sophisticated tool for fine tuning the incentives households face than a utility which uses the fairly standard two-part tariff. It is prudent to note that the rate experiments conducted in this section are specific to the households sampled for the utility in question, and may not be very useful or applicable for other service areas.

I begin with consumption targets. When a utility feels it necessary to target consumption, it is likely that the target is a lower level of consumption, or a conservation target. To achieve a conservation target via prices only, the utility may raise only p_1, only p_2, both by the same percentage, or both but by different percentages, or possibly, raise one block price while lowering the other. There is a tradeoff in achieving conservation between raising p_1 and p_2, although this tradeoff is not likely to be linear. Figure 1 shows the range of changes in p_1 and p_2, holding all other variables constant (except for their impact on d_2), that achieve two particular conservation targets: 10% and 20%.[24] Note the change in curvature from the 10% iso-conservation curve to the 20% curve. Also, the 20% iso-conservation curve asymptotically approaches the vertical axis—if this utility is to achieve a 20% conservation target, all households can expect to face increased prices, regardless of their discrete choice.

Not shown in Figure 1 is the impact these rate changes have on utility revenue, which varies along the curves. Revenue declines from southeast to northwest along the curve, although consumption is at a constant level. The explanation for this lies in noting which households are conserving

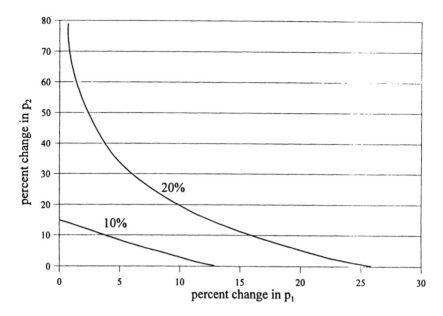

Figure 1. Iso-Conservation Rate Changes

at various points. Toward the northwest end, water conserved is primarily due to conservation of households originally in the second block, while toward the southeast end, the conserved water is due to a combination of the significantly higher price (p_1) for first block households, a somewhat higher price at the margin (p_2) for second block households, and a reduction in income (through d_2) for second block households as they pay the significantly higher p_1 on the inframarginal units. As the per-unit price of water is lower in the first block than the second block, the impact on utility revenue is less negative toward the southeast end.

The revenue impact associated with points along the iso-conservation curves gives further evidence that the standard revenue/elasticity relationship no longer holds. Although the revenue impact is negative everywhere along the 20% curve (ranging from −0.3% to −7%), the impact on revenue is positive, zero, and negative along the 10% iso-conservation curve. At the southeast endpoint the revenue impact is +0.3%, and at the northwest end, it is −3.8%. The revenue-neutral rate change that induces 10% conservation is a 12% increase in p_{11} combined with a 0.8% increase in p_{12}.

VI. PREDICTING THE IMPACT OF BLOCK RATES WHEN BLOCK RATES AREN'T CURRENTLY EMPLOYED

The previous sections assume that block rates are currently in place. How might a utility predict the impact of restructuring rates from uniform to block rates, when their customers have no experience with block rates? To describe how a utility might undertake such prediction, I will assume households have the same utility function as above, so that the Marshallian demand function is the same, although there is only one price (p) and *difference* variable ($d = -FC$). The demand equation is: $x = \exp(Z\delta)p^{\alpha}(y + d)^{\mu}\nu$, where ν is the sole identifiable error term. If the logarithmic version of this equation were estimated, using OLS and assuming that $E[\nu^*] = E[\ln \nu] = 0$, then the parameters recovered from estimation are δ, α, μ, and σ_{ν}. Although the parameters δ, α, and μ are necessary for prediction according to (5), so too are σ_{ε} and σ_{η}, which cannot be gleaned from σ_{ν} alone. Two methods for nonetheless predicting consumption under block rates present themselves. Both are feasible; I will argue that the second approach requires fewer ad hoc assumptions at only a slightly higher cost in terms of estimation of demand based on uniform rate data.

The first approach is essentially to bend the standard demand estimation results so that (5) may be employed directly for prediction. This approach is based on noting that $E[\eta]$ appears in each of the terms in (5), where the expectation is over the support of η. As η is multiplicative, a convenient assumption is that $E[\eta] = 1$. If one makes this assumption, then one needs only the distribution of ε, the household heterogeneity error, to be able to calculate (5). An obvious approach is to assume that the distributions of ν and ε are identical, and replace σ_{ε} with σ_{ν} in calculating (5). Clearly, household heterogeneity error is embedded in ν. However, if $E[\eta] \neq 1$, then substituting σ_{ν} for σ_{ε} is likely to introduce misspecification.[25] As will be shown, the second approach provides a means by which one can test the justification of the restrictions implied by the first approach.

The second approach is essentially to modify the estimation of demand under uniform rates so the estimated parameters match directly with those required for calculating (5), that is, to estimate a variant of the two-error D/C choice model. However, with uniform rate data, there would seem to be little rationale for a two-error likelihood, as there appears to be no discrete choice component to demand.[26] The view that there is no discrete choice component to demand may well be attributed to inertia, or the implicit assumption of no discrete component that standard estimation has always proceeded upon. I argue that there is a discrete choice in water consumption under uniform rates, and that discrete choice is whether to consume water or not. Such a discrete choice suggests that a tobit model of consumption, or a multiplicative error version of the tobit, should be estimated.[27]

The tobit model was developed in the context of predicting demand for durable goods, wherein there are many zero observations, and it is typically used only when the econometrician is clearly confronted with censoring (that is, many zero or near zero observations). However, zero or near zero observations need not be present in significant numbers to justify a tobit model. Nonnegativity or nontriviality of consumption are also sufficient causes for employing a tobit likelihood. In both cases the error term has a continuous distribution with the left tail truncated, justifying the tobit likelihood irrespective of the number of zero or nonzero observations. Of course, the severity of the truncation depends on the observed data and unknown parameters. If the independent variables explain much of the variation in the dependent variable, the truncation will not be severe, and hence the difference between parameter estimates derived from a regression model and a tobit model will not be significant. However, the econometrician cannot know a priori that such is the case; hence it is prudent to allow for a truncated error distribution.[28]

The argument just given can be interpreted as treating the censoring as a direct consequence of the D/C choice demand problem, rather than as a stochastic phenomenon necessary only when zero or near zero observations occur. The household chooses to consume either a zero amount of water or a positive amount, and given the discrete choice of positive amount, marginal price and virtual income $(y + d)$ explain the conditional continuous demand. Thus, price and virtual income are irrelevant explanatory variables for corner solutions, *except* to the extent that they influence the discrete choice to be the corner solution. A complete expression of the Marshallian demand for x, when x is censored at c, is

$$x = \begin{cases} c & \text{if } x(p, y + d) \le c \\ x(p, y + d) & \text{if } x(p, y + d) > c \end{cases} \tag{7}$$

Although (7) looks much like a tobit model, it is not one, for there are no error terms in (7). The critical distinction between this Marshallian demand and the standard expression, $x = x(p, y + d)$, is the inclusion of the range constraint implied by nonnegative consumption as a direct part of the utility maximization problem. How error terms are incorporated in this demand model is the next step.

Stochastic expressions vary with assumptions regarding the source of error terms. I will maintain the previous interpretations of ε as household heterogeneity error and η as perception error—both multiplicative—in developing the uniform rate version of the D/C choice model. When both errors are present, it is $x(\cdot)\varepsilon$ that drives the discrete choice, while η is a part of the continuous choice only:

$$x = \begin{cases} c\eta & \text{if } x(p, y + d)\varepsilon \leq c \\ x(p, y + d)\varepsilon\eta & \text{if } x(p, y + d)\varepsilon > c \end{cases} \qquad (8)$$

A heuristic expression of the two-error likelihood is as follows:

$$Pr(x) = f_\eta (x) \, F_\varepsilon[c/x(p, y + d)]$$

$$+ f_{\varepsilon\eta}[x/x(p, y + d)] \, \{1 - F_\varepsilon[c/x(p, y + d)]\} \qquad (9)$$

This likelihood is similar to (3) in that there is no sample separation due to the perception error; although each observation is nonnegative, the discrete choice cannot be directly observed. Compared to the heuristic expression of the two-error likelihood for the block rate example in (3), the parameters of this likelihood appear to be no less identified than in the former situation: there are terms in which the distributions of ε and η appear and those in which the distributions of $\varepsilon\eta$ and ε appear, in both (3) and (9). That is, the lack of a kink point (x_1) implies a similar likelihood function, though with fewer terms.

Several points regarding (9) deserve mention. First, this model will be somewhat more costly to estimate than the standard demand expression, $x = x(p, y + d)\nu$. Although the parameters in (9) appear to be identified from the standpoint that there are no redundant parameters, identification also depends on the information matrix being nonsingular. The nonsingularity of the information matrix depends in turn on the data and how well the model is conditioned to the data. In essence, data that are not well matched to a model will result in low predictive power in the regression context, but may prevent estimation in the two-error tobit context. While lack of diligence with respect to the match of data and model is only costly and not prohibitive in the regression context, it is no less prudent to exercise diligence in the regression context; consequently, less stringent data concerns are a weak argument for the regression approach.

Secondly, the two-error tobit model is the unrestricted version of the model of the first approach, whose restrictions take the form: $\sigma_\varepsilon = \sigma_\nu$ and σ_η such that $E[\ln \eta] = 0$ while $E[\eta] = 1$ (for the lognormal η). The first restriction is a test of parameters across two non-nested models, though the latter restriction is a nested model test. If the nested restriction statistically significant diminishes the log-likelihood, one can probably safely forego the non-nested test and conclude that the two-error tobit approach is most appropriate.

Thirdly, the astute reader will note that extending the two-error tobit model of (8) and (9) to the case of a two-block increasing block rate does not yield the model of (2) and (3), whose estimation is reported here. The two-error tobit extended to the block rate case would yield a model such as in (2) supplemented with the first line of (8), and (3) supplemented by the first term of (9). Such a model is likely to be identified (in the fullest sense) given that the model in (2) is identified. Of course, identification can only be determined on a case-by-case basis.

Finally, there is another reason to echo the exhortation to exercise diligence in gathering data for use in estimating the two-error tobit. This reason arises from wondering aloud whether ε and η will indeed possess the same distribution under uniform and block rates. To answer this, we must consider that ε and η are included to account for the effects of unobserved and omitted variables as well as functional misspecification in the case of ε, and these plus measurement and optimization error in η. Thus, a necessary condition for ε and η to possess similar distributions under uniform and block rates is that the independent variables under uniform data be capable of explaining why certain households would consume in the second block for the block rate structures under consideration.

To predict behavior under block rates when only uniform rate data is available, one would estimate the unknown parameters of demand using (9), and then predict using the estimated parameters and (5).

VII. SUMMARY

This study has demonstrated the range of demand and revenue elasticities that can be calculated from a discrete/continuous choice model of demand under block rates. Previously, the calculation of revenue elasticities has only been done under very restrictive assumptions previously (*e.g.*, Houston 1982). The range of elasticity calculations includes designing rates to achieve particular goals with respect to consumption and revenue. Behavior under block rates can be predicted even when a utility's customers have no experience with block rates. Such prediction does depend on having explanatory variables sufficient to explain the heterogeneity of households, and estimation of a discrete/continuous choice demand model.

NOTES

1. Excess supply is no less an economic problem: it implies that resources devoted to water supply would be more fruitfully devoted to supply of other goods or services. Utility customers are less likely to be aware of excess supply than excess demand, and may even think there is little wrong with excess supply. The problem of excess supply involves either myopia, poor information, or externalities, and is beyond the scope of this chapter.

2. The example given is of an increasing block rate with two blocks. More complex rate structures are possible. Utilities may employ multiple thresholds, may supplement such rates with fixed charges, and the marginal prices may vary dramatically. The analysis below can be modified to account for these complexities.

3. To straightforwardly supplement billing data with tax assessment data requires being able to match water utility customer account numbers with tax assessment data. This not always an easy task.

4. Although a simultaneous equations approach including both demand price and supply price equations would appear to accomplish the same, a difficulty such estimation encounters is the specification bias from assuming that the price schedule is stochastic or contains unknown parameters, when in fact, it is known with certainty.

5. Occasionally, $\bar{x}^k$ will be used as shorthand notation for $x^*(p_k, y + d_k)$.

6. The discrete choice could be directly observed under different pricing schemes that are commonly employed. An example of such a pricing scheme is to require households to purchase an option for water at specific prices and amounts in the future (see Hirshleifer, Dehaven, and Milliman 1960, pp. 101–103; Morris 1990).

7. The original motivation for including the perception error in Burtless and Hausman (1978) was that with a smooth distribution of household heterogeneity, one would expect a higher frequency of households observed at the kink point, but that this does not occur in actuality. See Hewitt (1995) for an alternate view of the motivation for including perception error.

8. Note that actual consumption is not necessarily identical to utility-generating consumption. For instance, the household may not benefit from the water "consumed" due to a leak. Furthermore, actual consumption is really the consumption for billing purposes. If the amount happens to be rounded downwards, then utility-generating consumption is higher, for example.

9. Income as measured here essentially reflects permanent income rather than the sum of permanent and transitory income. Permanent income is more likely to be the

determining factor for water consumption than transitory income fluctuations. The assessment data is from the year 1984 and is in 1984 dollars. Other variables expressed in dollars are converted to 1982–1984 dollars using the CPI-U, all items, all consumers, indexed to 1982–1984 = 100 (U.S. Department of Commerce 1989).

10. For some observations, a one-story house assumption led to negative lawn size, and so a two-story assumption was maintained for all houses, in the absence of more detailed information on variation in structure.

11. The two-error model has been used extensively in labor supply studies, and it is that literature which suggests the $\sigma_\varepsilon \cdot < \sigma_\eta \cdot$ expectation. This expectation is not driven by economic theory. For a survey on the labor supply literature, see Moffitt (1986).

12. This $\hat{x}$ is not simply the expectation of equation (4), which is in logarithm form. Alternatively, this may be accomplished by taking the exponential of (4), where $\varepsilon = \exp(\varepsilon^*)$ and $\eta = \exp(\eta^*)$, and taking expectations.

13. This may remain a counterintuitive point: how can a low-consumption household, one that has never consumed close to or over the block threshold of 20,000 gallons per billing period, ever be affected by a rate change that occurs outside of their range of consumption? The answer lies in the faulty premise of this question, which is that the household that has never consumed in the second block can be presumed never to do so in the future.

14. Hirschberg (1991) develops a method for calculating elasticities for multipart tariffs from an estimate of single-price elasticity. As he notes, his methodology does not address consistent estimations of the needed elasticities.

15. A computationally easier option is to evaluate these elasticities at explanatory variable values of a representative household. However, this option requires making some assumptions about the characteristics of a household that is representative—a consequence of which is to throw away information on the diversity of households and prejudice predictions.

16. This numerical procedure produces arc elasticities, rather than the point elasticities produced by the representative household approach. However, water utility management will likely be more interested in arc elasticities.

17. This point is developed further in note 23.

18. Although the utility cannot implement a change in the third grouping, management may nonetheless wish to know how exogenous changes will affect consumption and revenue.

19. They do not exactly add up, due to the change in d_2 caused by changes in p_1 and p_2. The influence of price through *difference* is very small, as *difference* is very small relative to y, and the income effect is itself small. In the empirical examples below, the effect of a change in p_1 through d_2 appears only in the fourth decimal place or beyond. Nevertheless, the *difference* effect is included.

20. The change in x_1 does affect the discrete choice probabilities, however.

21. As potential evapotranspiration not met by rainfall, weather is a rather complicated variable, depending upon temperature, direct sunlight, wind speed, and rainfall. Thus, increasing the weather variable by 1% may not be a particularly meaningful change in actual weather. A more useful method of projecting water demand would be to estimate a probability distribution of consumption based upon a probability distribution of potential evapotranspiration not met by rainfall, which would in turn be based on probability distributions of the various weather components.

22.   Again, the elasticity on the number of bathrooms may not be particularly useful. Number of bathrooms is recorded in half units, and a more meaningful increase in number of bathrooms is likely to be multiples of half units for some households and zero for others. Whether this elasticity realistically reflects an aggregate increase of 1% in the number of bathrooms is not clear.

23.   Suppose one were to totally differentiate E[Bill] with respect to prices, set this expression equal to zero, and manipulate the equation to solve for the demand "elasticity" level which represents the boundary between rising and falling revenue when prices are increased. The elasticity would be a conditional elasticity, but would equal -1 plus a term which can't be generally signed, and is observation-dependent. Thus, -1 no longer represents the boundary between elastic and inelastic demands.

24.   These rate changes were found by fixing p_1 at various levels and searching for the change in p_2 which achieves the particular target.

25.   Although based on the two-error D/C choice model, the parameter estimates in Table 2 represent a situation in which it was assumed that $E[\eta^*] = 0$, but $E[\eta]$ was allowed to vary from 1. The additional restriction that $E[\eta] = 1$ may reduce the model fit in a significant fashion.

26.   Furthermore, the motivation used by Burtless and Hausman (1978), who developed the two-error D/C choice model for labor supply estimation, for including the second error term was that it was necessary to improve model fit. A model based upon household heterogeneity error alone would predict a spike at the kink point in the frequency distribution of consumption. Yet such a discontinuity is rarely observed in actual data. The second error serves to smooth out the frequency distribution of consumption to better fit the observed data.

27.   Despite the argument just given, I am unaware that a tobit model has ever been employed to estimate water demand under uniform pricing. Another problem with the typical estimation of demand (under uniform and block rates) is the fact that many analysts treat the fixed charge as a separate regressor, rather than an adjustment to income. Such studies generally cite Taylor (1975) and Nordin (1976) as justification; the difficulty with treating fixed charge as a separate regressor is discussed in Hewitt and Hanemann (1995).

28.   Furthermore, common sense suggests that variables omitted from the data set here nonetheless influence consumption (e.g., number of household members and their ages, presence of water-using appliances, etc.). Omission of these variables suggests greater variability in the error distribution, and hence, truncation of a larger portion of the left tail of the error distribution when truncation is built into estimation. Ignoring truncation is likely to be more problematic when the independent variables do not fully explain the dependent variable.

REFERENCES

Billings, R.B., and D.E. Agthe. 1980. "Price Elasticities for Water: A Case of Increasing Block Rates." *Land Economics* 56: 73–84.

Burtless, G., and J.A. Hausman. 1978. "The Effect of Taxation on Labor Supply: Evaluating the Gary Income Maintenance Experiment." *Journal of Political Economy* 86: 1101–1130.

Foster, H.S., Jr., and B.R. Beattie. 1981. "Urban Residential Demand for Water in the United States: Reply." *Land Economics* 57: 257–265.

Hausman, J.A. 1979. "The Econometrics of Labor Supply on Convex Budget Sets." *Economics Letters* 3: 171–174.

Hewitt, J.A. 1995. "Three Stochastic Specification of a Discrete/Continuous Choice Model of Demand Under Block Rate Pricing." Staff Paper 94-6, Department of Agricultural Economics and Economics, Montana State University, Bozeman.

Hewitt, J.A., and W.M. Hanemann. 1995. "A Discrete/Continuous Choice Approach to Residential Water Demand under Block Rate Pricing." *Land Economics* 71 (2): 173–192.

Hirschberg, J.G. 1991. "Elasticities of Rate Schedule Parameters." *Journal of Regulatory Economics* 3 (2): 155–173.

Hirshleifer, J., J.C. DeHaven, and J.W. Milliman. 1960. *Water Supply: Economics, Technology, and Policy.* Chicago: University of Chicago Press.

Houston, D.A. 1982. "Revenue Effects from Changes in a Declining Block Pricing Structure." *Land Economics* 58 (3): 351–363.

Jones, C.V., and J.R. Morris. 1984. "Instrumental Price Estimates and Residential Water Demand." *Water Resources Research* 20: 197–202.

MaCurdy, T., D. Green, and H. Paarsch. 1990. "Assessing Empirical Approaches for Analyzing Taxes and Labor Supply." *Journal of Human Resources* 25 (3): 415–490.

Moffitt, R. 1986. "The Econometrics of Piecewise-Linear Budget Constraints: A Survey and Exposition of the Maximum Likelihood Method." *Journal of Business and Economics Statistics* 4 (3): 317–328.

Morris, J.R. 1990. "Pricing for Water Conservation." *Contemporary Policy Issues* 8: 79–91.

Nieswiadomy, M.L., and D.J. Molina. 1988. "Urban Water Demand under Increasing Block Rates." *Growth and Change* 19 (1): 1–12.

Nieswiadomy, M.L., and D.J. Molina. 1989. "Comparing Residential Water Demand Estimates under Decreasing and Increasing Block Rates Using Household Data." *Land Economics* 65 (3): 280–289.

Nordin, J.A. 1976. "A Proposed Modification of Taylor's Demand Analysis." *The Bell Journal of Economics* 7: 719–721.

Opaluch, J.J. 1982. "Urban Residential Demand for Water in the United States: Further Discussion." *Land Economics* 58: 225–227.

Schmidt, P. 1976. *Econometrics.* New York: Marcel Dekker, Inc.

Taylor, L.D. 1975. "The Demand for Electricity: A Survey." *The Bell Journal of Economics* 6(1): 74–110.

U.S. Department of Commerce. 1989. *Business Statistics: 1961–1988* (26th. ed.). A Supplement to the Survey of Current Business, Bureau of Economic Analysis.

WATER DEMAND ESTIMATION ON A STATE-BY-STATE BASIS

Robert M. Hordon, Kenneth D. Lawrence, and Sheila M. Lawrence

ABSTRACT

The demand for public potable water on a state-by-state basis was modeled using multiple regression techniques. Water use and population served data were obtained from the most recent publication (1990) of the U.S. Geological Survey which has been collecting water use data on a statewide basis at five-year intervals since 1950. Eighteen explanatory variables for each state were obtained from the 1990 census. Variable selection techniques were used to reduce the number of variables from 18 to the two most significant: population served and per capita income. The model will be used to forecast water demand at the state level.

I. INTRODUCTION

There have been numerous attempts over the years to estimate the demand for public potable water supply. The literature is replete with

Advances in Business and Management Forecasting, Volume 2, pages 101–112.

examples of different methodologies used for estimating demand for varying locations, seasons, and uses (Morgan 1974; Camp 1978; Danielson 1979; Hansen and Narayanan 1981; Terza and Welch 1982; Opaluch 1982; Schefter and David 1985; Martin and Thomas 1986; Williams and Suh 1986; Palencia 1988; Weber 1989; Metzner 1989; Griffin and Chang 1990). In short, there are all manner of spatial-temporal dimensions in water demand forecasting.

Given this situation, it is best to start with some basic definitions. Public potable water is defined herein as the amount of freshwater delivered to consumers by purveyors. These purveyors can be either public, as in the case of a municipal water department or a quasi-autonomous entity known as a municipal water authority, or private, as exemplified by investor-owned companies whose shares can be traded on the NASDAQ, the American Stock Exchange, or the New York Stock Exchange. The water supply can come from either surface or ground water sources, or a combination of the two.

The general procedure in water demand estimation is to identify water demand in million gallons/day (mgd) as the dependent variable (Y) and then obtain a number of explanatory variables $(X_1, X_2, \ldots X_k)$. A common form of forecasting is based on multiple regression techniques. The number of observations is governed by the number of locations in the study area. The locations could be residential or commercial subdivisions within a municipality, the entire municipality itself, a county, a sub-watershed or the whole watershed, a portion of the state, or, as in this paper, the entire state. Since the explanatory variables usually include many socioeconomic factors that come from the census, it is generally more convenient to use the same spatial unit of aggregation as the census. A watershed provides an excellent example of the hydrologic unity of a land area, yet census boundaries are rarely commensurate with watershed boundaries.

The study period can range from peak daily demand to average daily demand to monthly, seasonal, and annual usage. In this paper the study period will be the average annual water demand for 1990, as that is the most recent year for the acquisition of reliable water demand and socioeconomic data for all of the states in the nation.

Out of the wide array of explanatory variables that could have been included in an analysis of water demand by state, the following were selected for inclusion in a multiple regression equation:

1. Population served with public supplies of freshwater;

  2. Per capita personal income;
  3. Gross state production in $;
  4. Total state population;
  5. Population density;
  6. Median age;
  7. Number of households;
  8. Number of housing units;
  9. Size of the labor force;
10. Total number of business establishments;
11. Number of manufacturing establishments;
12. Per capita expenditures for health and hospitals;
13. Per capita expenditures for fire protection;
14. Per capita expenditures for waste treatment;
15. Total energy consumption (trillion BTU);
16. Metropolitan population;
17. Total number of hospital beds;
18. Total population in K–12 schools.

As expected in analyses of this type many of the variables were either redundant or added little explanation to the model. Variable selection techniques were employed to reduce the number of variables in the regression model. This process continued until two of the most significant variables were left: population served and per capita income.

At this point it would be useful to comment on the reliability of the data. The water demand and population served data came from a series of publications of the U.S. Geological Survey (USGS). As discussed more fully in the next section, the USGS acts as a central clearing house for water data as reported by each state. Some states keep better records than others, but at least the USGS provides a consistent procedure of categorizing water use. The socioeconomic data came from the census.

II. ESTIMATED USE OF WATER IN THE UNITED STATES

The U.S. Geological Survey has estimated water use for each state in the nation since 1950 at five-year intervals (MacKichan 1951,1957; MacKichan and Kammerer 1961; Murray 1968; Murray and Reeves 1972, 1977; Solley, Chase, and Mann 1983; Solley, Merk, and Pierce 1988; Solley, Pierce, and Perlman 1993). In all of the estimates the USGS gathers the data from state agencies such as health and environmental protection departments. Thus, the reliability of the data is governed by the record-keeping ability of each state, which, as might be expected, varies. For example, the population served in South Carolina reportedly dropped in 1970 and 1975 even though the total population increased at the same time. In the case of Oregon, the population served remained exactly the same in 1970, 1975, and 1980 (1,200,000) even in the face of the population increasing from 2,091,000 in 1970 to 2,614,000 in 1980. New Jersey reported for 1980 that the population served and total population were both 7,360,000 people which is clearly at variance with the other population-served values for the 1960–1990 period. As a final instance of strange reporting, Illinois used the same population-served estimate of 10,700,000 for 1970, 1975, and 1980. Indeed, the Illinois estimate for population served in 1975 actually exceeded the total estimated population for the state. To be fair to the states, they are dependent on information which is furnished to them from the public and private purveyors within their jurisdiction which of course vary in reliability. However, the probability of having the same population served for three consecutive five-year special censuses is rather remote.

On a national basis the average population served as a proportion of total population has increased from 75% in 1960 to 83% in 1990. This upward trend presumably reflects the increasing urbanization of the nation and the spread of water infrastructure in metropolitan areas. For the most recent reporting period available (1990), the population served as a proportion of total population ranges from a low of 54% for Arkansas to a high of 96% for Hawaii and Utah. Since there are no domestic wells in the District of Columbia, the population served is the same as the total population. Note that Washington, DC was initially included in the analysis but Puerto Rico and the Virgin Islands were not.

Water-use terminology has expanded over the years to cover the different aspects of water consumption. In this paper water demand will be based on the USGS estimate for public supply for freshwater use. The term "public supply" refers to water that is diverted from either surface or ground water sources and delivered to multiple users for domestic, commercial, industrial, and thermoelectric power users. The diverter can be either a public water system, such as New York City, or a private water system, such as the Elizabethtown Water Company in New Jersey which is investor-owned and has shares traded on the stock exchange. Public or private water systems are further defined by a minimum threshold of serving at least 25 people or having 15 hookups. Public systems, which deliver potable water to a variety of users, must comply with federal and state safe drinking water standards.

The source of raw water can be either surface or ground. Surface sources include run of river systems, such as the Torresdale intake on the Delaware River for Philadelphia, or stored water in reservoirs, such as the Quabbin Reservoir in Massachusetts which is used by the Boston Metropolitan District Commission. Lakes also serve as natural reservoirs and sources of surface water, as exemplified by Chicago and Milwaukee on Lake Michigan.

Ground water sources range from a few wells serving a small community or residential subdivision to a system of many wells serving a larger area, such as the Suffolk County Water Authority in Long Island, New York. The ground water source varies from unconsolidated materials, such as the sandy deposits along the Atlantic and Gulf Coastal Plain and the stratified sands and gravels of glaciated areas, to consolidated rocks, such as sandstone and shale where water is obtained from the fractures within the formation.

Domestic water use is defined as water that is used for normal household purposes, such as drinking, food preparation, bathing, washing dishes and clothes, toilet flushing, lawn and garden watering, and home car washing. It should be noted that those households that obtain their own water supply from an onsite well are not included in the population served numbers for public potable water systems. This self-supplied category is substantial. For example, the USGS estimates that 42.8 million people, or 17% of the U.S. population, were served by their own individual water system in 1990. Self-supplied domestic water systems are rarely metered and minimal data exist as to the magnitude of withdrawal. The usual method of estimating self-supplied water demand is to employ per capita use coefficients. Different jurisdictions use estimates which vary from 50 to 120 gallons/person/day (gpcd). For example, the state of New Jersey uses a conservative value of 100 gpcd for planning purposes.

Self-supplied domestic water use varies considerably from state to state. The USGS estimates that the total amount of self-supplied domestic water for the nation in 1990 was 3,390 million gallons/day (mgd) as compared to 21,900 mgd for domestic water deliveries by public systems (or 13.4% of the total domestic use). For consistency, water demand projections discussed in this paper will use only public supply values.

Commercial water use includes water for motels, hotels, office buildings, commercial facilities such as shopping centers and fitness centers, institutions such as schools and prisons, and military bases. As with self-supplied domestic water use, self-supplied commercial water use varies enormously from state to state. For example, the range is 0% in Montana to 91.4% in Oregon. The average for the United States is 28.8%. In order to maintain consistency, only the water delivered to commercial facilities by public systems will be used in this study.

Industrial water use includes water that is necessary for processing, washing, and cooling in factories that make a variety of products. Industries that are major users of water include, but are not limited to, steel, chemical, paper, and petroleum refining. For the nation, self-supplied diversions of water for industrial purposes account for 92.2% of the total amount of withdrawals. Water demand projections discussed in this paper will include only the industrial water delivered by public systems.

The thermoelectric category includes water used for electric power generation with either fossil fuel, nuclear, or geothermal energy. Most of the water used by thermoelectric plants goes for condenser and reactor cooling. Only a small fraction of the water used in this category comes from public water system deliveries.

The public use subcategory includes water used for fire-fighting, street washing, municipal parks, and swimming pools. Water lost in the collection and distribution system by leakage forms another subcategory for public water systems. Taken together, the two subcategories form a public use and losses category which will be included in the analysis.

Other categories of water use that were not included in this demand analysis were irrigation, livestock, and mining. These categories are specialized and beyond the scope of this study.

In sum at this point, the distribution of diversions by public water systems by user category for the nation in 1990 was as follows: domestic, 57%; commercial, 15%; public use and losses, 14%; industrial, 13%; and thermoelectric power, 0.2%. It should be recognized that the percentages by user type will vary from state to state based on local factors.

Another important variable that was collected by the USGS was the estimated population served by public water systems. The population served in 1990 by public systems was 210 million or 83.1% of the total population. The remaining 16.9% represent those people (42.8 million) on self-supplied domestic systems.

Per capita consumption in gallons/day is obtained by simply dividing the total amount of surface and ground water diversions by the population served by public systems. Note that the total diversions by public systems include the total deliveries to domestic, commercial, industrial, and thermoelectric power users. Public use and losses are also included as part of the deliveries by public systems. Based on these assumptions, per capita consumption varied from a low of 109 gallons/capita/day (gpcd) for Rhode Island to a high of 344 gpcd for Nevada in 1990. The national average is 184 gpcd (Solley, Pierce, and Perlman 1993). Generally, the per capita values are higher in the western states, presumably reflecting the effects of higher evapotranspiration rates, lower precipitation, and residential vegetation needs.

III. FORECASTING WATER DEMAND WITH A MULTIPLE REGRESSION MODEL

A. Model Building

In forecasting, building multiple regression models that relate the dependent variable (in this case, water demand) to the multiple independent variables is a very effective modeling technique. Such multiple regression models provide a powerful analytical and predictive tool that can relate the cause and effect relationship between the dependent and independent variables. Multiple regression is an important methodology in building forecasting models because it measures the simultaneous influence of a number of independent variables upon one dependent variable (Frees 1996; Neter, Kutner, Nachtsteim, and Wasserman 1996).

The regression modeling analyses of the study involved the use of several variable selection techniques that are available within the Proc Reg of SAS. After the application of the procedures, it became clear that the best explanatory variables for estimating water demand out of the initial set of 18 variables were population served and per capita income. It also became apparent after the application of various regression modeling structures and data analysis relating water demand to population and per capita income that segmentation of the conterminous 48 states involved in the analysis should be attempted. The segmentation required a separate regression model for each group of states.

A variety of empirically based disaggregation procedures were used in the segmentation process, such as the size of the population served and the division reflecting the macro-level differences of precipitation between the eastern and western states. It turned out that the best results in the regression model were achieved in the 48 states by using a combination of the aforementioned procedures, as follows (see Tables 1–3):

> Segment #1: 24 states that had population served greater than the median value of 2,800,000;
>
> Segment #2: 12 eastern states that had population served less than 2,800,000;
>
> Segment #3: 12 western states that had population served less than 2,800,000.

In order to forecast with the three-segmented regression models, forecasts of the explanatory independent variables population served and per capita income were needed. Population served was derived for each of the 48 states, by developing a separate regression model based on

Table 1. Water Demand Forecasts for Segment #1

State	1990 Actual Demand (mgd)	2000 Forecast (mgd)	Change from 1990–2000 (%)
1. Alabama	706	732	3.7
2. Arizona	706	736	4.2
3. California	5,815	5,924	1.9
4. Colorado	638	579	−9.2
5. Florida	1,922	2,547	32.5
6. Georgia	964	1,193	23.8
7. Illinois	1,858	1,833	−1.3
8. Indiana	604	697	15.4
9. Louisiana	618	663	7.3
10. Maryland	558	694	24.4
11. Massachusetts	712	958	34.6
12. Michigan	1,403	1,396	−0.5
13. Minnesota	514	504	−1.9
14. Missouri	677	892	31.8
15. New Jersey	1,038	1,302	25.4
16. New York	2,913	3,071	5.4
17. North Carolina	804	926	15.2
18. Ohio	1,299	1,788	37.6
19. Pennsylvania	1,728	1,704	−1.4
20. Tennessee	694	801	15.4
21. Texas	3,072	3,503	14.0
22. Virginia	710	963	35.6
23. Washington	1,071	773	−27.8
24. Wisconsin	596	581	−2.5

Table 2. Water Demand Forecasts for Segment #2

State	1990 Actual Demand (mgd)	2000 Forecast (mgd)	Change from 1990–2000 (%)
1. Arkansas	308	253	–17.9
2. Connecticut	372	464	24.7
3. Delaware	84	79	–6.0
4. Iowa	318	336	5.7
5. Kentucky	427	492	15.2
6. Maine	135	139	3.0
7. Mississippi	320	405	26.6
8. New Hampshire	106	138	30.2
9. Rhode Island	102	130	27.5
10. South Carolina	352	458	30.1
11. Vermont	58	51	–12.1
12. West Virginia	159	195	22.6

historical data that related population served for each state with the total population of the state. Note that those households that have their own wells would obviously not count as part of the population served by public potable water systems. For each of the 48-state regression models, the population values provided by the regional input-output forecasts of the Bureau of Economic Analysis of the U.S. Department of Commerce were substituted for the year 2000. These substitutions provided forecasts of the population served for each of the states for the year 2000.

Table 3. Water Demand Forecasts for Segment #3

State	1990 Actual Demand (mgd)	2000 Forecast (mgd)	Change from 1990–2000 (%)
1. Idaho	231	181	–21.6
2. Kansas	373	363	–2.7
3. Montana	135	154	14.1
4. Nebraska	299	245	–18.1
5. Nevada	384	270	–29.7
6. New Mexico	272	226	–16.9
7. North Dakota	77	125	62.3
8. Oklahoma	515	366	–28.9
9. Oregon	470	347	–26.2
10. South Dakota	76	165	117.1
11. Utah	508	294	–42.1
12. Wyoming	101	118	16.8

The forecasts of per capita income were also taken from the Bureau of Economic Analysis regional input-output model forecasts.

Thus, the forecast of water demand for the year 2000 was developed by substituting the appropriate explanatory variable forecasts into the appropriate segmented regression forecasting model.

Transformations were applied to the data with the three-segmented model structures under a variety of conditions. When the most appropriate transformations were found, a process of iteratively reweighted least squares was applied to the given segmented model structures. The need for iteratively reweighted least squares was indicated by a number of significant Cook's D distances for particular observations (states in this model) shown in the regression runs.

The forecasting regression models indicated by the iteratively reweighted least squares technique were as follows:

$$Y = b_0 + b_1 X_1 + b_2 X_2$$

where Y = water demand in million gallons/day (mgd)

$$X_1 = \text{population served}$$

$$X_2 = \text{per capita income}$$

Segment #1: $Y = 105.425 + 0.000197 X_1 - 0.014143 X_2$
Adjusted $r^2 = .9878$

Segment #2: $Y = 55.5507 + 0.000162 X_1 - 0.00448 X_2$
Adjusted $r^2 = .9824$

Segment #3: $Y^{0.5} = 1.0133 + 0.0078 X_1^{0.5} - 0.0402 X_2^{0.5}$
Adjusted $r^2 = .9298$

B. An Analysis of the Forecasts

In viewing the forecasts by segments in Tables 1–3 with regard to a high level of apparent over- and under-forecasting values that are substantially different from the 1990 levels of water demand, we see the following in Table 4.

It appears that there is a significant degree of over-forecasting in 16 out of the 48 states which have forecasts for the year 2000 over 20% of the actual 1990 water demand. The degree of under-forecasting is only significant in segment #3 where four out of the 12 states have forecasts

Table 4. A View of Apparent Over and Under Forecasting

Segment #	Forecasted Values Greater than X% of the 1990 Values					
	-20%	-30%	-40%	+20%	+30%	+40%
1. (24 states)	1	0	0	3	5	0
2. (12 states)	0	0	0	4	2	0
3. (12 states)	4	0	0	0	0	2

for the year 2000, 20% less than the actual values for 1990. Segment #2 has an apparent degree of over-forecasting where six states out of 12 have forecasts for the year 2000 over 20% of the actual 1990 water demand.

Further investigation of the amount of water demanded in particular states as well as the population served needs to be undertaken to validate the data used in the study. There appears to be a degree of question with regard to a number of states that have a large degree of difference between the actual water demand in 1990 and the forecasted values for the year 2000.

In segment #1 the data for Florida, Massachusetts, Missouri, Ohio, and Virginia should be reviewed. In segment #2 the data for New Hampshire and South Carolina should be reviewed. Without question, the data for Nevada, Oklahoma, South Dakota, and Utah needs to be reviewed for segment #3.

This review process should involve the validation of the data supplied to the U.S. Geological Survey by each of the states for water demand and population served.

REFERENCES

Camp, R.C. 1978. "The Inelastic Demand for Residential Water: New Findings." *Journal of the American Water Works Association* 70: 453–458.

Danielson, L.C. 1979. "An Analysis of Residential Demand for Water Using Micro Time-Series Data." *Water Resources Research* 15 (4): 763–767.

Frees, E.W. 1996. *Data Analysis Using Regression Analysis*. Englewood Cliffs, NJ: Prentice-Hall.

Griffin, R.C., and C. Chang. 1990. "Pretest Analyses of Water Demand in Thirty Communities." *Water Resources Research* 26 (10): 2251–2255.

Hansen, R.D., and R. Narayanan. 1981. "A Monthly Time Series Model of Municipal Water Demand." *Water Resources Bulletin* 17 (4): 578–585.

MacKichan, K.A. 1951. *Estimated Use of Water in the United States, 1950*. U.S. Geological Survey Circular 115.

MacKichan, K.A. 1957. *Estimated Use of Water in the United States, 1955.* U.S. Geological Survey Circular 398.

MacKichan, K.A., and J.C. Kammerer. 1961. *Estimated Use of Water in the United States in 1960.* U.S. Geological Survey Circular 456.

Martin, W.E., and J.F. Thomas. 1986. "Policy Relevance in Studies of Urban Residential Water Demand." *Water Resources Research* 22 (13): 1735–1741.

Metzner, R.C. 1989. "Demand Forecasting: A Model for San Francisco." *Journal of the American Water Works Association* 81, 56–59.

Morgan, W.D. 1974. "A Time Series Demand for Water Using Micro Data and Binary Variables." *Water Resources Bulletin* 10 (4): 697–702.

Murray, C.R. 1968. *Estimated Use of Water in the United States in 1965.* U.S. Geological Survey Circular 556.

Murray, C.R., and E.B. Reeves. 1972. *Estimated Use of Water in the United States in 1970.* U.S. Geological Survey Circular 676.

Murray, C.R., and E.B. Reeves. 1977. *Estimated Use of Water in the United States in 1975.* U.S. Geological Survey Circular 765.

Neter, J., M.H. Kutner, C.J. Nachtsheim, and W. Wasserman. 1996. *Applied Linear Regression Models* (3rd ed.). Homewood, IL: Irwin-McGraw-Hill.

Opaluch, J.A. 1982. "Urban Residential Demand for Water in the United States: Further Discussion." *Land Economics* 58 (2): 225–227.

Palencia, L.C. 1988. "Residential Water Demand in Metro Manila." *Water Resources Bulletin* 24 (2): 275–279.

Schefter, J.E., and E.L. David. 1985. "Estimating Residential Water Demand Under Multi-Part Tariffs Using Aggregate Data." *Land Economics* 61 (3): 272–280.

Solley, W.B., E.B. Chase, and W.B. Mann, IV. 1983. *Estimated Use of Water in the United States in 1980.* U.S. Geological Survey Circular 1001.

Solley, W.B., C.F. Merk, and R.B. Pierce. 1988. *Estimated Use of Water in the United States in 1985.* U.S. Geological Survey Circular 1004.

Solley, W.B., R.B. Pierce, and H.A. Perlman. 1993. *Estimated Use of Water in the United States in 1990.* U.S. Geological Survey Circular 1081.

Terza, J.V., and W.P. Welch. 1982. "Estimating Demand under Block Rates: Electricity and Water." *Land Economics* 58 (2): 181–188.

Weber, J.A. 1989. "Forecasting Demand and Measuring Price Elasticity." *Journal of the American Water Works Association* 65: 57–65.

Williams, M., and B. Suh. 1986. "The Demand for Urban Water by Customer Class." *Applied Economics* 18: 1275–1289.

WATER DEMAND MANAGEMENT:
THE EFFECTIVENESS OF PRICE AS A
CONSERVATION TOOL

Michael Nieswiadomy

ABSTRACT

This paper examines the impact of water rates on conservation in an urban environment. The literature includes over 100 water demand studies that have been published in the past three decades. Overwhelmingly these studies have demonstrated that water pricing is a powerful conservation tool. This paper focuses on the effect of rising water rates by examining various recent (since 1980) water demand price elasticity estimates. Most studies have found the elasticity of demand to range between −0.2 and −0.5. Elasticities are found to be greater in the long run than the short run and greater in the summer than in the winter. The effectiveness of various pricing techniques such as uniform, decreasing, or increasing block rates is also examined. Most researchers find that increasing block rates (as well as seasonal rates) tend to encourage conservation and can be structured to protect poorer consumers. Proper dissemination of information concerning the price structure is also a key to a successful conservation campaign.

Advances in Business and Management Forecasting, Volume 2, pages 113–129.
Copyright © 1998 by JAI Press Inc.
All rights of reproduction in any form reserved.
ISBN: 0-7623-0002-7

I. INTRODUCTION

During the summer of 1996 many states suffered through one of the worst droughts in many decades. The scarcity of water became alarmingly apparent as crops withered in the fields and cities rationed water. In contrast, in normal years very few residential consumers give much attention to water, or to their water bill. Many do not know what price they pay for water, yet consumers can recall how much they paid per gallon of gas. Why is this? One obvious reason is that the price of gas is clearly displayed on the pump while no such display exists for our water meters at home. But the primary reason that consumers do not know the price of water is that historically it has been so cheap. Even today the average price of 1,000 gallons is $2.00, or expressed alternatively, it is only $0.002/gallon. In some places, water is sold for much less.

Consumers' lack of knowledge about water prices is not the only perception problem. For years water planners operated under the belief that per capita water usage (i.e., "need") was constant. Thus, planners predicted future water demand by multiplying projected population by the per capita water "need." In making these forecasts, planners were assuming that water demand was not influenced by other economic factors such as income or the price of water. In economic terms, these forecasters assumed that the water demand curves were "perfectly inelastic."

However, there is a significant body of economics research that has shown that the demand for water is not perfectly inelastic, that is, it has been shown the consumers do react to higher water prices by reducing consumption. This literature will be surveyed in this report. One early study deserves mentioning because it clearly dispels the notion that the average amount of water used per person is constant. Hanke (1970) analyzed the quantity of water used before and after meters were installed in Boulder, Colorado in 1961. He found that residential customers were using more than 150% of the botanically ideal (the minimum amount needed to maintain aesthetic quality) for lawn watering. However, after meters were installed and customers were charged for each unit of water used, customers applied only 75% of botanically ideal amounts. Clearly water users were willing to tolerate less than perfect lawns when water prices increased.

Water has always been a scarce resource in the eyes of economists, but is only now being considered scarce by the general public. Water suppliers and consumers now face the need for conservation brought about by supply constraints. Since very little can be done to augment the existing supply of water, demand-side measures are needed to promote long-term changes in water consumption to meet the necessary conservation goals. These problems clearly imply that we must analyze water as an economic good, subject to the laws of supply and demand. Although all aspects of water management are important, this paper will focus on an understanding of the importance of implementing an efficient rate schedule, and its effects on water consumption. It might seem that the rate schedule is only one small aspect of water management, since several demand-side measures are available: public information, plumbing retrofits, residential audits, landscape measures, among others. None of these measures, however, will create the long-term behavioral changes among water consumers necessary to meet future conservation goals. This inadequacy is due primarily to the lack of an incentive powerful enough to change behavior. Price can provide that incentive. This paper will provide an overview of water demand studies conducted since 1980. To be accessible to both economists and noneconomists, the use of economic and econometric terminology will be kept to a minimum.

II. DEMAND, PRICE, AND ELASTICITY

The United Nations has determined that the minimum quantity of water needed to maintain a healthy person is 23 gallons per day. So in effect, any water consumption beyond that amount can be considered discretionary, and so subject to normal economic forces. Understanding these forces will allow a water agency to meet agency objectives, including conservation goals (Mitchell, Cubed, and Hanemann 1994).

Modeling residential water consumption requires an understanding of the concept of demand. Economists define demand as the quantity of a good consumers are willing and able to purchase at alternative prices. The law of demand holds true for water just as it does for other consumption goods: a higher price for water leads to a reduction in water purchases. A demand curve will depict this relationship for a given point in time, given the influence of several other factors such as household income, household size, time of the day or year, and climate, among others (Nieswiadomy 1992; Hewitt and Hanemann 1995; Mitchell, Cubed, and Hanemann 1994). All of these factors, including price, explain the variance in water consumption, but the importance of price is heightened because it is often the only factor that a water supplier can directly affect (Boland, Dziegielewski, Baumann, and Opitz 1984), either through increasing rates, or through altering the rate structure.

There are several ways to design a rate structure, but regardless of the final form of the structure, it will serve several goals. The primary goals are revenue sufficiency, that is, generating enough revenues to cover costs, and allocation of the costs of the agency to various user classes. Finally, and most importantly, the rate structure will provide incentives to consumers to modify their behavior (Mitchell, Cubed, and Hanemann 1994).

Theoretically, the most economically efficient structure would base pricing on marginal costs, allowing consumers to compare the benefits of consuming an additional unit of water with the costs of consuming that additional unit. This would promote the allocation of water to its highest valued use, and reduce the quantity of water assigned to secondary and less essential uses. The marginal cost of water, however, is seldom observed. There are, however, ways to approximate the marginal costs of water, and rate structures can be designed which promote conservation, that is, consumers will receive the correct signal about the scarcity of water, and adjust their behavior accordingly.

Both seasonal rates, and increasing block rates, send the appropriate price signals to the consumer via variable charges. The seasonal rate structure applies a higher rate during the peak season than during the off-peak season. The increasing block rate structure (see Figure 1) charges a higher price per additional unit of consumption as the number of units consumed increases. Either of these rate structures may also contain fixed charges, but as these are independent of water usage, fixed charges do not provide any incentive to conserve water. As the importance of water conservation has grown, water utilities have increasingly turned away from traditional decreasing block rate structures (which encourage use). A recent study by Ernst & Young (1992) showed that across the United States, decreasing block structures are falling out of favor. In the western United States, which has faced some of the severest water shortages, less than 10% of water utilities still use decreasing block rates.

A seasonal rate structure may have two different rate schedules, one for winter (off-season), and another for summer, or it may just have a base rate schedule with surcharges applied to peak-seasonal consumption. Increasing block rates, according to McCollum and Ricks (1996), are justifiable when distinct customer groups that impose different levels of cost on the agency can be identified. They note that any number of

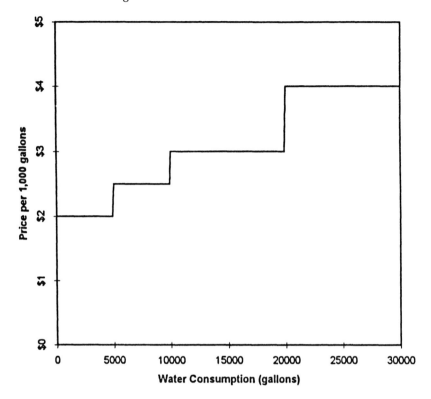

Water Use (gallons)	Price per 1,000 gals.
0-5,000	$2.00
5,000-10,000	$2.50
10,000-20,000	$3.00
20,000+	$4.00

Figure 1. An Increasing Block Rate Schedule

blocks can be specified, but that the first block must be large enough that it will entirely encompass the usage of at least some customers. These increasing block rates send clear price signals to consumers. The price signal that consumers respond to is a further question. Theory and empirical results make it clear that real, not nominal, prices are important (Billings and Agthe 1980). A price may be increasing in nominal terms, but after adjusting for inflation, may be declining in real terms, as was the case in Martin and colleague's (1984) study of Tucson. A more important price consideration is whether consumers respond to average price or marginal price. Average price faced by the consumer is the total amount spent for water divided by the total amount of water purchased per billing period. Marginal price faced by the consumer is the price associated with the last unit of water consumed. Under an increasing block rate structure, high-volume users will face a marginal price higher than the average price they paid for the water in that billing period.

Several studies have addressed this very issue. Obtaining marginal price information from bills can be costly for consumers. If the benefit to be gained from calculating the marginal price does not compensate for the cost of doing so, the customer may choose to respond to other price information instead (Shin 1985). The leading candidate is average price. Shin found that by constructing a *perceived price* variable, he could better explain customer response to price increases in electricity rates. He found that the perceived price was the average price paid by consumers (for his data set), not the marginal price. He limited his study though to decreasing block rates for electricity. Nieswiadomy and Molina (1991), using data for Denton, Texas from 1975–1985, extended Shin's approach to increasing block rate structures, and found some evidence that marginal price is what consumers are responding to under such a rate structure. Nieswiadomy (1992) applied Shin's price perception model to 1984 American Water Works Association survey data of 430 water utilities in the United States and found that in all regions consumers were more responsive to changes in average price than to marginal price. Using the same survey data, Nieswiadomy and Cobb (1993), in a study of elasticities across pricing block structures found that average price models are more appropriate for analysis. However, Billings and Agthe (1980) concluded that the use of average price models alone produces less accurate predictions on consumer behavior. All of these studies, as discussed below, still found that consumers were responsive to price.

Of course, the primary function of a water agency's rate structure is revenue sufficiency. To evaluate the impact of any price change on total revenues, the impact on quantity demanded of the price change must be determined. Economists use the concept of elasticity to describe the impact of a change in price on quantity demanded. The price elasticity of demand for water is defined as the percentage change in quantity demanded resulting from a 1% increase in the price. Formally, price elasticity (E_d) is defined as:

$$E_d = \%\Delta Q / \%\Delta P$$

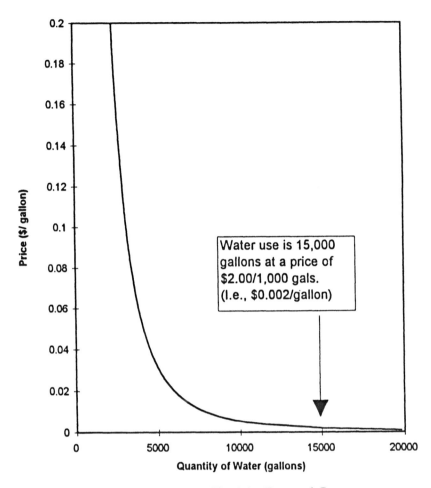

Figure 2. A Constant Elasticity Demand Curve

A larger than proportional change in quantity demanded implies that water is price elastic ($E_d < -1.0$), whereas a smaller than proportional change implies that water is price inelastic ($E_d > -1.0$). Figure 2 represents a typical water demand curve with constant price elasticity. If water is price elastic, an increase in price would result in a proportionally larger decrease in quantity demanded, and would cause revenues to decline. If water is price inelastic, an increase in price would result in a proportionally smaller decrease in quantity demanded, and would cause total revenues to actually increase, even though the quantity of water consumed has fallen. If water is perfectly price inelastic ($E_d = 0.0$), quantity demanded will not respond to a change in price at all. Therefore, estimating the price elasticity of demand would be the first priority in designing a price-based conservation program.

III. RESULTS OF PREVIOUS STUDIES

Many studies investigating the responsiveness of water demand to changes in price have been done, beginning with Howe and Linaweaver (1967). While these studies have varied in their level of statistical sophistication, the models estimated, the periods and regions covered, and the quantity and quality of data available, all have reached very similar conclusions. Most studies (e.g., Mitchell, Cubed, and Hanemann 1994) have found that with a 10% increase in price, a reduction in quantity demanded of 2 to 5% can be expected. These studies have also shown that outdoor use is more responsive to price than indoor use, primarily because outdoor use represents seasonal demand (irrigation during the summer months). Some studies have also shown that long-term water consumption is more responsive to price changes than short-term consumption. It has been hypothesized that this is due to the long time horizon required to invest in water saving appliances or to adjust landscape characteristics (Carver and Boland 1980).

In a review of the rate and price literature (Boland et al. 1984) covering 50 studies from 1926 up until the early 1980s, long-run residential average price elasticity was found to fall within a range of from –0.20 to –0.40. In the same study the range for short-run residential average price elasticity was found to be –0.00 to –0.30. The long run is defined as that period long enough to allow the substitution of old appliances and fixtures for newer, more efficient ones, or to xeriscape the property. This review also noted that water demand was more elastic during the summer months. Although Boland and colleagues (1984) survey up through the early 1980s, many new studies using more modern estimating techniques have appeared subsequently. This paper will present the findings of the major water demand studies conducted since 1980, in alphabetical order. These studies' results are summarized in Table 1.

Ben-Zvi (1980) studied residential water use along the Red River Basin, covering an area from northwest Texas to northwest Louisiana. The study incorporated cross-sectional data on residential water use for 20 communities, and indoor, outdoor, and annual average water use were modeled separately for each of three subregions. The highest price elasticities were reported for the eastern region, with indoor response

Table 1. Summary of Estimated Price Elasticities

Study	Location	Summer	Winter	Short Run	Long Run
Ben-Zvi (1980)	Red River, TX	-0.82	-0.79	—	-0.73
Billings and Agthe (1980)	Tucson, AZ	—	—	—	-0.49
Brown and Caldwell (1993)	SW Florida	—	—	—	-0.25/-0.57
Chicoine et al. (1986)	Rural Illinois	—	—	—	-0.42
Cuthbert (1989)	Tucson, AZ	—	—	—	—
Fox (1996)	San Antonio, TX	—	—	—	—
Griffin and Chang (1991)	Texas	—	—	—	-0.35
Hansen and Narayanan (1981)	Salt Lake City	—	—	—	-0.47
Hewitt and Hanemann (1995)	Denton, TX	—	—	—	-1.57/-1.63
Holloway and Hall (1991)	Texas	—	—	—	-0.04/-0.54
Howe and Linaweaver (1967)	U.S.	West:-0.73 East:-1.57	—	—	—
Howe (1982)	U.S.	West:-0.43 East:-0.57	-0.06	—	—
Jordan (1984)	Spalding Co., GA	—	—	—	-0.19
Martin et al. (1984)	Tucson, AZ	—	—	—	-0.26
Mitchell (1994)	Los Angeles, CA	—	—	—	—
Moncur (1987)	Honolulu, HI	—	—	—	-0.35
Morris and Jones (1980)	Denver, CO	-0.73	-0.09	—	—
Nieswiadomy (1992)	U.S.	—	—	—	-0.29/-0.40
Nieswiadomy and Cobb (1993)	U.S.	—	—	—	Inc: -0.64 Dec: -0.46
Nieswiadomy and Molina (1991)	Denton, TX	—	—	—	-0.36/-0.86
Ozog (1996)	Midwest U.S.	—	—	-0.21	-0.27
Palencia (1988)	Manila, Phillipines	—	—	—	-0.29
Stevens, Miller and Willis (1992)	Massachusetts	—	—	—	-0.10/-0.69
Williams and Suh (1986)	U.S.	—	—	—	-0.29/-0.49

being –0.794, outdoor response being –0.821, and annual average response being –0.734.

Billings and Agthe (1980), in a study of Tucson, Arizona from January 1974 to September 1977, examined the question of alternative price specifications in water demand models. They modeled household water demand (using both a linear and double-log models) as a function of two price variables, marginal price and Nordin's difference construct, an implicit marginal sewer charge, income, evapotranspiration minus rainfall. Nordin's difference variable is defined as the difference between a consumer's actual utility bill, and what the bill *would* have been if all units of the commodity were purchased at the marginal price. Billings and Agthe found the combined elasticity to be –0.39 for the double-log model, and –0.63 for the linear model. In addition, the authors estimated both models using first nominal data (unadjusted for inflation), and then deflated price and income data. The statistical results were much more powerful using real data than with nominal data, indicating that consumers responded to real prices and changes in income, not nominal ones.

Briggs (1989) discusses the impact of a 50% premium assessed on water consumption in excess of 15,000 gallons per month for residential users in Orange County, Florida adopted in February 1987. Briggs found that the surcharge program reduced consumption in excess of 15,000 gallons in service areas comprising average-priced homes (approximately $92,000) by approximately 25%, and in service areas comprising expensive homes (approximately $146,000), found excess consumption reduced by 11%. The surcharge program was considered successful in promoting water conservation, and was cost effective because it cost little to implement the program, as opposed to substantial sums that might have been spent on alternative conservation programs.

Brown and Caldwell (1993) estimated the water demand for 10 counties of the Southwest Florida Water Management District, using more than 42,000 observations. Within the district, single-family residences formed the single largest class of users, comprising more than 66% of the total. For water prices more than $1.50, the study found elasticity increases with increases in property value. For example, at a price of $3.00, price elasticities were –0.25, –0.43, and –0.57 for low, medium, and high property value homes, respectively. Several explanations were provided for this relationship. First, high value homes, which exhibit significantly higher levels of water consumption, have more discretionary water use due to irrigation. Also, wealthy consumers can more readily afford water efficient devices, or even alternative sources of water. Below $1.50, the price elasticities for each group are very similar.

Chicoine, Deller, and Ramamurthy (1986) developed and estimated a study of demand under block rate pricing for potable water using a simultaneous equation approach. The data came from a sample of rural water district water users in Illinois in 1982, where all households faced decreasing block rate pricing structures with no seasonal variation. They estimated the price elasticity with respect to marginal price to be −0.42.

Cuthbert (1989) revisited the case of Tucson (studied by Martin et al. 1984), examining a period from 1978 to 1986. The increasing block rate structure placed the burden of the rate increases on customers with above-average consumption of water. Average use overall for single-family residential customers had declined, with much of the decline coming in seasonal (summer) water consumption. Additionally, the portion of total system water use accounted for by this class fell from 60 to 53%.

Fox (1996) discusses the implementation of a conservation rate structure by the city of San Antonio, which is completely dependent on a ground water source, the Edwards Aquifer. The heavy use of the aquifer, as well as litigation over the protection of endangered species habitat, led the city to adopt an aggressive conservation plan. The final design resulted in four blocks. The first block covered 50% of residential customers and the winter average of 7,500 gallons per month. The second block covered 80% of residential customers and average water use of approximately 12,000 gallons per month. The third block covered 90% of residential customers as well as the typical customer's landscape use. The fourth block, covering the remaining 10% of residential customers (who use in excess of 17,200 gallons per month) has rates sufficiently high to discourage this amount of consumption. A new 30% surcharge over the base rate for seasonal use (July 1–October 31), replaced a previous 10% surcharge. The new rate structure was published via a redesigned monthly water bill, explaining how the bill was calculated, historical data on the customer's usage, and their usage relative to the community. After implementing the rate structure, residential water use was found to be 12% beneath the historic trend, and $5 million was generated for 1995–1996 Fiscal Year.

Griffin and Chang (1991) studied 221 communities across Texas over a period of five years from 1981 to 1985. Using a new climate variable to refine the estimates, they find that summer elasticities generally exceed winter price elasticities by 30%. Griffin and Chang also note that for the type of data they are using (pooled monthly) that generalized

Cobb-Douglas and augmented Fourier forms are better alternatives. The study finds that price elasticity is approximately −0.35 for most of the models, with the most price elastic months being April, May, June, and July. Because of the seasonality of price response, the authors suggest that peak load pricing will be a more effective conservation measure.

Hansen and Narayanan (1981) presented a time-series model designed to examine monthly fluctuations in municipal water demand. Using data covering the years 1961–1977 from the Salt Lake City Water Department, a double-log model was estimated that generated a price elasticity estimate of −0.47.

Hewitt and Hanemann (1995) are the only researchers to model the consumer choice problem as a discrete/continuous problem, where the consumer must decide which block to consume in, and secondly how much water to consume within the block. They find demand to be price elastic (−1.6) unlike most other studies which find demand to be price inelastic. This method deserves further investigation, but is rather costly and complex to estimate.

Holloway and Hall (1991) conducted a study of the general downward trend in per capita water consumption for 28 Metropolitan Statistical Areas and 72 cities in the state of Texas for the period 1978 to 1988. To better capture climatological and topographical differences, the MSAs were divided into nine regions. Holloway and Hall (1991) found the price elasticities of demand ranged from −0.042 to −0.543.

Jordan (1994) analyzed the results of a conservation (increasing block) rate structure adopted by the Spalding County, Georgia, Water Authority on January 1, 1991. The new rate resulted in a reduction in per capita water consumption of 5%, while revenues increased by 21%. The increasing rate structure price structure forced the heaviest consumers of water to pay a higher price, thus reducing per capita water demand while increasing revenues. The implied price elasticity based on an increase in revenues of 21% with a decrease in per capita water usage of 5% is −0.19.

Martin and colleagues (1984), made an extensive study of water conservation in Tucson, Arizona covering a 42-month period following July 1976. It had been commonly accepted that the high level of public information was the primary cause of reduced per capita water consumption, but Martin and colleagues (1984) showed that price was also a major factor. Martin and colleagues (1984) estimated a log-linear model with the log of quantity of water delivered to a household as the dependent variable, and marginal price (adjusted for inflation), evapotranspiration minus rainfall per month, and full cash value of the home as the independent variables. Based on the mean price, the estimated price elasticity was –0.26.

Mitchell, Cubed, and Hanemann (1994) discuss an increasing block rate structure adopted by the city of Los Angeles in January 1993 in the face of severe drought. A committee, appointed by Mayor Bradley, analyzed the Los Angeles Department of Water and Power's costs and proposed an increasing block rate structure designed to encourage conservation by targeting consumers with higher than average use (Hall 1996). Committed to the principle of marginal cost pricing, the committee also wanted to ensure revenue sufficiency, especially with the expected increase in the marginal costs of new supplies of water. The committee felt that an increasing block rate structure, coupled with automatic rate adjustments, would accomplish these goals. The L.A. City Council adopted a two-tier rate structure that accepted most of the committee's recommendations (see Table 2). Staff from the LADWP estimated that 71% of single-family residences would have a lower annual bill in normal years, even though some users might experience higher monthly bills during the peak summer season. Over the first 12 months under the new rate structure actual events came close to the predicted outcome.

Moncur (1987), in a study of the Honolulu water pricing program, using data on single-family residential customers from 1977 to 1983, including a drought spanning 1977–1978, estimated a model including variables for price, rainfall, lagged consumption, income, household size, as well as an indicator variable for the presence of drought restrictions. He found that a 10% reduction in usage could be achieved by a 29% rate increase (implying that the price elasticity was –0.35), in the absence of any other measures, such as voluntary restrictions or public

Table 2. Normal Year Rates, LADWP

Users	Price in Low Block	Switch Point	High Block:Winter	High Block:Summer
Residential Single Family	$1.14/CCF	575 gal/day	$2.33/CCF	
		725 gal/day		$2.98/CCF
Multi-Family	$1.14/CCF	125% of winter use	NA	$2.92/CCF
Nonresidential	$1.21/CCF	125% of winter use	NA	$2.98/CCF

information campaigns. With such measures, the same sort of reduction in water consumption could be achieved with a less drastic price increase.

Morris and Jones (1980) studied single-family residential demand in the Denver metropolitan area for 1976. The indoor price elasticity was found to be −0.09, which confirms previous hypotheses that indoor use does not represent discretionary water consumption. The outdoor price elasticity was −0.73, and while still inelastic, shows consumers are much more responsive to price for discretionary uses.

Nieswiadomy (1992) estimated water demand equations using 1984 American Water Works Association (AWWA) survey data from 430 of the 600 largest U.S. utilities. Nieswiadomy estimated three different models using marginal price, average price, and Shin's price perception construction. Finding that average price was the best specification, Nieswiadomy reported price elasticities ranging from −0.29 for the North Central region to −0.40 in the South region.

Nieswiadomy and Cobb (1993) provided an empirical analysis of differences in price elasticities of demand across water pricing block structures and examined their conservation potential. Using data from the 1984 AWWA survey, they estimated water demand under increasing and decreasing block structures. The results indicated that price elasticity of demand under increasing block structures was greater (−0.64) than under decreasing block structures (−0.46), implying that the increasing block structure is more conservation oriented. Nieswiadomy and Molina (1989) studied monthly water use of 101 individual customers in Denton, Texas. The data set was unique because it contained time series observations on the same set of customers facing for the first half (1976–1980) of the time series a decreasing block rate schedule, and for the second half (1981–1985) an increasing block rate schedule. The study was also unique in that it was the first to use a weather variable including evapotranspiration matched to the billing cycle of each consumer. Performing estimation via ordinary least squares, an instrumental variable technique, and two-staged least squares, they report statistically significant price elasticities ranging from −0.36 to −0.86.

Ozog (1996), in a study of an unidentified midwestern utility attempting to convert from groundwater to surface water, estimated separate regression models for the period 1979 to 1993 for each of three sectors: residential, apartment, and commercial. The dependent variable in all three models was logged monthly water consumption, and depending on sector, the explanatory variables included the log of average price, lagged log of consumption, maximum temperature, maximum relative humidity, percentage of sunshine, and income. Demand was price inelastic for all three sectors in the short run, and for all sectors but the commercial sector, which was elastic, in the long run. For the residential sector, he reported short-run elasticity to be −0.21, and long-run elasticity to be −0.27.

Stevens, Miller, and Willis (1992) analyze residential water demand for 85 Massachusetts communities to compare the responses to increasing versus decreasing block rates. Using a two-stage least squares method proposed by Nieswiadomy and Molina (1989) they estimate price elasticities in the range of −0.10 to −0.69. They do not find a significant difference in price elasticities for customers facing increasing versus decreasing block rates.

IV. CONCLUSION

Recent research has demonstrated that water consumers do respond to higher prices, although residential water demand is price inelastic. A few of the reasons for the price inelasticity of water are the difficulty of substituting away from water and the high costs to a household of monitoring usage. Exacerbating this tendency is that consumption of water precedes payment (often by a substantial amount of time), and so a disconnection exists between water consumption and payment for the water consumed. Finally, the price of water is very low relative to other goods, and so consumers are reluctant to make the up-front investment necessary to reduce their water requirements.

Research has also shown that consumers are more price responsive (elastic) in the long run than the short run, and in the peak season than in the off-peak season. This indicates that water agencies can use price as a conservation measure while still meeting revenue requirements. Increasing block rate and/or seasonal rate structures are the most effective conservation pricing schemes. While it is still unclear empirically exactly to which price signal (average or marginal) consumers are responding to, as a practical matter they are responding to price signals by conserving water. Several of the studies also point out that education about the rate structures increases their effectiveness. Mitchell, Cubed, and Hanemann (1994) point out that public education and information programs ("moral suasion"), unaccompanied by financial incentives, are not nearly as effective as when the two are combined.

REFERENCES

Ben-Zvi, S. 1980. *Estimates of Price and Income Elasticities of Demand for Water in Residential Use in the Red River Basin.* Tulsa, OK: U.S. Army Corps of Engineers.

Billings, R.B., and D.E. Agthe. 1980. "Price Elasticities for Water: A Case of Increasing Block Rates." *Land Economics* 56 (1): 73–84.

Boland, J.J., B. Dziegielewski, D. Baumann, and E.M. Opitz. 1984. *Influence of Price and Rate Structures on Municipal and Industrial Water Use.* Contract Report 84-C-2. Planning and Management Consultants, Ltd. Fort Belvoir, VA: Institute of Water Resources, U.S. Army Corps of Engineers.

Briggs, R.K., Jr. 1989. "Evaluating a Water Conservation Surcharge Program in Orange County, Florida." *Government Finance Review* 5 (2): 7–10.

Brown and Caldwell Consulting Engineers. 1993. *Water and Price Elasticity Study.* Southwest Florida Water Management District.

Carver, P.H., and J.J. Boland. 1980. "Short- and Long-Run Effects of Price on Municipal Water Use." *Water Resources Research* 16 (4): 609–16.

Chicoine, D.L., S.C. Deller, and G. Ramamurthy. 1986. "Water Demand Estimation Under Block Rate Pricing: A Simultaneous Equation Approach." *Water Resources Research* 22 (6): 859–63.

Cuthbert, R.W. 1989. "Effectiveness of Conservation-Oriented Water Rates in Tucson." *Journal American Water Works Association* 81 (3): 65–73.

Ernst & Young. 1992. *Ernst & Young's 1992 National Water and Waste Water Rate Survey.* National Environmental Consulting Group, Ernst & Young.

Fox, T.P. 1996. "Analysis, Design and Implementation of a Conservation Rate Structure." Pp. 47–51 in *Proceedings of CONSERV96: Responsible Water Stewardship.* Orlando, FL: American Water Works Association.

Griffin, R.C., and C. Chang. 1991. "Seasonality in Community Water Demand." *Western Journal of Agricultural Economics* 16 (2): 207–17.

Hall, D. 1996. *Advances in the Economics of Environmental Resources: Marginal Cost Rate Design and Wholesale Water Markets.* Greenwich, CT: JAI Press Inc.

Hanke, S. 1970. "Demand for Water under Dynamic Conditions." *Water Resources Research* 6 (5): 1253–1261.

Hansen, R.D., and R. Narayanan. 1981. "A Monthly Time Series Model of Municipal Water Demand." *Water Resources Bulletin* 17 (4): 578–85.

Hewitt, J.A., and W.M. Hanemann. 1995. "A Discrete/Continuous Choice Approach to Residential water Demand under Block Rate Pricing." *Land Economics* 71 (2): 173–192.

Holloway, M.L., and B.S. Hall. 1991. *Understanding Trends in Texas Per Capita Water Consumption.* Austin, TX: Southwest Econometrics. Texas Water Development Board.

Howe, C.W., and F.P. Linaweaver. 1967. "The Impact of Price on Residential Water Demand and Its Relation to System Design and Price Structure." *Water Resources Research* 3 (1): 13–32.

Howe, C.W. 1982. "The Impact of Price on Residential Water Demand: Some New Insights." *Water Resources Research* 18 (4): 713–6.

Jordan, J.L. 1994. "Rates: Consider Conservation Water Pricing." *Opflow* 20 (4): 1,4.

Martin, W.E., H.M. Ingram, N.K. Laney, and A.H. Griffin. 1984. *Saving Water in a Desert City.* Washington, DC: Resources for the Future.

McCollum, K., and K. Ricks. 1996. "Water Pricing and Resource Management: The Central Utah Project's Water Pricing Policy Study." Pp. 867–871 in *Proceedings of CONSERV96: Responsible Water Stewardship.* Denver, CO: American Water Works Association.

Mitchell, D.L., M. Cubed, and W.M. Hanemann. 1994. *Setting Urban Water Rates for Efficiency and Conservation: A Discussion of Issues.* California Urban Water Conservation Council.

Moncur, J.E.T. 1987. "Urban Water Pricing and Drought Management." *Water Resources Research* 23 (3): 393–98.

Morris, J.R., and C.V. Jones. 1980. *Water for Denver: An Analysis of the Alternatives.* Denver, CO: Environmental Defense Fund.

Nieswiadomy, M., and D. Molina. 1989. "Comparing Residential Water Demand Estimates Under Decreasing and Increasing Block Rates Using Household Data." *Land Economics* 65 (3): 280–289.

Nieswiadomy, M., and D. Molina. 1991. "A Note on Price Perception in Water Demand Models." *Land Economics* 67 (3): 352–59.

Nieswiadomy, M.L. 1992. "Estimating Urban Residential Water Demand: Effects of Price Structure, Conservation, and Education." *Water Resources Research* 28 (3): 609–15.

Nieswiadomy, M.L., and S.L. Cobb. 1993. "Impact of Pricing Structure Selectivity on Urban Water Demand." *Contemporary Policy Issues* 11 (3): 101–113.

Ozog, M.T. 1996. "Price Elasticity and Net Lost Revenue." Pp. 485–489 in *Proceedings of CONSERV96: Responsible Water Stewardship.* Orlando, FL: American Water Works Association.

Shin, J–S. 1985. "Perception of Price When Price Information is Costly: Evidence from Residential Electricity Demand." *Review of Economics and Statistics* 67 (4): 591–98.

Stevens, T.H., J.Miller, and C. Willis. 1992. "Effects of Price Structure on Residential Water Demand." *Water Resources Bulletin* 28 (4): 681–685.

Williams, M., and B. Suh. 1986. "The Demand for Urban Water by Customer Class." *Applied Economics* 18: 1275–1289.

DEMAND SYSTEMS FOR ENERGY FORECASTING:
PRACTICAL CONSIDERATIONS FOR ESTIMATING A GENERALIZED LOGIT MODEL

Weifeng Weng and Timothy D. Mount

ABSTRACT

Generalized logit models of demand systems for energy and other factors have been shown to work well in comparison with other popular models, such as the "almost ideal demand system and translog model. The main reason is that the derived price elasticities are robust when expenditure shares are small, as they are for electricity and fuels. A number of different versions of the generalized logit model have been applied in the literature, and the primary objective of the paper is to determine which one is the best. Using annual data for energy demand in the United States at the state level, the final model selected is similar to a simple form that was originally proposed by Considine. A second objective of the paper is to demonstrate that the estimated elasticities are sensitive to the units specified for prices, and to show how price scales should be estimated as part of the model.

Advances in Business and Management Forecasting, Volume 2, pages 131–153.
Copyright © 1998 by JAI Press Inc.
All rights of reproduction in any form reserved.
ISBN: 0-7623-0002-7

I. INTRODUCTION

Generalized logit models (GL) have been used in a number of different applications to estimated demand systems for energy. Recently, Rothman, Hong, and Mount (1994) have shown that a GL model of consumer demand performed much better than the popular almost ideal demand system, proposed by Deaton and Muellbauer (1980a) (DM), or the translog model, proposed by Christensen, Jorgenson, and Lau (TL). This analysis was based on United Nations data for a cross-section of 53 different countries. Although all three models gave similar estimates of price elasticities at the mean of the sample, the economic consistency of the DM and TL models tended to breakdown when expenditure shares differed from the mean values. For a nine commodity system the estimated demand equations were consistent with theory for only 9 and 26% of the countries using the DM and TL models, respectively. In contrast, the GL model gave consistent demand equations for 96% of the countries. The simplest explanation of why the GL model performed better is that the price elasticities in the DM and TL models are sensitive to situations in which some expenditure shares are close to zero. This issue is discussed more fully in Section II.

Reasons for using a GL model are not limited to judging its relative performance with other models. The structure of the GL model also enhances the types of analysis that can be conducted by making it possible to consider extreme situations which are not observed directly in the sample. For example, Dumagan and Mount (1992, 1993, 1996) show how a GL model of a demand system, which includes electricity, natural gas, and oil, can be used to represent an all-electric customer who is not affected by changes in the prices of natural gas or oil. In this case, the issue is how price elasticities behave when some expenditure shares are zero.

The basic tradeoff between using a DM model of consumer demand (or a TL model of factor demand) and a GL model is that the structure of the GL model is more difficult to estimate. Hong (1994) has shown that a generalized Barnett model, which was much harder to estimate than a GL model, also performs better than the DM and TL models using the data from 53 countries, but characteristics of the corresponding price elasticities were very difficult to interpret. Fortunately, the expressions for the price elasticities derived from a GL model are simple functions of the parameters and easy to interpret.

The main complication of estimating a GL model compared to the DM model, for example, is that weighting functions for prices must be specified to approximate the symmetry restrictions derived from economic theory. A variety of different parameterizations of the weighting function have been specified for GL models in the literature. The primary objective of this paper is to specify a general form of weighting function, and to determine which specific parameterization is supported best by the data. It should be noted that one parameterization gives price elasticities which are almost identical to the DM and TL models. A secondary objective of the paper is to introduce a new issue concerning how to scale the price variables. This issue is shown to affect the economic properties of the estimated elasticities in a significant way. The empirical results are presented in Section III and IV using annual data for energy demand in the United States at the state level. Separate GL demand systems are estimated for the residential, commercial, and industrial sectors.

II. ECONOMIC PROPERTIES OF THE GENERALIZED LOGIT MODEL

This section describes the basic structure of a linear regression model which can be applied to both consumer demand and factor demand systems. Using this general form, the structures of the TL model of factor demand and the DM model of consumer demand are compared to the corresponding GL models. This comparison is used to identify reasons for preferring the properties of the price elasticities in a GL model. Since a factor demand system is simpler in structure than a consumer demand system, factor demand is discussed first and consumer demand is treated as an extension of the factor demand system.

A. Model Specification for Factor Demand

The general form of a demand system for n input factors can be written as a series of $(n - 1)$ linear regression equations:

$$y_i = \alpha_{i0} + \alpha_{i1}x_{i1} + \ldots + \alpha_{in-1}x_{in-1} + \beta_{i1}z_{i1} + \ldots + \beta_{im}z_{im} + e_i$$

$$= \alpha_{i0} + \sum_{j=1}^{n-1} \alpha_{ij}x_{ij} + \sum_{k=1}^{m} \beta_{ik}z_{ik} + e_i \quad i = 1, 2, \ldots, n - 1 \quad (1)$$

where y_i is the dependent variable, x_{ij} is a price variable, z_{ik} is a non-price variable (e.g., dummy variables for different locations), and e_i is a residual. Important restrictions on the price coefficients (α_{ij}) can be derived from economic theory. These restrictions tend to increase the efficiency of the estimation (i.e., reduce the standard errors of estimated coefficients) as well as ensure that the demand responses are consistent with theory.

The Translog Demand System

One of the most widely used models of factor demand is the TL model developed by Christensen, Jorgenson, and Lau. If C is the total cost of all input factors, p_i is the price of factor i, and q_i is the quantity of factor i, then the dependent variable in (1) is the expenditure share of factor i, and the price variables are the logarithms of price ratios:

$$y_i = w_i = p_i q_i / C; \quad 1 \geq w_i \geq 0; \quad \sum_{i=1}^{n} w_i = 1$$

$$x_{ij} = \log(p_j/p_n) \qquad j = 1, 2, \ldots, n-1$$

The main restrictions from economic theory imply symmetry of the price coefficients in the demand system ($\alpha_{ij} = \alpha_{ji}$ for all i and j). Using price ratios in x_{ij} ensures that the expenditure shares are not affected by pure inflation (the same proportional change in all prices). Economic theory also implies that the Hicksian price effects should be consistent with conditions for concavity of the cost and utility functions.

The standard (Hicksian) price elasticities (holding production fixed) have a relatively simple form, but they are functions of the expenditure shares (note that

$$\alpha_{in} = -\sum_{j=1}^{n-1} \alpha_{ij}).$$

Cross-price

$$E_{ij} = \alpha_{ij}/w_i + w_j, \quad \text{for all } i \neq j \tag{2a}$$

Own-price

$$E_{ij} = \alpha_{ii}/w_i + w_i - 1 \qquad (2b)$$

The TL model is widely used, but there is a practical problem associated with it when an expenditure share w_i is close to zero. The value of the price elasticities are very sensitive to small changes of w_i when $w_i \to 0$, and if $\alpha_{ii} > 0$ (price inelastic), the own-price elasticity will violate economic logic by becoming positive. Since expenditure shares on fuels and electricity are often quite small, the TL model for energy demand is vulnerable to this problem. Thus, it is desirable to find an alternative model which is more suitable for situations when expenditure shares are small. The GL model is one way to solve the problem.

The Generalized Logit Demand System

The GL model is a simple modification of the standard regression equation in (1):

$$y_i = \alpha_{i0} + \sum_{j=1,j\neq i}^{n} \alpha_{ij}x_{ij} - \sum_{j=1}^{n-1} \alpha_{nj}x_{nj} + \sum_{k=1}^{m} \beta_{ik}z_{ik} + e_i \qquad (3)$$

where

$$y_i = \log(w_i/w_n) \qquad i = 1, 2, \ldots, n-1,$$

$$x_{ij} = \theta_{ij}\log(p_j/p_i) \quad \text{for all } j \neq i,$$

where θ_{ij} is a known function of w_i and w_j (discussed below). In both the TL and GL models, the restrictions $\alpha_{ij} = \alpha_{ji}$ are implied by economic theory.

Even though the form of the regression equations in the GL model is more complicated than it is for the TL model, the expressions for the Hicksian price elasticities for the GL are simple.

Cross-price

$$E_{ij} = \alpha_{ij}\theta_{ij} + w_j \quad \text{for all } i \neq j \qquad (4a)$$

Own-price

$$E_{ii} = - \sum_{k=1,\, k \neq i}^{n} \alpha_{ik}\theta_{ik} + w_i - 1 \qquad\qquad (4b)$$

Unlike the TL elasticities, the GL elasticities are not sensitive to small expenditure shares ($w_i \rightarrow 0$) if the form of θ_{ij} is specified appropriately.

B. Model Specification for Consumer Demand

In models of factor demand the logarithm of production can be included as an explanatory variable (one of the z_{ik}) if returns to the scale of production are not constant. In consumer demand the equivalent assumption to constant returns to scale is that all income elasticities are unity. In most applications this simplification is not realistic for consumer demand. When income elasticities are allowed to differ from unity, a problem arises in specifying a demand system that is consistent with economic theory because the Hicksian price elasticities are defined holding utility constant. Unlike the level of production in models of factor demand, utility is not observable and cannot be included as an explanatory variable. As an alternative the observed level of income is included, and Marshallian price elasticities (holding income constant) are generally reported for consumer demand. Nevertheless, the important symmetry restrictions derived from economic theory are still defined in terms of the Hicksian price elasticities, and there is a simple relationship linking the Hicksian to the Marshallian elasticities:

$$E_{ij} = E_{ij}^m + w_j E_{il}^m \quad \text{for all } i \text{ and } j \qquad\qquad (5)$$

where E_{ij}^m is the Marshallian price elasticity, and E_{il}^m is the Marshallian income elasticity.

The model of consumer demand corresponding to the form of the TL model of factor demand is the DM model proposed by Deaton and Muellbauer (1980b). In the DM model the logarithm of real (deflated) income is included ($z_{i1} = \log(I/QPI)$, where I is nominal income and QPI is a quadratic price index of $\log(p_i)$, $i = 1, 2, \ldots, n$). In the GL model of consumer demand the logarithm of real income is also included but the deflator is the standard Stone price index (see Appendix). The dependent variables, the price variables, and the symmetry restrictions ($\alpha_{ij} = \alpha_{ji}$) have the same forms as the TL and GL models of factor demand, defined above. Under these specifications the income elasticities have the following simple forms:

DM Model

$$E_{iI} = 1 + \beta_{i1}/w_i \qquad (6a)$$

GL Model

$$E_{iI} = 1 + \beta_{i1} - \sum_{k=1}^{n} \beta_{k1} w_k \qquad (6b)$$

The Hicksian price elasticities for consumer demand, corresponding to (3) and (4), can be written as follows (the Marshallian price elasticities can be derived using (5) and (6), but the expressions are relatively complicated):

DM Model
Cross-Price

$$E_{ij} = \alpha_{ij}/w_i + w_j + \beta_{i1}\beta_{j1}\log(i/QPI)/w_i \quad \text{for } i \neq j \qquad (7a)$$

Own-Price

$$E_{ii} = \alpha_{ii}/w_i + w_i + \beta_{i1}^2 \log(I/QPI)/w_i - 1 \qquad (7b)$$

GL Model
Cross-Price

$$E_{ij} = \alpha_{ij}\theta_{ij} + w_j \quad \text{for } i \neq j; \qquad (8a)$$

Own-Price

$$E_{ii} = - \sum_{j=1, j\neq i}^{n} \alpha_{ij}\theta_{ij} + w_i - 1 \qquad (8b)$$

The forms of the elasticities for the GL model are identical for factor demand (4) and consumer demand (8) but the elasticities in the DM model of consumer demand (7) have an additional term compared to the TL model of factor demand (2) (this extra term is zero if real income is normalized to one at the point of evaluation). More importantly, the price elasticities for the DM model still exhibit the undesirable property of being sensitive to small expenditure shares ($w_i \to 0$).

III. FUNCTIONAL FORM OF THE CROSS-PRICE WEIGHT IN THE GL MODEL

The functional form of θ_{ik} in a GL model (3) is critical in determining the properties of the price elasticities. All elasticity expressions in (4) and (8) have been derived conditionally on the value of θ_{ij}. Using this simplification, any form of θ_{ij} must satisfy the property $w_i\theta_{ij} = w_j\theta_{ji}$ (for $i \neq j$) to ensure that the symmetry conditions required by economic theory are met.

When $w_j \rightarrow 0$, it is desirable to have the cross-price elasticity $E_{ij} \rightarrow 0$ because it implies that the demand for commodity i is unresponsive to changes in prices for commodities that are not purchased. The following forms of weighting scheme have been used in previous studies:

(i) $\theta_{ij} = w_j$. With this form, the cross-price elasticities in (4) and (8) are simple linear functions of w_j (Considine).

(ii) $\theta_{ij} = (w_j^{1-\gamma})/(w_i^\gamma)$ where $0 \leq \gamma \leq 1$ is a parameter (Dumagan). This is a general form of the weight in (i), but the problem is that as $w_i \rightarrow 0$, $\theta_{ij} \rightarrow \infty$. If $\gamma = 1$, the cross-price elasticities in (4) have a similar form to the TL elasticities for factor demand (3), and therefore, this form of θ_{ij} can be used to test the appropriateness of the TL model.

(iii) $\theta_{ij} = w_i^{-\gamma}w_j^{1-\gamma}$ and $\gamma \leq 0$. This form is similar to the weight in (ii) but since $\gamma \leq 0$, the problem associated with $w_i \rightarrow 0$ is eliminated, and $\theta_{ij} = 0$ if $w_i = 0$ or $w_j = 0$.

(iv) $\theta_{ij} = w_i^{-\gamma}w_j^{1-\gamma}(1 - w_i - w_j)$ and $\gamma \leq 0$. The term $(1 - w_i - w_j)$ is added to (iii) to deal with complementarities (when any α_{ij} has a negative value large enough to make $E_{ij} < 0$). It ensures that all pairs of commodities must be substitutes, as theory requires, if any two commodities dominate expenditures ($w_i + w_j \rightarrow 1$). This form of θ_{ij} has been shown to perform well in comparison to other models (see Rothman, Hong, and Mount (1994)).

(v) $\theta_{ij} = (w_j)/((w_i + \delta)^\gamma(w_j + \delta)^\gamma))$ and $\delta > 0$. This form is closely related to (ii), but because $\delta > 0$, it does not explode when $w_i \rightarrow 0$. Forms (i), (ii), and (iii) can be viewed as special cases of (v). To ensure that θ_{ij} increases monotonically with w_j, the restriction $\gamma \leq 1 + \delta$ must hold.

For standard data sets which are characterized by substitution among commodities, forms (i), (ii), and (iii) are possible choices for θ_{ij}, and all three can be approximated by (v) when $\delta \rightarrow 0$. All three cases exhibit the desirable property $E_{ij} \rightarrow 0$ when $w_j \rightarrow 0$. However, the behavior of E_{ij} when $w_i \rightarrow 0$ is determined by the sign of γ, and this has implications for the economic logic of the model. One would expect that the elasticity for

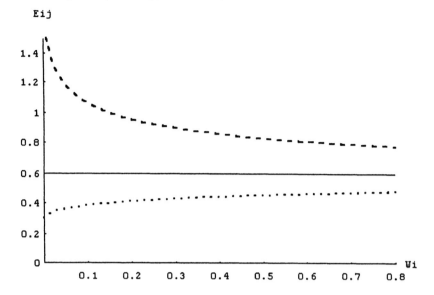

Figure 1a. Hicksian Cross-price Elasticity E_{ij} (holding $w_j = .2$ constant) $\gamma = -.2 \cdots, \gamma = 0 \text{——}, \gamma = .2 ---$

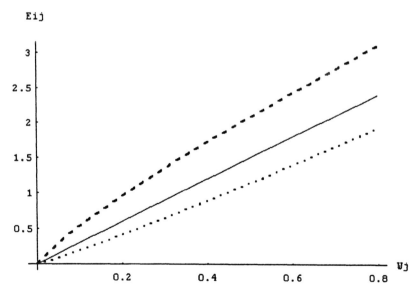

Figure 1b. Hicksian Cross-price Elasticity E_{ij} (holding $w_i = .2$ constant) $\gamma = -.2 \cdots, \gamma = 0 \text{——}, \gamma = .2 ---$

changing price j (for a given w_j) would be larger if w_i was small. Consequently, GL models with $\gamma > 0$ should be preferred. These results are illustrated in Figure 1, and the dashed lines ($\gamma = .2$) have the desirable properties in both 1a and 1b, but the dotted line ($\gamma = -.2$) in 1a is counterintuitive. In the next section the value of γ is estimated, and as a result, it will be possible to determine whether the data support the TL or DM model ($\gamma = 1$), Dumagan's GL model ($\gamma = .5$), Considine's GL model ($\gamma = 0$), or Rothman, Hong, and Mount's GL model ($\gamma = -1$).

IV. ESTIMATION AND PRICE SCALING

In most previous applications of the GL model, the form of the cross-price weight θ_{ij} is fully specified, including the values of the parameters γ and δ. The models estimated by Dumagan are exceptions. One objective of this paper is to allow the data to determine the best form of θ_{ij}. Before this can be done, however, another important question must be discussed. Why are the results sensitive to the units of prices in the GL model but not in TL or DM model? The reason is that in the TL or DM model changing the scale of any price results in offsetting changes of the intercepts. For the GL model, the presence of the cross-price weights makes the model more complicated. If $c_j > 0$ is a scalar (e.g., for normalizing price j to a given year), then $\alpha_{ij}x_{ij} = \alpha_{ij}\log((c_jp_j)/p_n) = \alpha_{ij}\log(c_j) + \alpha_{ij}\log(p_j/p_n)$ for the TL and DM models, and $\alpha_{ij}x_{ij} = \alpha_{ij}\theta_{ij}\log((c_jp_j)/p_i) = \alpha_{ij}\theta_{ij}\log(c_j) + \alpha_{ij}\theta_{ij}\log(p_j/p_i)$ for the GL model. The estimated price coefficients (α_{ij}) are unaffected in the TL and DM models by the choice of the price scalar (c_j), but these parameters should be estimated in the GL model because θ_{ij} is a variable. The alternative is to adopt a specific way to normalize the prices in a GL model, and the results are then conditional on that choice.

GL models with and without price scaling are estimated by using a range of values of γ and a specified value of $\delta = .005$. By varying γ from -1 to 1, the goodness of fit and the economic validity of the model can be determined and the effects of scaling prices assessed. First, any set of estimated price elasticities should be logical and consistent with economic theory (the Eigen values of the Hicksian price effects should be nonpositive). For estimation, the best value of γ is selected by finding the smallest determinant of the variance-covariance matrix of residuals across equations, which corresponds to the best fit of the model. A finer grid of γ values is used close to the best fit ($\gamma = 1, 0.5, 0.1, 0.05, 0.01, 0,$ $-0.01, -0.05, -0.1, -0.5, -1$).

The data used for estimation are a pooled cross-section of 48 states and an annual time series from 1970 to 1992 (residential) and 1978 to 1992 (commercial and industrial) using data from the Energy Information Administration and the Bureau of Economic Analysis (see Weng and Mount 1996). A separate GL demand system is fitted for the residential, commercial, and industrial sectors, and the factors included are:

Residential	Commercial	Industrial
Electricity (EL)	Electricity (EL)	Electricity (EL)
Natural Gas (NG)	Natural Gas (NG)	Natural Gas (NG)
Oil (OL)	Oil (OL)	Oil (OL)
Other (OT)	Capital (CE)	Coal (CL)
	Labor (LB)	Capital (CE)
		Labor (LB)

Figure 2 gives a summary of the estimated own price elasticities in the residential sector for different values of γ. The first observation is that the price elasticities, particularly for electricity in the model without price scaling, are sensitive to the value of γ. Demand is generally more price responsive at the extreme values of γ and less responsive for values close to zero. The second observation is that price scaling matters. In the model without price scaling, two of the cases violate economic logic and give price elasticities for electricity that are positive. In addition, the value of gamma with the best fit ($\gamma = 0.01$) is close to the invalid models ($\gamma = .05$ and $.1$). The model with price scaling is consistent with economic theory for all values of γ, and the corresponding price elasticities are much more robust to different values of γ. Thus, the model with price scaling is preferred, and this conclusion is also reached in the commercial and industrial sectors.

For $\delta = .005$, the best fit is obtained at $\gamma = .01, .075$, and $.05$ for the residential, commercial, industrial sectors, respectively. In order to get an economically valid model for the industrial sector, weak separability among fossil fuels was imposed. This type of simplification is easy to impose using the restrictions $\alpha_{ik} = \alpha_{jk}$ for all i, j that belong to the fossil-fuel group and all k that do not belong to that group.

The estimated values of γ in the cross-price weights for the three sectors are all positive and close to zero. The positive signs are consistent with

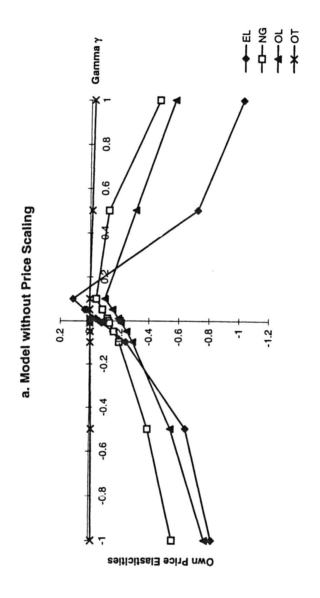

a. Model without Price Scaling

Gamma γ

EL
NG
OL
OT

Own Price Elasticities

142

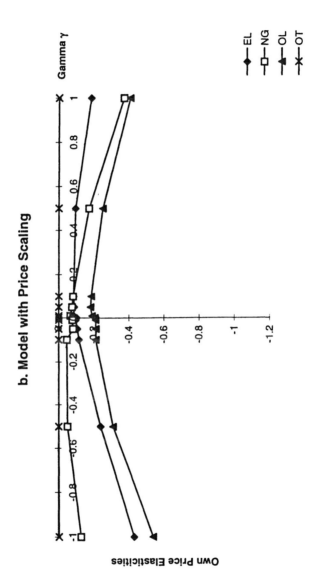

b. Model with Price Scaling

Figure 2. The Estimated Elasticities for Different Values of Gamma

143

the desired properties of the cross-price elasticities shown in Figure 1. The small values provide support for Considine's simple weighting scheme with $\gamma = 0$ versus the TL and DM models ($\gamma = 1$) or Dumagan's (1991) ($\gamma = .5$) and Rothman, Hong, and Mount's (1994) ($\gamma = -1$) GL model. For comparative purposes, Considine's form of GL model ($\gamma = \delta = 0$) was estimated with price scaling. For the industrial and commercial sectors, the fit with $\gamma = \delta = 0$ was worse (4 and 3% increase in the error, respectively), and the model for the commercial sector violated the concavity requirements of economic theory. For the residential sector, the fit with $\gamma = \delta = 0$ was slightly better (0.1% decrease in the error) and the estimated price elasticities were virtually identical. Estimated elasticities for the three sectors with price scaling, $\delta = .005$ and an estimated γ are presented in the final section.

V. RESULTS AND CONCLUSIONS

The matrices of estimated elasticities for the three sectors using the GL model are presented in Tables 1–3. Since the models include a dynamic adjustment process (see Appendix), estimates of both the short-run and long-run elasticities are given (the restrictions derived from economic theory and the expressions in Section II refer to the short-run elasticities). The reported elasticities use the data for New York State in 1991 as the base point. The estimated regression models are summarized in the Appendix.

In general, own price elasticities for all sources of energy in all three sectors are price inelastic in the short run and in the long run. Cross-price elasticities between sources of energy are very small ($|E_{ij}| < 0.1$) in the residential and industrial sectors, but generally exhibit strong substitutability ($E_{ij} > 0.1$) in the commercial sector. Complementary relationships between energy and non-energy exist in the residential sector. Strong substitutability between energy factors and capital exists in both the commercial and industrial sectors. In contrast, all but one of the relationships between energy and labor are complementary. Labor and capital are strong substitutes in both the commercial and industrial sectors. One surprise in the residential sector is that the long-run income elasticity for oil is highly negative. This may reflect a general movement away from using oil for heating homes during the eighties.

One issue about the form of the GL models deserves further elaboration, and this relates to the relatively large number of negative estimates of the cross price coefficients (α_{ij}). Given the chosen form of the cross

Table 1. The Estimated Demand Elasticities for Residential Sector

Short-Run Mairshallian Income and Price Elasticities

	Electricity	N Gas	Oil	Other	Income
Electricity	-0.09767	0.03979	-0.00071	-0.84035	0.89894
N gas	0.07112	-0.07349	-0.00784	-0.80765	0.81787
Oil	0.00429	-0.00923	-0.19312	-0.13134	0.32939
Other	-0.01060	-0.00630	-0.00322	-0.98490	1.00502

Short-Run Hicksian Elasticities

	Electricity	N Gas	Oil	Other
Electricity	-0.08780	0.04539	0.00287	0.03954
N gas	0.08010	-0.06840	-0.00459	-0.00711
Oil	0.00791	-0.00718	-0.19181	0.19107
Other	0.00044	-0.00005	0.00078	-0.00118

Long-Run Marshallian Income and Price Elasticities

	Electricity	N Gas	Oil	Other	Income
Electricity	-0.47167	0.17652	0.01189	-0.28263	0.56586
N gas	0.39810	-0.35114	-0.02373	-0.27262	0.24940
Oil	0.16085	0.06583	-0.89820	2.81973	-2.14868
Other	-0.00912	-0.00638	-0.00040	-1.00666	1.02245

Long-Run Hicksian Elasticities

	Electricity	N Gas	Oil	Other
Electricity	-0.46066	0.18275	0.01587	0.69618
N gas	0.40908	-0.34490	-0.01975	0.70619
Oil	0.17184	0.07205	-0.89414	3.79854
Other	0.00187	-0.00015	0.00358	-0.02775

price weight (θ_{ij}), the cross price elasticities for the GL model in (4) and (8) can be written:

$$E_{ij} = w_j \left[\alpha_{ij} / \left((w_i + \delta)^\gamma (w_j + \delta)^\gamma \right) + 1 \right] \tag{9}$$

Consequently, the sign of α_{ij} determines whether E_{ij} increases more than ($\alpha_{ij} > 0$) or less than ($\alpha_{ij} < 0$) proportionally with w_j. If α_{ij} is sufficiently negative, then E_{ij} is also negative and the relationship is complementary.

Since the effect of α_{ij} in (9) is largest, for any given w_j and $\gamma > 0$, when $w_i = 0$, the discussion will focus on how E_{ij} changes as w_j increases from 0 to 1 holding $w_i = 0$. If $\alpha_{ij} > -\delta^{2\gamma}$, E_{ij} is always positive (substitute), and if $\alpha_{ij} < -(1 + \delta)^\gamma \delta^\gamma$, E_{ij} is always negative (complement). For $-(1 + \delta)^\gamma \delta^\gamma < \alpha_{ij} < -\delta^{2\gamma}$, $E_{ij} < 0$ for small w_j and $E_{ij} > 0$, as economic theory requires, if $w_j \rightarrow 1$. Given these desirable properties, one could consider using $-\delta^{2\gamma}$ as a lower bound for α_{ij}, but the problem with this restriction is that the magnitude of $|E_{ij}|$ is too small to capture strong complementary relationships. Hence, the presence of $\alpha_{ij} \leq -(1 + \delta)^\gamma \delta^\gamma$ must be accepted as a possibility, and the economic logic of the model would only hold for a limited range of w_i and w_j in this case (i.e., $w_i + w_j < c < 1$). This may not be a serious limitation in many applications if it is unlikely that any pair of factors will dominate expenditures. It is interesting to note that capital and labor are found to be substitutes in Tables 2 and 3. Since these two factors generally account for almost 90% of total expenditures, finding complementary relationships would have posed a potential problem. If complementaries are important in a particular application, as they are in the cross country study reported by Rothman, Hong and Mount (1994), then modifying form (v) of θ_{ij} could be considered using the same rationale adopted to convert form (iii) to form (iv) in Section III.

In summary, this paper has focused on two practical issues related to estimating GL models of demand. The first issue is price scaling, which has not been discussed before in the literature. The results show that the estimated models are sensitive to price scaling, and that the estimated elasticities are more robust and consistent with economic theory when price scales are estimated. We conclude that price scaling should be adopted when estimating GL models.

Table 2. The Estimated Demand Elasticities for Commercial Sector

Short-Run Price Elasticities					
	Electricity	N Gas	Oil and Coal	Capital	Labor
Electricity	−0.04744	0.02598	0.01556	0.03275	−0.02685
N gas	0.13502	−0.18649	0.05598	0.12371	−0.12821
Oil and Coal	0.08633	0.05974	−0.19266	0.38053	−0.33394
Capital	0.00244	0.00177	0.00510	−0.34246	0.33315
Labor	−0.00060	−0.00055	−0.00135	0.10054	−0.09803
Long-Run Price Elasticities					
	Electricity	N Gas	Oil and Coal	Capital	Labor
Electricity	−0.04682	0.05601	0.02884	0.03356	−0.07164
N gas	0.40422	−0.41604	0.13057	0.24739	−0.36625
Oil and Coal	0.33236	0.18585	−0.40085	0.93375	−1.05142
Capital	−0.01774	−0.00083	0.00713	−0.83853	0.84996
Labor	0.00331	0.00004	−0.00174	0.24746	−0.24906

Table 3. The Estimated Demand Elasticities for Industrial Sector

Short-Run Price Elasticities

	Electricity	N Gas	Oil	Coal	Capital	Labor
Electricity	-0.19054	-0.00010	-0.00018	-0.00003	0.10498	0.08586
N gas	-0.00038	-0.11256	.00217	0.00211	0.18996	-0.08132
Oil	-0.00038	0.00124	-0.10676	-0.00276	0.18996	-0.08132
Coal	-0.00038	0.00731	-0.01665	-0.09894	0.18996	-0.08132
Capital	0.01047	0.00509	0.00890	0.00147	-0.59988	0.57395
Labor	0.00367	-0.00094	-0.00163	-0.00027	0.24613	-0.24697

Long-Run Price Elasticities

	Electricity	N Gas	Oil	Coal	Capital	Labor
Electricity	-0.35704	-0.01227	-0.00974	-0.00234	0.35870	0.02261
N gas	0.00225	-0.35350	-0.00039	-0.00332	1.07140	-0.71659
Oil	0.00806	0.08300	-0.26201	-0.01121	0.09881	0.08325
Coal	0.00431	0.06738	-0.01212	-0.24444	0.44219	-0.25744
Capital	0.02815	0.02207	0.00655	0.00357	-1.44409	1.38371
Labor	0.00300	-0.00676	0.00291	-0.00035	0.58817	-0.58694

The second issue in the paper considers the form of the cross-price weights (θ_{ij}) in the GL model. In this paper a general form is chosen that can approximate a range of models discussed in the literature, including the popular DM and TL models. The key parameter (γ) that determines the form of θ_{ij} is estimated using a grid search over the range -1 to 1. The estimated values are positive and close to zero in all three sectors. These results do not support the form of elasticity derived from a DM or TL model ($\gamma = 1$), and are closest to the GL model proposed by Considine ($\gamma = 0$). They are consistent with the economic expectation of how price elasticities should change when expenditure shares change ($\gamma > 0$). In this respect, the results provide more evidence that the GL model can provide a satisfactory way to represent demand systems for energy.

ACKNOWLEDGMENTS

The authors wish to thank the New York Department of Public Service, the Cornell Institute for Social and Economic Research (CISER), and the College of Agriculture and Life Sciences for supporting this research. The responsibility for all conclusions rests exclusively with the authors, and the conclusions do not necessarily reflect the view of the sponsors. The authors are, of course, solely responsible for all errors.

APPENDIX

Regression Equations for the GL Model

Most empirical models of energy demand incorporate some form of dynamic response to price changes, implying that short-run responses are generally smaller than the long-run responses. This can be done in the GL model by adding the lagged value of $\log(q_i/q_n)$ as an explanatory variable. If the cross-price weights θ_{ij} remained constant, the long-run elasticities could be derived analytically. However, cross-price weights are functions of the expenditure shares, and the long-run elasticities must be computed by simulation.

The Hicksian price elasticities can be derived from the share elasticities for factor demand . Since the logarithm of an expenditure share can be written as

$$\log w_i = \log p_i + \log q_i - \log C,$$

the long-run Hicksian own-price elasticities can be computed as

$$E_{iiLR} = \frac{(w_{iT} - w_{i0})/w_{i0}}{(p_{iT} - p_{i0})/p_{i0}} + w_{i0} - 1$$

and the long-run Hicksian cross-price elasticities can be computed as

$$E_{ijLR} = \frac{(w_{iT} - w_{i0})/w_{i0}}{(p_{jT} - p_{j0})/p_{j0}} + w_{j0} \quad \text{for all } i \neq j.$$

where p_{i0} and p_{iT} are the initial and final price of factor i, and w_{i0} and w_{iT} are the corresponding expenditure shares. The long-run Marshallian price elasticities can be computed directly

$$E_{ijLR}^m = \frac{(q_{iT} - q_{i0})/q_{i0}}{(p_{jT} - p_{j0})/p_{j0}} \quad \text{for any } i \text{ and } j;$$

and the long-run Mashallian income elasticities can be computed as

$$E_{iiLR}^m = \frac{(q_{iT} - q_{i0})/q_{i0}}{(I_T - I_0)/I_0}.$$

The specific approach used to calculate the long-run elasticities reported in Tables 1–3 is to (1) use the data for New York State in the year

1991 as the initial values (the intercepts of the estimated equations are determined through calibration to the initial values); (2) change (decrease or increase) one of the prices (or income) by 1% in 1992 and hold it at that level; (3) hold all other explanatory variables at their initial levels; (4) compute annual forecasts to 2010 (the forecasts in 2010 are the final values); and (5) use the average values of the elasticities computed by decreasing and increasing each price as the reported long-run elasticities.

For the regression models, s is the state, t is the year, HDD is heating degree days, and CDD is cooling degree days. The distributed lag parameter for the lagged quantities is λ, c_i is the price scale for p_i, and the α_{ij} parameters correspond to (3). The form of the cross-price weight θ_{ij} is:

$$\theta_{ij} = \frac{w_j}{(w_i + \delta)^\gamma (w_j + \delta)^\gamma}$$

The estimated residential model is given in (A1), where $i = 1$ is electricity, 2 is natural gas, 3 is oil, n is other, non-energy goods.

$$\log(w_{its}/w_{nts}) = (\alpha_{i0s} - \alpha_{n0s}) + \sum_{j=1, j \neq i}^{n} (\alpha_{ij}\theta_{ij(t-1)s} \log(p_{jts}/p_{its}))$$

$$- \sum_{j=1}^{n-1} (\alpha_{nj}\theta_{nj(t-1)s} \log(p_{jts}/p_{nts})) + \sum_{j=1, j \neq i}^{n} (\alpha_{ij}\theta_{ij(t-1)s} \log(c_j/c_i))$$

$$- \sum_{j=1}^{n-1} (\alpha_{nj}\theta_{nj(t-1)s} \log(c_j/c_n))$$

$$+ (\beta_i - \beta_n)\log(I_{ts}/SPI_{ts}) + \lambda(\log(q_{i(t-1)s}/q_{n(t-1)s}))$$

$$+ \gamma_{i1} HDD_{ts} + \gamma_{i2}CDD_{ts} + (e_{its} - e_{nts}),$$

$$i = 1, 2, 3; \tag{A1}$$

subject to $\alpha_{ij} = \alpha_{ji}$, $c_n = 0$, $\beta_n = 0$ and $\alpha_{n0s} = 0$. SPI_{ts} is a Stone price index using lagged expenditure shares defined as

$$\log SPI_{ts} = \sum_{j=1}^{n} w_{j(t-1)s} \log p_{jts}.$$

The estimated commercial and industrial models correspond to (A2), where $i = 1$ is electricity, 2 is natural gas, 3 is oil in both sectors, 4 is capital, 5 is labor in the commercial sector and 4 is coal, 5 is capital, 6 is labor in the industrial sector.

$$\log(w_{its}/w_{nts}) = (a_{i0s} - a_{n0s}) + \sum_{j=1, j\neq i}^{n} (\alpha_{ij}\theta_{ij(t-1)s} \log(p_{jts}/p_{its}))$$

$$- \sum_{j=1}^{n-1} (\alpha_{nj}\theta_{nj(t-1)s} \log(p_{ts}/p_{nts}))$$

$$+ \sum_{j=1, j\neq i}^{n} (\alpha_{ij}\theta_{ij(t-1)s} \log(c_j/c_i))$$

Table A1. The Estimated Demand Models for Residential Sector (SAS Output)—Generalized Logit model using form (v) with delta = 0.005 and gamma = 0.01

Nonlinear ISTUR Summary of Residual Errors

Equation	DF Model	DF Error	SSE	MSE
ELEC	5.333	1051	2.112	0.0020
NGAS	5.333	1051	9.202	0.0088
OIL	4.333	1052	25.232	0.0240

Nonlinear ISTUR Parameter Estimates

Para.name	Est. Value	Std. Error	T Ratio	Prob > |T|
RC12	5.77198	0.79794	7.23	0.0001
RC13	-0.25621	0.49223	-0.52	0.6028
RC14	-0.92057	0.01931	-47.66	0.0001
RC23	-1.96355	1.21077	-1.62	0.1052
RC24	-0.96289	0.02256	-42.69	0.0001
RC34	-0.76762	0.02484	-30.9	0.0001
RC1Y	-0.10608	0.01869	-5.67	0.0001
RC2Y	-0.18715	0.0411	-4.55	0.0001
RC3Y	-0.67563	0.06216	-10.87	0.0001
RB1	-0.25638	2.45514	-0.1	0.9169
RB2	1.08547	2.45441	0.44	0.6584
RB3	2.03102	2.99777	0.68	0.4982
RL11	0.78922	0.01497	52.71	0.0001
WE12	0.00017	9.82E-06	17.69	0.0001
WE21	0.00001	5.11E-06	2.24	0.0256

$$- \sum_{j=1}^{n-1} (\alpha_{nj} \theta_{nj(t-1)s} \log(c_j/c_n))$$

$$+ \lambda(\log (q_{i(t-1)s}/q_{n(t-1)s}))$$

$$+ \gamma_{i1} HDD_{ts} + \gamma_{i2} CDD_{ts} + (e_{its} - e_{nts}),$$

$$i = 1, 2, \ldots, n - 1; \tag{A2}$$

Table A2. The Estimated Demand Models for Commercial Sector (SAS Output)—Generalized Logit model using form (v) with delta = 0.005 and gamma = 0.075

Nonlinear ISTUR Summary af Residual Errors

Equation	DF Model	DF Error	SSE	MSE
ELEC	5.75	554.3	1.915	0.0035
NGAS	4.75	555.3	4.814	0.0087
OIL	4.75	555.3	28.495	0.0513
CAPITAL	3.75	556.3	5.126	0.0092

Nonlinear ISTUR Parameter Estimates

Para.name	Est. Value	Std. Error	T Ratio	Prob > |T|
CC12	3.67407	1.216510	3.02	0.0026
CC13	2.15639	1.724310	1.25	0.2116
CC14	-0.57539	0.039190	-14.68	0.0001
CC15	-0.76135	0.024560	-30.99	0.0001
CC23	8.47007	3.028450	2.8	0.0053
CC24	-0.28369	0.060380	-4.7	0.0001
CC25	-0.79996	0.032350	-24.73	0.0001
CC34	0.42453	0.168230	2.52	0.0119
CC35	-0.98541	0.047150	-20.9	0.0001
CC45	-0.48788	0.017800	-27.4	0.0001
CB1	-1.65737	0.290490	-5.71	0.0001
CB2	-0.18124	0.281050	-0.64	0.5193
CB3	-0.33217	0.243760	-1.36	0.1735
CB4	3.42573	0.349550	9.8	0.0001
CL11	0.58897	0.014930	39.44	0.0001
WE11	0.00001	0.000005	1.3	0.1952
WE12	0.00008	0.000018	4.45	0.0001
WE21	0.00002	0.000007	2.56	0.0109
WE31	0.00002	0.000018	0.9	0.3692

subject to $\alpha_{ij} = \alpha_{ji}$, $c_n = 0$, $\beta_n = 0$ and $\alpha_{n0s} = 0$.

Models for the residential, commercial, and industrial sectors have been estimated by iterated seemingly-unrelated-regression (ITSUR) using SAS. A summary of the estimated parameters and the fit of the equations are included in Table A1 to Table A3. The relationship of the names of the parameters in the SAS output to those in (A1) and (A2) are as follows: $RCij$, $CCij$ and $ICij$ correspond to α_{ij} (R = residential sector, C = commercial sector, i = industrial sector); $RCiY$ corresponds to β_i ($\beta_4 = 0$ is used for normalization); $RL11$, $CL11$, and $IL11$ correspond to λ; $WEi1$ corresponds to γ_{i1}; $WEi2$ corresponds to γ_{i2}. RBi, CBi, and IBi

Table A3. The Estimated Demand Models for Industrial Sector (SAS Output)—Generalized Logit model using form (v) with delta = 0.005 and gamma = 0.05

Nonlinear ISTUR Summary of Residual Errors

Equation	DF Model	DF Error	SSE	MSE
ELEC	3.55	402.5	1.642	0.0041
NGAS	5.3	400.7	6.390	0.0160
OIL	4.3	401.7	4.475	0.0111
COAL	4.3	401.7	15.465	0.0385
CE	2.55	403.5	8.244	0.0204

Nonlinear ISTUR Parameter Estimates

Para.name	Est. Value	Std. Error	T Ratio	Prob > |T|
IC12	−0.68700	0.06332	−10.85	0.0001
IC15	−0.50055	0.08993	−5.57	0.0001
IC16	−0.71993	0.03327	−21.64	0.0001
IC23	−0.55101	0.10780	−5.11	0.0001
IC24	−0.02649	0.41055	−0.06	0.9486
IC25	−0.25129	0.08946	−2.81	0.0052
IC26	−0.88416	0.03233	−27.35	0.0001
IC34	−1.43896	0.46956	−3.06	0.0023
IC56	−0.12467	0.04377	−2.85	0.0046
IB1	−1.97709	0.89683	−2.2	0.0281
IB2	2.77073	0.46545	5.95	0.0001
IB3	−0.32021	0.55037	−0.58	0.561
IB4	1.80407	0.49588	3.64	0.0003
IB5	5.28239	0.97854	5.4	0.0001
CL11	0.59277	0.01677	35.35	0.0001
WE12	0.00001	0.00002	0.37	0.7082
WE21	0.00001	0.00002	0.56	0.5755
WE22	−0.00007	0.00004	−1.69	0.0924

(for $i = 1, 2, \ldots, n - 1$) correspond to log c_i. In the industrial model, $IC13 = IC14 = IC12$, $IC35 = IC45 = IC25$, and $IC36 = IC46 = IC26$ hold to reflect weak separability of the three fossil fuels.

REFERENCES

Considine, T., and T.D. Mount. 1984. "The Use of Linear Logit Models for Dynamic Input Demand Systems." *The Review of Economics and Statistics* 66 (3): 434–444.

Deaton, A., and J. Muellbauer. 1980a. "An Almost Ideal Demand System." *American Economic Review* 70 (3): 312–326.

Deaton, A., and J. Muellbauer. 1980b. *Economics and Consumer Behavior.* Cambridge: Cambridge University Press.

Dumagan, J.C. 1991. "Measuring Welfare Changes and Modeling Demand Systems: Theory and Applications to Energy Efficiency and Environmental Externalities in New York State Residential Energy Demand." Ph.D. Dissertation, Agricultural, Resource and Managerial Economics Cornell University.

Dumagan, J.C., and T.D. Mount. 1992. "Measuring the Consumer Welfare Effects of Carbon Penalties: Theory and Applications to Household Energy Demand." *Energy Economics Journal* 14 (2): 82–93.

Dumagan, J.C., and T.D. Mount. 1993. "Welfare Effects of Improving End-Use Efficiency: Theory and Application to Residential Electricity Demand." *Resource and Energy Economics Journal* 15 (2): 175–201.

Dumagan, J.C., and T.D. Mount. 1996. "Global Properties of Well-Behaved Demand Systems: A Generalized Logit Model Specification." *Economic Modelling* 13: 235–256.

Green, R., and J. Alston. 1990. "Elasticities in AIDS Models." *American Journal of Agricultural Economics* 72 (2): 442–445.

Hong, J-H. 1994. "The Performance of Alternative Flexible Functional Forms in Model Demand Systems: Theory and Application to Consumer Energy Demand." Ph.D. Dissertation, Agricultural, Resource and Managerial Economics, Cornell University.

Rothman, D.S., J.H. Hong, and T.D. Mount. 1994. "Estimating Consumer Energy Demand Using International Data: Theoretical and Policy Implications." *The Energy Journal* 15 (2): 67–88.

Weng, W., and T.D. Mount. 1996. "New York Energy Demand Model: Demand." CCMU Model Documentation, ARME, Cornell University.

PART III

APPLICATIONS OF FORECASTING

FORECASTING STATE TAX REVENUES:

A NEW APPROACH

Kenneth Lawrence, Asokan Anandarajan, and

Gary Kleinman

ABSTRACT

Developing methods to accurately forecast state tax revenues is a topic that has been discussed extensively in the fields of public policy, econometrics, and public finance. Forecasting state tax revenues is important because the forecasted numbers influence public policy which in effect impacts many parties dependent on the availability of government funding. Budgeting uncertainties in the last decade have led many state governments to rely on ever more sophisticated forecasting methods to provide them with more accurate information for policy making. These methods have been criticized as not being cost effective (the benefits in terms of superior accuracy not outweighing the costs). The objective of this paper is to show the power of relatively simpler statistical techniques in predicting state and local taxes. This paper uses information that is readily available from the New Jersey Department of Labor's internet site at URL and develops a simple, parsi-

Advances in Business and Management Forecasting, Volume 2, pages 157–170.
Copyright © 1998 by JAI Press Inc.
ISBN: 0-7623-0002-7

monious regression model that eliminates bias. The simplicity and parsimony of the model developed has the added advantage that it enables more users (and not simply those with more advanced statistical training) to understand how the numbers have been derived.

I. OBJECTIVE

Developing methods to accurately forecast state tax revenues has been an issue of great interest to students and practitioners of public policy, econometrics, and public finance for many years. The issue draws such interest due to the reliance of so many parties on the availability of government funding. The objective of this study is to show the power of relatively more available statistical techniques in predicting state and local taxes. We believe that this is important because the broader availability, and higher understandability, of such techniques should promote more informed public debate on public finance issues than would the use of such arcane techniques as ARIMA and Box-Jenkins.

II. INTRODUCTION

Budgeting uncertainties in the last decade have led many state governments to rely on ever more sophisticated forecasting methods to provide them with more accurate information for policy making. Because of the magnitude of the fiscal problem facing many states, forecasting has assumed a more central role in the policy-making process. Currently revenue forecasts are closely examined and precision is considered to be essential. This is because revenue forecasting is an important component of the budget development process. The revenue forecast influences the aggregate level of the budget and therefore indirectly affects allocation decisions among various budget categories.

Currently the vote on the balanced budget amendment makes the need for accurate and unbiased forecasting tools imperative. This is because federal and subsequently state policies will be affected by the amendment. State policies in turn will be determined by the tax revenues forecasted. The literature (refer to Section III) indicates that forecasts are significantly biased based on the nature of the party in power. In this scenario it is essential to develop accurate forecasting methods that can eliminate bias and prevent manipulation of policy based on the political dictates of the state and local government parties.

Such a forecasting method, to serve its purpose, should be (a) relatively accurate, (b) require minimal assumptions, and (c) be relatively simple to understand. The relative lack of bias means that the model predicts well, that is, without seasonal or period failures. The minimal assumptions requirement is based on the desire to avoid any avoidable assumptions that people can disagree about, making political bias more difficult. Relative simplicity of understanding suggests that less statistically trained individuals can evaluate the model's output in coming to decisions about future state revenues.

III. LITERATURE REVIEW

The research on forecasting state tax revenues has been limited. In general, however, the published research can be broadly classified into three categories:

- Investigation of the existence and role of bias in revenue forecasts.
- Analysis of the predictive abilities of different forecasting tools for state tax revenue.

Each category will now be considered individually.

A. Investigation of the Existence and Role of Bias in Revenue Forecasts

The main findings of this line of research are shown in Figure 1. This research is based on the premise that political needs lead to manipulation of forecasts. The biased forecasts are then used to justify specific strategies, relating in particular to tax and spending. Research in the last decade has particularly investigated the existence and role of bias in the sales tax revenue forecasts used in government budgeting (Larkey and Smith 1984; Bretschneider and Schroeder 1985; Kamlet, Mowery, and Su 1987; Feenberg, Gentry, Gilroy, and Rosen 1989; Cassidy, Kamlet, and Nagin 1989; Gentry 1989; Shkurti and Winefordner 1989; Bretschneider Gorr, Grizzle, and Klay 1989).

Larkey and Smith argued that the political decision maker responsible for developing a budget has an "asymmetric loss function" with regard to deviations from a balanced budget in the face of economic uncertainty. By this they mean that the greater the deviation, the greater the perceived losses in the form of (a) political embarrassment and (b) lack of flexibility to choose policies that could win the next election. Larkey and Smith noted that forecasting numbers will be biased to provide an "optimum

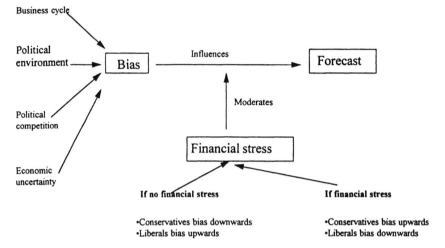

Figure 1. Summary of Tax Forecasting Literature

budget." An optimal budget in their definition is one that generates a small surplus, not large enough to cause political embarrassment but still sufficient to provide a buffer against revenue shortfalls due to downward economic cycles and rising expenditure needs.

Bretschneider and Schroeder (1985) developed a theoretical model of budget decisions that focused on the relationship between risk-taking propensity and revenue forecast bias. The model predicted that budget officials are conservative in their attitude to risk, and revenue forecasts are based accordingly. Feenberg and colleagues (1989) empirically corroborated the model of Bretschneider and Schroeder. They examined the forecasts of state governments' own source tax collections (sales tax, inheritance tax, and so on). They found that the predicted growth of tax revenues were conservatively biased in all three states. Gentry tested the Bretschneider and Schroeder model for individual tax collection revenue and also found a statistically significant bias.

While the samples of the above studies were limited, Cassidy, Kamlet, and Nagin (1989) used a broader sample comprised of more states. They examined 128 state government general fund revenue forecasts representing 23 states for a varying number of years from 1978 to 1986. They found a significant bias in forecasts but noted that the bias was not necessarily conservative. They noted that the bias was a function of (a) anticipated economic outlook and (b) the party in power. In particular, they noted that the Republican states had a propensity for conservative revenue forecasting (ostensibly to cut spending); Democratic states had a propensity for optimistic revenue forecasting (ostensibly to increase spending).

In general, the findings of Cassidy, Kamet, and Nagin suggest that fiscal stress is a moderating variable. If no fiscal stress exists, conservative regimes would conservatively bias forecasts to keep expenses down. Liberal regimes do the opposite. If fiscal stress exists, conservatives switch the direction of their bias and forecast optimistically to "balance the budget on paper" and forestall a tax increase. Liberals do the opposite and forecast conservatively in order to maximize the budget gap and any resultant tax increases.

Bretschneider and Gorr (1992) found that political competition between the branches of state governments in the form of different political parties in control of a state's senate, house, and or governor's office resulted in countervailing pressures that reduced bias.

The summary conclusions of the research are:

1. Bias does exist in forecasting
2. The behavioral aspects of factors that influence the bias are complex.

B. Analysis of the Predictive Abilities of Different Forecasting Tools for State Sales Tax Revenues

It has been noted that state governments use econometric models to forecast revenues. These models employ regression equations that estimate revenues based on predicted levels of economic variables associated with revenue generation. Most local governments do not use econometric analysis but rely instead on simpler trend analysis and "guesstimates." Econometric models have been criticized as not cost beneficial. Grizzle and Klay (1994) attempted to compare the relative predictions of alternative forecasting methods for sales tax revenues. The methods studied were: (a) penultimate, (b) average change, (c) exponential smoothing, (d) linear exponential smoothing (e) linear regression, (f) curve fitting, and (g) combination techniques.

The results indicated that:

1. The performance of the moving average was by far the worst.
2. The error rates covaried with the effort required to make the forecast. The average change and penultimate method, which

hardly required much statistical manipulation, produced the highest error rates.

3. The curve-fitting technique was the most resource intensive in terms of time and effort but produced the lowest error rates.

4. A combination technique using exponential smoothing and linear regression produced an even lower error rate than the curve-fitting technique.

The general conclusion was that for governments not using econometric models combining forecasts from different extrapolative methods might be a more cost effective way of increasing forecast accuracy than going to the expense of developing econometric models.

Fullerton (1989) studied the predictive ability of composite forecasting models. (Composite forecasting models are defined as combinations of two or more different forecasts. It is a technique that incorporates the information provided by several forecasts.) Fullerton compared the predictive ability of composite models with projections provided by an econometric model and an ARIMA univariate time-series model in terms of their ability to predict sales revenues. The results indicate that a composite model built with econometric and univariate ARIMA projections of retail sales tax revenues provide better forecasts than either model. The combined forecasts were also found to be more accurate than the executive branch forecasts actually utilized.

The most recent research developed a system for forecasting corporate tax revenue based on fuzzy logic and fuzzy-set theory (Shnaider and Kandel 1992). The forecast errors using fuzzy logic were considered to be of "acceptable magnitude" when compared to the actual published tax revenues. (Though no definition of acceptable magnitude exists in the literature, it appears to be in the range of less than 5%. The forecasting errors of Shnaider and Kandel, for example, ranged from -1.68% to $+4.6\%$ with a mean error of 1.96%.)

The general conclusion of this line of research is that the superiority of forecasting techniques increases with increased levels of sophistication. The best results may be obtained from using composite forecasts. Newer techniques incorporating fuzzy-set theory provide lower error rates but the reduction in error rates is not superior to the predictive ability of composite techniques (mean forecast errors approximately marginally higher than 2%) despite the increase in sophistication.

IV. LIMITATIONS OF EXTANT RESEARCH

The research that is pertinent to this study relates to that cited earlier. The published research in that section has the following drawbacks:

- It has to be noted that the period studied in the most recent published article ends in 1984/1985. This period contains the deep 1981 and 1982 economic recessions. The deep recessionary cycle present in the data raise some questions about the generalizability of the results. The models developed may most likely reflect some levels of financial stress above the norm.
- The data in these studies relate to a single revenue source (e.g., sales tax revenues). Changes in policy associated with other revenue devices will affect or limit the generalizability of these findings to them.

V. CONTRIBUTION

This study makes a contribution to the extant literature cited earlier in the following respects:

- The relevant sample data relates to the period 1982 to 1994. Even though this does straddle the deep recessionary period of 1991 it also incorporates the period of recovery.
- A common criticism in the published literature is that the benefits from advanced sophisticated techniques such as econometric modeling do not justify their cost (Grizzle and Klay 1994). Arguments were made for simpler more cost effective models. This research develops a model that is not complex and is comparatively cost effective.

The next section discusses the data and the research methodology.

VI. METHODOLOGY

A. Sample

The sample comprised economic performance data on various sectors of the New Jersey economy for the years 1982 to 1995. The data was retrieved from the state of New Jersey Department of Labor's internet site at URL www.state.nj.us/labor/lra. The data at this site consisted primarily of industry indicators and overall economic indicators (comprising both raw and seasonalized data). This data is periodically adjusted (or re-benchmarked as it is popularly called) and the adjustment is then applied retroactively to all prior years. Thus, this data is amenable for use in time-series analysis (the method undertaken in this study). Similar data is provided by the N.J. Department of Labor publication "New Jersey Economic Indicators." However, this data was not used in this study since this it is not retroactively re-benchmarked.

This study examined 14 years of monthly New Jersey economic data. The monthly data was then averaged to create quarterly economic data. Quarterly data on New Jersey gross income tax receipts was received from the New Jersey Office of Tax Analysis. In summary, this study used 56 observations (14 years at four quarterly observations per year) in the data analysis. Table 1 presents descriptive information of the variables examined in this study. The labels in Table 1 are taken from the N.J. Department of Labor's description of the items. Table 1 presents means, standard deviations, skewness, and kurtosis information for the variables selected for this study.

B. Data Analysis

The actual data analysis proceeded in stages using quarterly gross income and tax receipts as the dependent variable. The first stage of the analysis consisted of attempting to predict New Jersey gross income tax collections using numerous economic indicators as the dependent variables. At this first stage of the study only data for the years 1982 to 1994 was used; economic data and New Jersey gross income tax receipts for

Table 1. Description of Variables

Name
Employment to population ratio in %
Gross income tax receipts
Manufacturing employment (in 000s)
Manufacturing workweek (in 000s)
Manufacturing payroll employment (in 000s)
New business incorporations
Private sector non-farm payroll employment
Sales of retail stores (in millions)
Weekly earnings of manufacturing workers in 1982
NJ total personal income (in current $)

1995 was withheld from the model in order to enable us to use 1995 for testing its predictive accuracy.

Various options were adopted in order to more fully understand the available data. These options included the forward and backward stepping regression sequences and instructions that the R-squared value be maximized and separately minimized. The statistical technique initially used was stepwise regression. The variables used in this initial analysis constituted a broad cross-section of economic statistics in the state of New Jersey. These variables are defined in Table 1. Based on our analysis of the regression outputs and collinearity diagnostics, the subsequent set of data analyses were reduced to the following six variables:

1. Insured unemployment in construction;
2. Manufacturing employment;
3. Manufacturing payroll employment;
4. Sales retail stores (millions);
5. Weeks claimed weekly average insured unemployment benefits;
6. Construction payroll employment.

VII. RESULTS

After examining the regression runs using the variables shown in Section VI, we isolated three variables that appeared to have potential. These variables were *SORSTO* (sales of retail stores), *MPEERO* (manufacturing payroll employment), and *MFGERO* (manufacturing employment). These three variables in their untransformed state generated an adjusted R-squared of .8696, an F-value of 114.37, and a model probability of .0001.

It has to be mentioned that certain characteristics of untransformed data may militate against its providing the best prediction of the dependent variable. For example, the skewness in the original data may let extreme observations unduly influence the calculation of the regression weights.

In order to overcome the drawbacks of using untransformed data, two common data transformations were used and the impact of these data transformations on the predictive ability of the model was examined. These transformations were applied to the dependent and all three independent variables. The two transformations were (a) transforming to the natural log of the four variables, and (b) inversion of the variables.

Table 2 provides a summary of the three models generated (namely, the model with the untransformed data and the two models with different transformations). We evaluated Durbin Watson Statistical test for all models. It did not appear from this evaluation that there was autocorrelation.

Column 1 of Table 2 contains descriptions of the statistics generated (i.e., model F, model P, the adjusted R-squared, and the names of the independent variables used in the regression equation). Each of the three models (untransformed, natural log, and inverted) occupies two columns apiece (refer to columns 2 through 9). The first column for each model presents the model statistics and variable parameters (i.e., beta values). The second column shows the p-values associated with the model's variable parameters.

Inspection of the model's adjusted R-squared values suggests that the natural log transformation and the model developed from the inverted variable values are evenly matched with adjusted values of .9309 and .9374 respectively. Both clearly dominate the non-transformed variable model.

While the adjusted R-squared values suggest strongly that both models are equally valuable in accounting for the longitudinal variation in New

Table 2. Results of Regression for the Three Models

	Model 1	Model 2	Model 4
	Non Transformed	Natural Log Transformation	Inverse Transformation
Intercept	759.07	1.3708	0.000126
P values	0.0205	0.53007	0.7833
MFGERO	−3.2799	−1.9795	−1.14556
P values	0.0678	0.0096	0.0188
MPEERO	0.6723	0.8851	1.1378
P values	0.5433	0.228	0.1303
SORSTO	0.1699	1.3264	12.3755
P values	0.0001	0.0001	0.0001
F values	114.37	229.96	255.689
Model P value	0.0001	0.0001	0.0001
R-squared	0.8773	0.9349	0.9411
Adjusted R-squared	0.8696	0.9309	0.9374

Notes: MFGERO = Manufacturing employment.
MPEERO = Manufacturing payroll employment.
SORSTO = Sales of retail stores.

Jersey gross income tax receipts, a better test of the models can be obtained by examining which best predicts New Jersey gross income tax receipts for a year that had not been used in the model building (namely, 1995).

To test the ability of the models generated to predict 1995 gross income tax receipts, we multiplied the 1995 data values for the three independent variables by the beta values in each model, adding the respective intercept values. The predicted values for 1995 quarterly gross income tax were then subtracted from the actual values. The resulting deviation scores were then divided by the actual 1995 quarterly values to derive quarter by quarter prediction deviations as a percentage of the actual value. The results of these calculations are shown in Table 3.

A comparison of the natural log prediction accuracy (refer columns headed DVLGR95) with the inverted model's prediction accuracy (refer columns headed DVIGR95) reveals that the approximate equality of the adjusted *R*-squared values was not a good indicator of the predictive value of the models. Table 4 clearly shows that the natural log model dominates the other two models in all four quarters of 1995. As our interest is in our model's predictive ability, we conclude that the natural log model is superior.

Table 3. Comparison of Actual and Predicted Gross Income Receipts
1995 Tax Year
(Dependent variable predicted as the deviation of the predicted
variable from the actual)

Observation	GRSINC	DVSGR95	DVLGR95	DVIGR95	DVGR95
1	1,011.30	−0.23728	0.008878	−1.10328	0.04201
2	1,329.80	0.11656	0.020507	−0.04661	0.16582
3	871.5	−1.13747	−0.045805	0.35748	−0.30556
4	1,124.50	−0.36924	−0.016716	0.27005	−0.05694

Notes: GRSINC = Actual gross income receipts for quarter.

   DVSGR95 = Deviation of predicted squared gross income receipts from the square of GRSINC, divided by square of GRSINC.

   DVLGR95 = Deviation of predicted natural log gross income receipts from the natural log of GRSINC, divided by natural log of GRSINC.

   DVIGR95 = Deviation of predicted inverted gross income receipts from the inversion of GRSINC, divided by inverted GRSINC.

   DVGR95 = Deviation of predicted gross income receipts (untransformed) from the GRSINC, divided by GRSINC.

Table 4. A Comparison of Actual and Predicted Model Values and
Further Evidence for the Models' Goodness of Fit

Panel A

Gross Income Tax Receipts and Model Quality, Using Untransformed Data for 1995

Quarter	GRSINC	GR95	DGR95	DVGR95
1/1995	1,011.30	968.2	42.481	0.04201
2/1995	1,329.80	1,109.29	220.51	0.16582
3/1995	871.5	1,137.80	−266.298	−0.3056
4/1995	1,124.50	1,188.53	−64.035	−0.0569

Panel B

Natural Log of Gross Income Tax Receipts and Model Quality, Using Data for 1995

Quarter	LGRSINC	LGR95	DLGR95	DVLGR95
1/1995	6.9189	6.8757	0.06143	0.008878
2/1995	7.19278	7.04528	0.1475	0.020507
3/1995	6.77022	7.08033	−0.31011	−0.045805
4/1995	7.02509	7.14253	−0.11743	−0.016716

Panel C

Inversion of Gross Income Tax Receipts and Model Quality, Using Data for 1995

Quarter	IGRSINC	IGR95	DIGR95	DVIGR95
1/1995	0.000988	0.001091	−0.000102	−0.10328
2/1995	0.000752	0.000787	−0.000035	−0.04661
3/1995	0.001147	0.000737	0.000410	0.35748
4/1995	0.000889	0.000649	0.000240	0.27005

LEGEND:

In Panel A:

GRSINC = Gross income tax receipts as reported by the New Jersey Division of Taxation (in millions)

GR95 = Predicted gross income. It was calculated by multiplying the regression weights for each of the three variables in the model by the 1995 quarterly data values, and then summing the results.

DGR95 = Is the difference between actual gross income and predicted gross income (GRSINC - GR95)

DVGR95 = Is calculated by dividing DGR95 by GRSINC. It serves as a crude measure to fit.

In Panel B:

LGRSINC = The natural log of gross income (GRSINC above)

LGR95 = The predicted natural log of gross income. It was calculated by multiplying the regression weights for each of the three variables in the model by the 1995 quarterly data values, and then summing the results.

DLGR95 = Is the difference between the natural log of actual gross income and predicted gross income (LGRSINC - LGR95)

DLVGR95 = Is calculated by dividing DLGR95 by LGRSINC. It serves as a crude measure of fit.

Table 4. (Continued)

In Panel C:

IGRSINC = The inversion of gross income (GRSINC above). It was calculated by dividing 1 by GRSINC.

IGR95 = The predicted inverted gross income value. It was calculated by multiplying the regression weights for each of the three variables in the model by the 1995 quarterly data values, and then summing the results.

DIGR95 = Is the difference between the inverted actual gross income and predicted gross income (IGRSINC – IGR95)

DVIGR95 = Is calculated by dividing DIGR95 by LGRSINC. It serves as a crude measure of fit.

VIII. CONCLUSION

The objective of this paper was to facilitate the improvement of practices in public finance with reference to the selection and use of forecasting models for tax revenues. It is the belief of the authors that the best model is one that possesses certain attributes, namely:

- ability to predict accurately;
- requires minimal assumptions for making the prediction;
- be relatively simple to understand.

The minimal assumption requirement in particular is important because users of forecasts frequently disagree about the relevancy of various assumptions. The greater the disparity of opinion on various assumptions used, the less the credibility placed on the resultant forecasts. Further the use of an increasing number of assumptions may result in the introduction of bias. As noted in the literature review section, bias can be used to produce numbers that conform to the political dictates and support the policies of the state government.

The purpose of this paper is to develop a model that eliminates politics from the forecasting process. The only way bias can be removed is to be parsimonious with the number of assumptions and variables used. Parsimony can be incorporated by keeping the model simple. This paper uses a simple, parsimonious regression model that eliminates bias. Regression is considered to simpler because of the following reasons:

- Regression in its various forms is taught in many different curriculums.

- Other forecasting techniques such as Box Jenkins and ARIMA are largely tools of those with more advanced statistical training.

The simplicity and parsimony of the model has the added advantage that it enables more users to understand how the numbers have been derived; the greater the comprehension the greater the potential for challenge and debate.

REFERENCES

Bretschneider, S., and L. Schroeder. 1985. "Revenue Forecasting, Budget Setting, and Risk." *Socio-Economic Planning Sciences* 19: 431–439.

Bretschneider, S., and W. Gorr. 1992. "Economic, Organizational, and Political Influences on Biases in Forecasting State Sales Tax Receipts." *International Journal of Forecasting* 7: 457–466.

Bretschneider,S., W.L. Gorr, G. Grizzle, and E. Kay. 1989. "Political and Organizational Influences on the Accuracy of Forecasting State Government Revenues." *International Journal of Forecasting* 5: 307–319.

Cassidy, G., M.S. Kamlet, and D.S. Nagin. 1989. "An Empirical Examination of Bias in Revenue Forecasts by State Governments." *International Journal of Forecasting* 5: 321–331.

Feenberg, D.R., W.M. Gentry, D. Gilroy, and H.S. Rosen. 1989. "Testing the Rationality of State Revenue Forecasts." *Review of Economics and Statistics* 71: 300–308.

Fullerton, T.M., Jr. 1989. "A Composite Approach to Forecasting State Government Revenues: Case Study for the Idaho Sales Tax." *International Journal of Forecasting* 5: 373–380.

Gentry, W.M. 1989. "Do State Revenue Forecasters Utilize Available Information?" Unpublished Manuscript, Princeton University.

Grizzle, G.A., and W.E. Klay. 1994. "Forecasting State Sales Tax Revenues: Comparing the Accuracy of Different Methods." *State and Local Government Review* 26 (3): 142–152.

Kamlet, M., D. Mowery, and T T. Su. 1987. "Whom do you Trust? An Analysis of Executive and Congressional Economic Forecasts." *Journal of Policy Analysis and Management* 6: 365–384.

Larkey, P.D., and R.A. Smith. 1984. "The Misrepresentation of Information in Governmental Budgeting." Pp. 63–92 in *Advances in Information Processing in Organizations*. Greenwich, CT: JAI Press.

Shkurti, W.J., and D. Winefordner. 1989. "The Politics of State Revenue Forecasting in Ohio, 1984–1987: A Case Study and Research Implications." *International Journal of Forecasting* 5: 361–371.

Shnaider E., and A. Kandel. 1992. "A System for Forecasting Corporate Tax Revenue Based on Fuzzy Logic and Fuzzy Set Theory." *Information Sciences* 63: 11–31.

FORECASTING AND MONITORING STATE TAX REVENUES THROUGHOUT THE BUDGET CYCLE

Ray D. Nelson, Gary C. Cornia, and
Douglas A. MacDonald

ABSTRACT

Unexpected revenue shortfalls and surpluses that develop during the annual execution of a public budget create problems for administrators, agencies, and the recipients of government services. This chapter develops and implements a state revenue monitoring process that builds on the techniques of statistical process control. The application of this model to a state agency's situation illustrates how the proposed methodology allows public managers to respond to unexpected revenue shortfalls and surpluses in a timely and rational manner.

Advances in Business and Management Forecasting, Volume 2, pages 171–191.
Copyright © 1998 by JAI Press Inc.
ISBN: 0-7623-0002-7

I. INTRODUCTION

As they do in all estimation exercises, state tax forecasters encounter challenges that cause uncertainty in their projections. Among the challenges identified by Shkurti and Winefordner (1989), Bretschneider, Gorr, Grizzle, and Klay (1989), and Bretschneider and Gorr (1992) are long lead times, numerous taxes, a variety of forecasting techniques, inadequate revenue data points, limited endogenous variables, and partisan state politics. Unfortunately, common operating practices in many states exacerbate the dangers of the uncertainty inherent in revenue forecasts. State agencies often disburse funds as though no uncertainty accompanies expected revenue receipts.

Monitoring tax revenue collections throughout the fiscal year shares features common to overseeing manufacturing. During the manufacturing process, production engineers and managers first specify a product's desired attributes. They then design an operation capable of yielding products which satisfy the specified characteristics. By using statistical process control (SPC) methodology, operations managers attempt to determine when a production process goes out of control. When problems arise, production managers react by adjusting the process. Even though SPC doesn't precisely fit the forecasting problems confronted by government planners, adaptation of its basic philosophy does result in a methodology which proves useful to tax revenue monitoring. This paper develops and describes a process to monitor state revenue forecasts throughout the entire budget process.

The development of tax revenue monitoring methodology first overviews potentially useful SPC-type models that have been adopted for business planning under uncertainty. Next, the paper provides the context for the model development. Adaptation of SPC and business planning models then generates methodology applicable to the state tax revenue monitoring situation. The discussion next focuses on the estimation challenges inherent in the trend and seasonal characteristics of tax collections. Finally, an application illustrates the implementation of these techniques for the motor fuel tax in Utah.

II. MONITORING METHODOLOGY

Operations managers attempt to determine when a production process is out of control by using SPC methodology. SPC techniques help detect deteriorating manufacturing processes before an excessive number of products either exceed or fail the standard specifications. Wu (1988) and Wu, Hosking, and Doll (1992) propose methodology that shares the philosophy and intent of SPC. Their models, however, do not focus on monitoring manufacturing but on the achievement of business objectives. Their techniques, hereafter referred to as the Wu methodology, share much in common with state revenue monitoring.

The Wu methodology begins by subdividing annual goals into a series of monthly quantities. These monthly amounts allow the development of historical and planner tracks that are the foundation of the Wu monitoring approach. The historical track identifies two sources of uncertainty. The first is mistakes in estimating the annual target. Wu and her colleagues define a parameter g to represent the error in setting the annual target. If $g = 1$, then the sum of the monthly target values exactly equals actual receipts. Thus, the g parameter measures the degree to which the target and actual revenues differ.

A second source of error is the allocation of the annual target into corresponding monthly values. The Wu framework apportions an annual target T into individual monthly components T_i using seasonal parameters. This suggests a second parameter τ_i, which represents the error due to the estimation of the seasonal parameters. Wu proposes that these seasonal coefficients be based on historical average percentages of annual receipts.

The annual target and two uncertainty components combine to equal the actual quantity Y_i in month i or

$$Y_i = gT_i + \tau_i \tag{1}$$

This equation provides the foundation for the construction of basic monitoring charts. The charts summarized in Table 1 depend on both the estimated track values and the variability of these estimates. The Wu model develops these charts to answer the questions listed in Table 1. The first or shipwreck chart monitors the difference between actual collections and track values. When actual revenue receipts accumulate slower than the expectation, the shipwreck chart evaluates whether future months might possibly make up the shortfall.

The second type of Wu chart gives business analysts high, expected, and low outlooks. These outlook charts reflect the evolution of information as actual receipts dissipate the uncertain expectations inherent in the original track. Initially, the individual track values T_i sum to equal the target T. As actual receipts become available, the outlook chart substi-

Table 1. Basic Wu Methodology Monitoring Charts

Chart Name	Type of Measure	Business Strategy Monitoring Questions
Shipwreck	Absolute Comparison	"Will we recover from our deficit by year's end?"
Outlook	Forecast	"What is our outlook range for the full year?"

tutes actual receipts for track values. Summing actual and track values then gives an updated forecast of actual receipts, which constitutes the expected value outlook for revenues. By assuming Poisson and normal distributions, Wu's methodology estimates a variance that allows calculation of the high and low outlooks as a confidence band around the forecast.

Unfortunately, some tax revenue collection patterns may not behave as regular, recurrent Poisson or normally distributed global processes. For example, the economy goes through business cycles which cause local rather than global trends.[1] Seasonal patterns often evolve rather than stay stationary from year to year. The Wu methodology recognizes these problems and suggests a weighted average estimation procedure consistent with an adaptive expectations framework.[2]

As mentioned, the historical tracks require the estimation of seasonal parameters to allocate the annual budget into expected values for each month. The Wu formulation has potential problems when a constant global trend does not exist throughout the entire historical sample. Wu relies on cumulative percentages of annual receipts to circumvent the problem of having trend in the data. In other words, when the receipts are growing, annual receipts are simply divided by a larger amount.

The distribution of the stochastic components of the Wu model may also cause concern in attempts to apply this approach to monitoring tax revenues. The Wu methodology models this problem with a parametric solution by assuming that the month-to-month variation in revenues comes from a Poisson distribution. Although this assumption allows the uncertainty associated with revenue collections to decrease as the end of the fiscal year approaches, this pattern may not accurately describe tax revenue receipts. Annual tax deadlines and quarterly report filings may cause more complicated seasonal patterns which are not compatible with the Wu methodology. Thus, rather than modeling the variation of the revenue stream by estimating the parameters of a given family of distributions, the simple alternative exists to show the distribution of errors through box plots, dot plots, or nonparametric density representations. This approach does not allow the formal calculation of a confidence interval, but it does avoid the need to make the possible erroneous assumption of normality in order to derive a familiar but unreliable confidence band.

III. REVENUE UNCERTAINTY

The unique characteristics of public institutions mean that forecasting errors that create surpluses and deficits have an impact on state governments in distinctive ways. Tax revenue forecasts influence the entire state government policy agenda. The role of forecasts is strong in each of five basic steps found in a state budgeting process. In the first step, state agencies receive budget guidelines from the executive branch which are based on initial estimated revenues and expenditures. In the second step, agencies respond to the governor with budget requests. In the third, agency hearings take place before the fourth step, in which the governor and staff submit the budget to the legislature. Finally, the legislature adopts the budget.

The time line presented in Figure 1 summarizes the principal aspects of the five-step state budgeting process. It divides the planning horizon into four planning intervals. The economic and revenue outlook of a state performs a critical role in Interval I. Initial and revised forecasts strongly influence the budget guidelines, agency budget hearings, the governor's budget proposal, and legislative deliberations. The legislature passes a budget at decision point A, as shown on the time line. Adoption of a budget by the legislature for the coming fiscal year moves planning and monitoring into Interval II. Although actual spendable revenues do not occur until the start of the fiscal year, additional economic information becomes available in the interim. This information allows updating of revenue outlooks. In Interval III the state revenue department reports actual receipts for the current fiscal year. This supplements other new economic and business information. Actual rather than projected values begin to replace the statistics used to monitor revenue receipts.

Unexpected shortfalls and surpluses can trigger supplemental spending decisions. At decision points B_i, the legislature can alter funding. Its revision of the target values for the three months remaining in the fiscal year moves the monitoring process into Interval IV. During this time, analysts continue to update the outlook and compare actual receipts

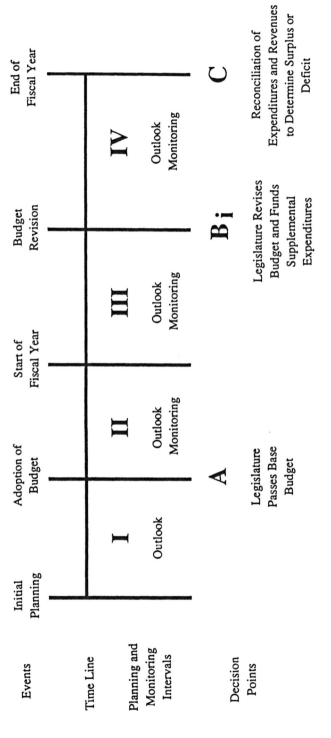

Events | Initial Planning | Adoption of Budget | Start of Fiscal Year | Budget Revision | End of Fiscal Year

Time Line

Planning and Monitoring Intervals | I — Outlook | II — Outlook Monitoring | III — Outlook Monitoring | IV — Outlook Monitoring

Decision Points | A — Legislature Passes Base Budget | B — Legislature Revises Budget and Funds Supplemental Expenditures | C — Reconciliation of Expenditures and Revenues to Determine Surplus or Deficit

Information Flows

Monthly Revenue Collection Reports from the Revenue Department
Monthly State and National Economic Forecasts from Commercial Sources
Monthly and Quarterly National Statistical Reports
State Quarterly Income Reports
State Monthly Labor Statistics

Figure 1. State Budgeting Time Line and Decision Points

against target values. As the fiscal year comes to a close at decision point C, government officials reconcile expenditures and revenues to ascertain formally the existence of a surplus or deficit.

IV. TAX REVENUE MONITORING METHODOLOGY

The proposed methodology for monitoring tax revenue collections combines ideas from the statistical process control and business planning under uncertainty literatures. This methodology focuses on providing government planners with information about two fundamental questions. The first question is how much revenue will tax receipts generate during the planning horizon? The answer to this question comes from an outlook chart which includes the effects of dynamic information flows. The second question is when do actual tax receipts signal significant departures from budgeted amounts? Proposed indicators of potential surpluses and deficits can alert planners to off-track or out-of-control situations. The graphs useful for providing information about this second question have their roots in the control charts mentioned previously.

Some modifications of the Wu model are needed to make it applicable to tax revenue monitoring. The proposed model differs from the original Wu framework in the following important ways. First, calculation of the track uses standard time series forecasting techniques. Second, variability in tax collections need not be constant throughout the year. Peak load constraints on tax receipt processing capacity can cause seasonal patterns in the variability of tax collections. Third, standard parametric families may not accurately reflect the stochastic ingredients of the tax revenue time series. Fourth, small sample sizes and nonstandard distributions make the use of resistant and robust statistics very important. Finally, modifications to Wu's charts add information to the intracycle revenue monitoring process.

A. Interval I

An adaptation of the Wu methodology begins with the following notation and definitions. Let Y_{ij} represent actual tax collections for the ith month of the jth year. The sum over 12 months gives $Y_{.j}$ or the actual spendable revenues in the jth year. The budgeting process requires a forecast $F_{.j/t}$ which anticipates $Y_{.j}$ and is based on the information available at time t. The fiscal year total can be calculated as $\sum_{i=1}^{12} F_{ij/t}$ where $F_{ij/t}$ represents anticipated monthly collections in the jth year and

ith month conditioned on the information available at time t. The difference between the actual and forecasted monthly collections is $\varepsilon_{ij/t}$, which means that

$$Y_{ij} = F_{ij/t} + \varepsilon_{ij/t} \qquad (2)$$

These definitions provide the basis for the outlook needed for Interval I.

B. Interval II

When the legislature passes the budget, then the forecasts become the target values. This means that the target revenues $T_{\cdot j/A}$ correspond to the anticipated revenue for the jth year when the legislature adopts the budget with the information available at decision point A. Formally, the targets come from the following expression

$$T_{ij/A} = F_{ij/A} \qquad (3)$$

The fiscal year total can be calculated as $\sum_{i=1}^{12} T_{ij/A}$ where $T_{ij/A}$ represents the anticipated monthly collections in the jth year and ith month conditional on the information available when time $t = A$. As already mentioned, Wu gives a useful representation between the target and the actual outcome. Defining the difference between the actual and on-track monthly collections as $\tau_{ij/A}$ means that

$$Y_{ij} = gT_{ij/A} + \tau_{ij/A} \qquad (4)$$

The variable g plays an especially important role, since it indicates whether the revenue receipts are on track to achieve the annual total budget $T_{\cdot j/A}$.

For Interval II, two measures help the analysis. The first gives the revenue outlook at any time t as

$$\sum_{i=1}^{12} F_{ij/t} \qquad (5)$$

A monitoring measure similar to the shipwreck chart calculates the potential surplus or deficit. This is simply the difference between the sum of the current forecasts and the forecasts used originally for the budget or

$$\sum_{i=1}^{12} F_{ij/t} - \sum_{i=1}^{12} T_{ij/A} \tag{6}$$

C. Interval III

As stressed before, monitoring monthly revenue receipts requires a clear understanding of the evolution of the uncertainty surrounding collection patterns. Progression toward the end of the fiscal year means that month by month, the uncertainty surrounding the annual totals diminishes. At the beginning of the fiscal year, the total collections can be represented by expression (5). As actual receipts come into the state's coffers, at time t, the actual receipts replace track and error terms to give the outlook estimate

$$\hat{Y}_{\cdot j/t} = \sum_{i=1}^{t} Y_{ij} + \sum_{i=t+1}^{12} F_{ij/t} + \sum_{i=t+1}^{12} \varepsilon_{ij/t} \tag{7}$$

This means that as more information becomes available, the amount of uncertainty about the annual tax collections diminishes since the number of terms $\varepsilon_{ij/t}$ declines.

The differences depicted in the shipwreck charts contrast the track values with the corresponding actual values. Modification of expression (6) means that in Interval III the sums range from the beginning of the year to time t, the month in which the monitoring occurs. This contrasts with the full year summations for Interval II. Difference comparisons give the potential surplus or deficit calculated for the shipwreck chart as given by

$$\sum_{i=1}^{t} Y_{ij} - \sum_{i=1}^{t} T_{ij/A} \tag{8}$$

D. Interval IV

A minor modification of the Interval III monitoring measures gives expressions appropriate for Interval IV. New targets from supplementary funding decisions replace the original budgeted amounts. This means

$$T_{ij/B} = F_{ij/B} \tag{9}$$

and that

$$T_{\cdot j/B} = \sum_{i=1}^{B} Y_{ij} + \sum_{i=B+1}^{12} F_{ij/B} \qquad (10)$$

The outlook formula for Interval IV is identical to expression (7) for Interval III. The new target values replace the corresponding variables in the formulas for the monitoring charts.

V. ESTIMATION AND FORECASTING CHALLENGES

The stochastic nature of the proposed measures means that their use in control-type charts requires an understanding of the distribution of each of these outlook and monitoring statistics. Wu's (1988) discussion of the quantification of variability gives very helpful direction to estimating the shape of these distributions. Quantifying the monitoring measures requires an adjustment of the track values.

First consider expressions for the forecast errors for each of the different planning intervals. Because the outlook chart reports the forecasted revenues based on the information at time t, the forecast errors are the difference between the actual outcome and forecast or $Y_{\cdot j} - F_{\cdot j/t}$. For any given time t in planning Intervals I and II, the annual forecast errors $\varepsilon_{\cdot j/t}$ result from simply summing the monthly errors. As indicated by equation (7), when t corresponds to a month within an actual fiscal year, actual revenue receipts replace their forecasted values in the outlook calculation. This means that uncertainty about the outlook exists only because of the unknown or forecasted future values. Therefore the outlook uncertainty, when t represents a month within Interval III or IV or a current fiscal year, is

$$\varepsilon_{\cdot j/t} = \sum_{i=t+1}^{12} (Y_{ij} - F_{ij/t}) \qquad (11)$$

The use of forecasts rather than adjusted track values causes this outlook measure to differ from the Wu variability measures. These calculations do not require that the $\varepsilon_{ij/t}$ terms share identical and independent distributions. The historical variability of $\varepsilon_{\cdot j/t}$ measures the uncertainty of the outlook values. Because in Intervals I and II, t precedes the beginning of the fiscal year, the sum covers all 12 months of the fiscal year. In Interval III and IV, the scale of $\varepsilon_{\cdot j/t}$ should decline as the number of stochastic terms in the summation decreases.

Now consider the adjustment of the historical data needed to ascertain the variability of the monitoring chart statistics. The monitoring charts warn when actual receipts deviate substantially from the track values given by the adopted budget. The reference values of zero for the monitoring charts allow government analysts to ask whether or not revenue receipts are on track. The differences in expressions (6) and (8) should neighbor zero when revenues are on track. The random nature of these differences, however, means that seldom will they exactly equal zero even if collections are indeed on track. The analyst must therefore question how far the statistic can deviate from the zero baseline value before concluding that revenues are off track.

Rarely will the sum of track values exactly match annual collections. Therefore, preliminary alterations must occur before asking questions that hypothesize that forecasts are on track. For this reason, off-track values must be modified. The g parameter allows a useful adjustment of the original track values which enables this calculation. If the forecast is on track for the jth year, this means that

$$\sum_{i=1}^{12} Y_{ij} = g_{j/t} \sum_{i=1}^{12} T_{ij/t} \tag{12}$$

and $g_{j/t} = 1$. In this instance, t represents either decision point A or B. Requiring that the forecasts be on track is the very same as saying $\sum_{i=1}^{12} \varepsilon_{ij/t} = 0$ for every year j and forecasting point t. The g parameters adjust each track value so that this condition holds. The estimate of the $g_{j/t}$ parameter which adjusts each historical track is

$$\hat{g}_{j/t} = \frac{\sum_{i=1}^{12} Y_{ij}}{\sum_{i=1}^{12} T_{ij/t}} \tag{13}$$

In the years in which $\hat{g}_{j/t}$ exceeds 1, a budget surplus occurs because actual receipts exceed the track or budgeted amounts. Values for this ratio less than 1 suggest budget shortfalls because receipts fall behind the track values. Multiplying the historical track values by $\hat{g}_{j/t}$ increases the track values when a surplus occurs. This adjustment also decreases the historical track to match the lower-than-expected revenues in the case of a deficit. These adjustments allow the calculation of how much variation exists if revenue estimates had actually been on track.

When revenue receipts are on track, then $\tau_{ij/t}$ represents the variation around the on-track values. Because the monitoring measures differ for Intervals II and III, they require separate formulas for measuring their variability. The monitoring measure for Interval II compares the updated forecasts with the track values. Substituting adjusted or on-track values into expression (6) for the actual track values gives the following equation

$$\tau_{ij/t} = \sum_{i=1}^{12} F_{ij/t} - \hat{g}_{j/t} \sum_{i=1}^{12} T_{ij/A} \tag{14}$$

The difference in expression (8) compares actual cumulative receipts to the cumulative track amounts in Intervals III and IV. Into this expression make a similar substitution of the on-track values to give

$$\tau_{ij/t} = \sum_{i=1}^{t} Y_{ij} - \hat{g}_{j/t} \sum_{i=1}^{t} T_{ij/t} \tag{15}$$

Remember that the $\hat{g}_{j/t}$ values adjust all of the original track values proportionately so that the adjusted track values sum to the actual collections. These calculations show the historical distribution of being on track. Against this background the actual observed values can be evaluated. Under the assumption that the revenues are on track, this statistic attempts to ascertain how much this ratio can deviate from zero before an analyst should reject the supposition that revenue collections will reach the anticipated amount.

Estimates for the variability of the outlook and monitoring statistics require that standard forecasting techniques replace the historical tracks used in the original Wu formulation. These forecasts must accommodate local trends and seasonality. Holt-Winters exponential smoothing and ARIMA models allow joint estimation of trend and seasonality. In addition, both these techniques seem appropriate for two principal reasons. First, both have proven relatively accurate for short-term forecasts.

Second, they mirror the dynamics of information flows, since both exponential smoothing and ARIMA can have an adaptive expectations interpretation.

The proposed graphical representations of the distribution of outlook and monitoring statistics differ markedly from the parametric approach of the Wu model. As mentioned, the Wu model assumptions allow uncertainty to decrease toward the end of the fiscal year. This differs from the observed collection patterns often created by annual tax deadlines and quarterly report filings. Rather than modeling the variation of the revenue stream by estimating the parameters of a given family of distributions, the simple alternative exists to show the distribution of errors through box plots, dot plots, or nonparametric density representations. Although such an approach does not allow formal calculation of a confidence interval, it does avoid the need to make possible erroneous distributional assumptions in order to derive confidence bands.

The graphical representations of the statistics provide an additional advantage over standard parametric approaches. The small sample sizes usually available to estimate the track and its inherent uncertainty not only make identification of an appropriate family of distributions difficult, but also make summary statistics such as mean and variance especially susceptible to outliers. A simple statistical display of all observations in a dot plot with grouping by month fosters managerial intuition about trend and seasonality. Alternatively, combining medians and inter-quartile ranges into a box plot gives measures of location and scale that are resistant to outliers. These graphics give better insights into the forecasts and differences reported in outlook and monitoring charts.

VI. APPLICATION AND ILLUSTRATION: UTAH MOTOR FUEL TAX

Utah's motor fuel tax provides an excellent illustration of how revenue forecasts, budget tracks, and tax receipts combine to give outlook and monitoring charts. This illustration first outlines the forecasting methodology that generates revenue estimates. These estimates give the basic data needed for outlook charts. The revenue estimates also give the budget or track values needed to construct the monitoring charts. The motor fuel tax example also illustrates the value of graphical, resistant statistical analysis of revenue patterns.

A. Estimation Procedures and Characteristics of Forecast Errors

An appropriate forecasting model must consider the dynamics of the information flows throughout the budget cycle. As new information becomes available, it should be incorporated into updated forecasts. From any given reference point, the estimation process should clearly distinguish between historical and future information. In other words, the model should not treat ex ante information as though it were ex post. This means that one model cannot be fit for the whole historical data set and then applied retroactively. For instance, the data set used in this example comes from the Utah Department of Transportation and covers fiscal years 1980–1994. Estimating forecasts for 1984 should use information only through 1983 rather than the entire available time series. The model for 1994 forecasts should use fiscal years 1980–1993. This estimation procedure, therefore, reflects the true information available at the time each forecast is made.

For this illustration a seasonal *ARIMA* model generates the necessary forecasts by estimation based on appropriate subsets of the fiscal years 1980–1994. The data have been adjusted for tax rate changes. Selection of an *ARIMA* model over Holt-Winters exponential smoothing occurs because *ARIMA* can generalize exponential smoothing. An *ARIMA* $(2, 1, 1)(0, 1, 1)^{12}$ fits this time series and is used for all the different forecasts. At each point in the series, the parameters of this model are reestimated on the basis of information available up to that point in history. Summing the monthly estimates gives the annual forecasts. Because the budget decisions occur in February when the Utah legislature meets, the February forecasts become the track or budgeted amounts.

As expected, the time from the end of the fiscal year for which the forecasts are made strongly influences the distribution of forecast errors. Since the planning process in Utah begins a full 12 months before the fiscal year begins, forecasts occur at the first of July, based on the information available by the end of June. Updating occurs at the first of August, based on the information which becomes available during July. This updating continues throughout the budget cycle until all uncertainty disappears at the end of the fiscal year. The box plots in Figure 2 show the distributions of forecast errors for each of these different forecasting horizons. The width of the inter-quartile ranges shows how the uncertainty about revenue receipts stays approximately the same until the beginning of the fiscal year. As actual receipts replace the forecasted values in equation (7), the distribution of error terms begins to narrow.

The range of forecasting errors, however, does not uniformly decrease. Political and legal practices often strain the tax receipts processing and reporting capacity of state governments. For example, peak load constraints during April, when the Utah State Tax Commission processes individual income tax returns, strongly affects the accounting of motor fuel taxes. The demands of closing the accounts for the fiscal year cause erratic June collections. The inter-quartile ranges and whiskers in the box plots in Figure 2 show that the error terms from the *ARIMA* model probably are not homoscedastic. The processing and accounting constraints at the Tax Commission undoubtedly contribute to larger variations in August, April, and May.

Another aspect of the forecasts that critically influences the construction of monitoring charts is whether the error terms behave in a standard, normal way. If the error terms are normally distributed, then hypothesis tests and confidence intervals proceed in well-established ways. If not, however, statements regarding degree of confidence can be very misleading. The box plots in Figure 2 suggest that the errors are positively biased. This means that the forecasts tend to underestimate receipts. Since the medians tend toward the lower hinge on the box plots, this also suggests positive skewness.

B. Outlook and Monitoring Charts

Because of the biased forecasts, seasonal patterns, and nonnormal errors, the use of the resistant statistics employed in box plots becomes all the more important. The outlook chart in Figure 3 shows the forecasts for fiscal year 1994. The solid line on the chart depicts the forecasts that come from the *ARIMA* methodology described previously. Adding the forecast errors used to construct the box plots in Figure 2 to the forecasts generates the background box plots. These graphs give analysts historical perspective on the range of possible outcomes at each point in time in the budgeting cycle. Since the forecasts lie below the medians depicted in the box plots, this method of representing the outlook chart reminds analysts that in this case, forecasts made early in the budgeting cycle tend to underestimate revenues.

The outlook chart shows that from the inception of planning in July, forecasts gradually increase until the Utah legislature adopts the budget in February. The gradual increase in the forecasted values continues into the fiscal year until September. At this point, strong motor fuel tax receipts cause the increase in the forecasts to accelerate. By February,

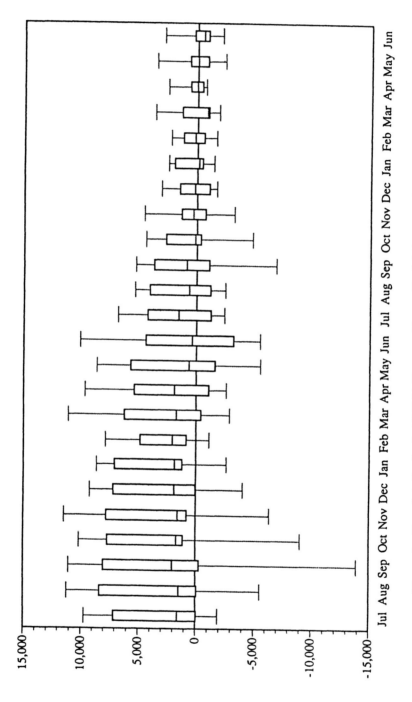

Figure 2. Boxplot-Outlook ARIMA Forecast Errors Utah Motor Fuel Tax 1984–1994

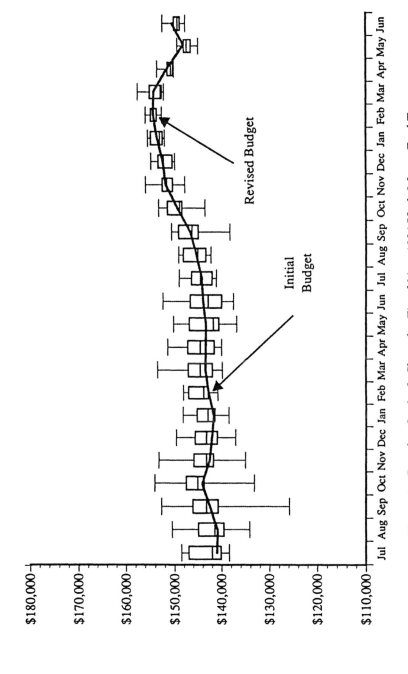

Figure 3. Boxplot-Outlook Chart for Fiscal Year 1994 Utah Motor Fuel Tax

when the legislature revises the budget, the forecast has risen from approximately $142 to $153 million. Unfortunately, just after the legislature alters the budget to accommodate an anticipated budget surplus, the forecasts begin to decline. The fiscal year ends with revenues of approximately $150 million.

Outlook charts drawn using a parametric approach similar to that used by Wu would fail to recognize the seasonal patterns in the variability of tax receipts. One would expect that as more and more information becomes available, the uncertainty of forecasts would decrease. The box plots in Figure 3 show that the variability of forecast errors does tend to decline between July and January. Beginning in March and continuing through April and May when income taxes strain the accounting facilities at the tax commission, however, the forecasting uncertainty actually increases. In other words, the income tax bulge in April and May causes erratic collection patterns. This makes it much harder to ascertain whether economic conditions or simply accounting problems cause increases or decreases in revenue receipts.

Given the seasonal variation found in the nonnormally distributed error terms that associate with the track, the modified shipwreck monitoring chart seems appropriate for the motor fuel tax. The points plotted on the solid line in Figure 4 come from expressions (6) and (8) and give the time path of the difference between actual cumulative tax receipts and the sum of the corresponding track values. The box plots show the relationship of the current year to the historical location and scale of the $\tau_{ij/t}$ values given by equations (14) and (15) at each time t.

The modified shipwreck chart gives a similar interpretation of the budgeting process for fiscal 1994 motor fuel receipts. This example also shows the value of the monitoring chart throughout the budgeting process. The diagram in Figure 4 shows that the difference between updated forecasts and budgeted track receipts stays well within the historical range of values up to the beginning of the fiscal year. The first comparison of actual to budgeted receipts happens at the beginning of August. The extreme variability in the August difference occurs because this statistic compares one month of actual receipts against one single track value. In September collections move outside the inter-quartile range, which indicates that revenues may be off track. Motor fuel tax collections exceed expectations; this alerts analysts to a potential surplus. The variability of the difference graphed in the monitoring chart decreases in September. This happens because, at this point in time, two months of cumulative receipts compare against two months of cumulative track

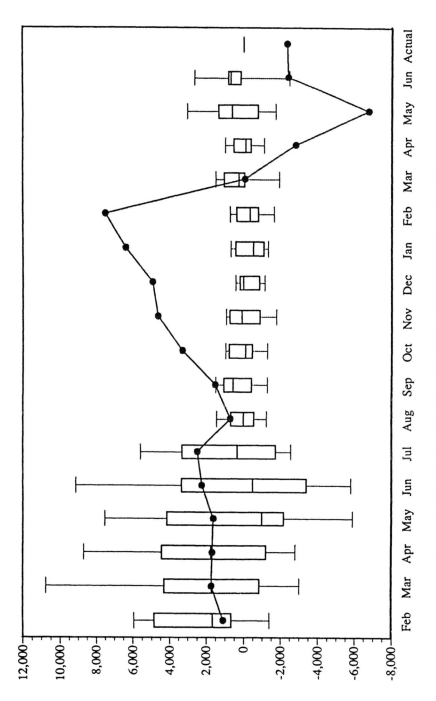

Figure 4. Monitoring Chart for Fiscal Year 1994 Utah Motor Fuel Tax

values. Because of strong collections, the monitoring chart continues to indicate a potential surplus from October through February. The variability of the difference continues to decrease because of the effect of cumulative collections on the statistics. During February the legislature revises the budget. This puts the receipts back on track with reference to the revised budget. The modified shipwreck monitoring chart, like the outlook chart discussed previously, shows that unfortunately motor fuel tax receipts immediately weaken following the legislative session. In the months that follow revenue receipts again give an off-track signal. This time, however, the chart suggests a deficit rather than a surplus.

VII. SUMMARY AND CONCLUSIONS

Without a doubt, statistical control methods contribute significantly to management solutions in an information age. Given their success in the private sector, it seems appropriate that these methodologies should find application in the public sector. Well-developed methodologies allow statistical monitoring of manufacturing processes and business plans. Adaptation of these techniques to fit the state budgeting process could lead to as important improvements in the public sector as those already achieved in business.

Many things make the budgeting process different from quality control in operations management and monitoring of business plans. The state budgeting process does not conform to the stationarity and constancy of a manufacturing process. Legislators and government officials often change and tweak tax codes. Continuous improvements by state tax agencies cause changes in collection and accounting procedures. For these reasons, application of statistical concepts to tax revenues often must rely on data sets with very small sample sizes. This points to the need to replace traditional classical statistical measures with their resistant counterparts. The graphical nature of dot plots and box plots replaces traditional expected values and confidence intervals on the shipwreck and outlook charts of the Wu methodology. Such displays give public officials the graphical feedback needed for good decision making.

The potential of this methodology depends on its regular and timely application. Operations engineers avoid significant costs by early detection of out-of-control manufacturing processes. Similarly, a more efficient allocation of public resources occurs when governmental officials ascertain the existence of revenue variances early in the budgeting process. The proposed methodology should achieve higher levels of efficiency for all government stakeholders if anticipated rather than unanticipated deficits and surpluses drive the decision process throughout the entire budget cycle.

NOTES

1. Newbold and Bos (1994) define global trends as those that remain fixed over the entire span of time for which the time series is observed. This contrasts with local trends, where nonconstant growth rates evolve smoothly over time.

2. Adaptive expectations or exponential smoothing refers to processes whereby decision makers adjust their expectations as information evolves. As new information appears, decision makers compare their previously held expectations with the new data, correcting their expectations or forecasts accordingly. When the expected value exceeds the observed data, the decision maker decreases the forecast. Similarly, when the observed data exceeds the expected value, the decision maker increases the forecast.

REFERENCES

Bretschneider, S., and W. Gorr. 1992. "Economic, Organizational, and Political Influences on Biases in Forecasting State Sales Tax Receipts." *International Journal of Forecasting* 7: 457–466.

Bretschneider, S.I., W.L. Gorr, G. Grizzle, and E. Klay. 1989. "Political and Organizational Influence on Forecast Accuracy: Forecasting State Sales Tax Receipts." *International Journal of Forecasting* 5: 307–319.

Newbold, P., and T. Bos. 1994. *Introductory Business and Economic Forecasting.* Cincinnati, OH: South-Western Publishing Co.

Shkurti, W.J., and D. Winefordner. 1989. "The Politics of State Revenue Forecasting in Ohio, 1984–1987: A Case Study and Research Implications." *International Journal of Forecasting* 5: 367–371.

Wu, L.S., J.R.M. Hosking, and J.M. Doll. 1992. "Business Planning Under Uncertainty: Will We Attain Our Goal?" *International Journal of Forecasting* 8: 545–557.

Wu, L.S. 1988. "Business Planning Under Uncertainty: Quantifying Variability." *The Statistician* 37: 141–151.

FORECASTING MIGRATION INTO
AND OUT OF NEW JERSEY

Sheila M. Lawrence and Charles Nanry

ABSTRACT

The objective of this study is to develop forecasting models regarding migration into, out of, and within the state of New Jersey. Included in the study were demographic, social, economic, and weather variables shown in the literature to impact the decision to migrate. The overall model was further disaggregated by age and by sex.

I. INTRODUCTION

The use of multiple regression models of migration has been dominant since the 1960s. Advances to the ordinary regression model, where some measure of migration is a function of various socioeconomic variables, have incorporated the distance structure of the gravity model, as well as stratification by age and sex.

Relationships were developed for estimating flows of migration as a motivation for social mobility among and between the 21 counties in

Advances in Business and Management Forecasting, Volume 2, pages 193–217.
ISBN: 0-7623-0002-7

New Jersey and the remaining states. The migration flows were in the aggregate and then disaggregated by age and sex. The data source was tapes from the 1980 Census of Population. Examples of the demographic, social, and economic variables shown in the literature to impact social mobility and to influence the decision to migrate, for the disaggregate analyses, included, for example, age, income, and educational attainment level.

Included in this research was a gravity modeling process to examine population interactions and distributions. Also included was the socioeconomic modeling process, to relate the occurrence or nonoccurrence of migration flows to a set of socioeconomic and weather variables.

The objective guiding the empirical work of this study was to develop a forecasting model regarding migration. This objective was tested via the construction of explanatory models of migration among New Jersey counties, from New Jersey's counties to the remaining states, as well as from the remaining states to New Jersey's counties. It was assumed that migrants do not wander aimlessly. Rather it was assumed that migrants make conscious decisions about where to settle.

The data was based on both secondary data (place-to-place migration from census data), as opposed to scanty data on the subjective perceptions of individual migrants, as well as based on statistical techniques.

The justification for studying determinants of migration was that though migration flows represent only one source of migration to and from New Jersey's counties, they contained an important advantage from an analytical standpoint. The migration process could be analyzed within an identifiable system of origin and destination places. This meant that socioeconomic characteristics of origin, as well as destination, could be taken into account when evaluating why people go where they do.

It was on the basis of these premises that when measured differences between the remaining states were correlated with migration among, to, or from New Jersey counties, that the factors affecting decision to migrate were evaluated.

II. MODELING PROCESS

A. The Classical Gravity Model

Thomas Robert Malthus (1766–1834), William Farr (1807–1883), and Ernest George Ravenstein (1834–1913) were three eminent nineteenth-century students of population. Each one made important contributions to population theory and analysis. Although their work was the subject of criticism both in their own lifetimes and since, their ideas have proved stimulating to social scientists and demographers even in the twentieth century.

Ravenstein's "laws of migration" are broad generalizations on the characteristics of migrants and their origins and destinations but chiefly on the characteristics of the migration streams. These "laws" have been discussed at length by a number of more recent scholars.

In the 1930s and 1940s the roles of population size and distance in determining interaction of all sorts became formalized in what have become known as gravity models. They are based on Newton's Law of Universal Gravitation. It states that two bodies in the universe attract each other in proportion to the product of their masses and inversely as the square of the distance between them. People may be regarded as predictable in their aggregate behavior on the basis of mathematical probability.

Zipf's P/D hypothesis is representative of the classic gravity model of social interaction pioneered also by Reilly, Young, Stewart and Warntz. Zipf regarded the movement of goods, information, and people within the social system as an expression of his "principle of least effort," whereby intercommunity movement is to minimize the total work of the system. He expressed the amount of movement (*M*) between any two communities (*i* and *j*) as being directly proportional to the product of their populations (*P*) and inversely proportional to the shortest transportation distance between them (*D*):

$$M_{ij} = k \frac{P_i * P_j}{D_{ij}} \tag{1}$$

where *k* is the proportionality constant.

The formula has an intuitive appeal with regard to the case of migration. Population size, at origin, is an acceptable index of people disposed to move and, at destination, of opportunities available. Similarly, distance deters migration because of the difficulties and expense of traveling, the wish to maintain social contacts at the place of origin, and the limited information available on long-distance opportunities.

Several attempts have been made in migration research at a more precise specification, through differential weighting, of the P/D relationship. It is now widely agreed that the impact of distance is not uniform, so that the relationship to migration is only rarely the simple inverse one specified in Zipf's formula. In order to fit different sets of migration data, exponential values have been adopted for D ranging from 0.4 to 3.0 (Hagerstrand 1957). The lower values generally apply at the more advanced stages of economic development. Thus, the frictional drag of distance is less powerful, so that migration fields are extensive and have gentle gradients. Anderson (1955) suggests that the distance exponent is a variable which is inversely related to population size. Likewise, Olson (1966) considers that sensitivity to distance diminishes with an increase in the hierarchical order of both origin and destination settlement. Stewart (1970) also suggests that there may be circumstances in which the P component in the formula should be raised to a power above unity, specifically at those stages of development when big cities exert a disproportionate pull on migrants.

B. Modified Gravity Models

The simple physical analogies of the gravity model have been qualified with time. In particular, the population size variables have been replaced or supplemented by largely economic variables designed to capture the relative drawing power or comparative advantages. A typical example is the expanded gravity model used by Rogers (1967) in his analysis of inter-regional migration in California ($R^2 = 0.92$).

$$M_{ij} = k \frac{U_i}{U_j} * \frac{WS_j}{WS_i} * \frac{LF_i LF_j}{D_{ij}}$$

where

M_{ij} = number of migrants from i to j
U = civilian unemployment rate
LF = labor force eligibles (i.e., of working age)
WS = per capita income
D_{ij} = highway distance between i and j.

It should be noted that distance is a proxy for time and cost of travel. Given the freedom and access of travel (i.e., planes, roads, etc.), distance is typically used.

In tests of models of this type the basic gravity components usually account for, by far, the greater part of migration variation. For instance, in Masser's (1970) analysis of migration between English conurbations, an R^2 of 0.91 was obtained from operationalizing a simple gravity model, compared with an R^2 of 0.95 from an extended model of the Lowry-

Rogers type. This is largely because the emphasis in these models is on absolute numbers of migrants, rather than migration rates.

Another variation (Hagerstrand 1957) adopted as a functional measure of population size the number of personal contacts between areas of origin and destination at the beginning of the migration period. Thus, the critical importance of friends and relatives in migration flows through the provision of information, initial house, and so on, was recognized. A common proxy for the number of personal contacts was the amount of previous migration between particular areas. This, however, raised the charge that a good fit in the model may simply reflect a constancy of migration-regulating conditions, rather than any functional role of "the friends and relatives multiplier."

C. Intervening Opportunity Models

In 1940 Stouffer introduced his influential "intervening opportunities" hypothesis. He argued that linear distance was less important a determinant of migration patterns than the nature of space; that distance should be regarded in socioeconomic rather than geometric terms; and that because migration is costly, socially as well as financially, that a mobile person will cease to move when he or she encounters an appropriate opportunity.

His basic hypothesis was that "the number of persons going a given distance is directly proportional to the number of opportunities at that distance and inversely proportional to the number of intervening opportunities" (Stouffer 1940). This may be expressed in a formula:

$$y = k \frac{W_x}{x} \tag{3}$$

where y is the expected number of migrants from a place to a particular concentric zone or distance band around that place, W_x is the number of opportunities within this band, and x is the number of opportunities intervening between origin and midway into the band in question.

In 1960 Stouffer refined his "intervening opportunities" model. He had been concerned with the operational inflexibility of the original model. It could only cope with migration flows from a given center to surrounding distance bands. He also realized that the take-up of opportunities in place B by inhabitants of place A through migration is inversely proportional not only to the opportunities intervening between A and B

but also to the number of competing migrants from elsewhere. His refined formula takes the following form:

$$y = \frac{X_0 * X_I}{X_B * X_C}$$

where

$y =$ the number of migrants from city 1 to city 2

$X_0 =$ all out-migrants from city 1

$X_I =$ opportunities in city 2, measured by total in-migrants

$X_B =$ opportunities intervening between cities 1 and 2, measured by total in-migrants to a circle having its diameter the distance from city 2 to city 1

$X_C =$ migrants potentially competing for opportunities in city 2, measured by total out-migrants from all cities within a circle having as its center city 2 and as its radius the distance from city 2 to city 1

Exponents for the terms in the formula can be determined empirically to improve the flexibility and goodness of fit of the model.

The real value of the gravity model is not so much the emphasis on distance as an explanatory variable. Rather it is on the deviations from the gross flows that might be expected between regions. The residuals can be examined for other possible explanations of the flows and are a useful device for understanding the overall patterns of flows.

III. ANALYSIS OF THE MODEL

A. A Brief Statement

This study analyzed the flows of migration among and between the 21 counties of the state of New Jersey and the remaining states of the United States. The modeling process was broken down into the following classes of data, based on the geographic locations of the particular points.

Migration Flows-

1. From the 21 counties of New Jersey to the 21 counties of New Jersey (Intercounty New Jersey)

2. From the 21 counties of New Jersey to the remaining states of the United States
3. From the remaining states of the United States to the 21 counties of New Jersey.

The historical basis of data was data tapes from the 1980 U.S. Census of Population. The data consisted of the migration flows in the period 1975–1980, excluding immigration. Obviously illegal immigration also is not captured in census data.

B. The Gravity Modeling Process

The law of gravity and the concept of potential force are utilized to examine population interaction and distributions. Any two places, i and j, will have an interaction (M) in proportion to their population size (P), and inversely proportional to the distance separating them (D).

$$M_{ij} = f(P_i, P_j, D_{ij})$$

The strong statistical association between migration and distance has been demonstrated in several studies. Taylor (1971) has evaluated a number of different models for fitting the migration distance function. The gravity approach may provide a good fit to a set of data, but the reliance on distance alone is not a true explanation for the migration pattern. It says nothing about the causes of migrant behavior or about the many variables that go into the decision-making process that individuals use in their relocation behavior. Hence, the initial model employed population and distance as the explanatory models, but subsequently additional variables were considered.

Both linear and log-linear forms of the model were considered. The log-linear form was preferred over the linear form because the parameters of this model can be directly interpreted as elasticities. Elasticity is the rate of change of dependent variable migration caused by any of the independent variables. In other words, elasticities gave the predicted percentage difference in migration caused by a 1% difference in the predictor variable.

Moreover, the parameters of this model can be directly compared with each other, while the same cannot be said about the parameters of the linear model. The elasticities were constant and, therefore, do not depend on the reference values of the dependent and independent variables. A comparison problem arose with the parameters of the linear model, since they depended on the units in which the independent variables are measured. Further, the dependent variable in the intrastate regression was a percentage which is bounded below by zero. Hence, the log transformation, or logistic regression, better satisfied the Ordinary Least Squares (OLS) assumptions. Therefore, the functional form of the model was developed based on a log-linear function, which was estimated by least-squares fitting techniques.

The first phase of the modeling process dealt with the most disaggregate level of the data. The modeling approach was based on a production constrained gravity model form. The basic form of this model consisted of terms representing the population size of both the origination/destination geographic points (by age, sex, and race), as well as a distance or impedance function. The nature of the impedance or distance function was developed directly from the fitting of the data at the most disaggregate level. (This function was again used in the second phase of the modeling process. In this phase the migration flow needed to be aggregated, due to the varying levels of granularity of the socioeconomic variables.)

To begin the modeling process, an appropriate data structure needed to be developed for each of the specific migration flow structures:

1. Intercounty New Jersey
2. From New Jersey counties to other states
3. From the other states to the New Jersey counties

The data was disaggregated by age and sex groupings.

For each of these data structure (geographic, age, sex, and racial classification), the number of migrants in each grouping was delineated. Next the proportion of migrants out of the total population of each group was calculated. The nature of the dependent variable can be more precisely defined:

$$P_{ijk} = \frac{m_{ijk}}{n_{ijk}}$$

$I = 1, 2,$ (male, female)
$j = 1, 2, ..., 9$ (age grouping)
$k = 1, 2, 3$ (migration group by geography)

where

P_{ijk}: is the proportion of the group migrating, the geographic age and sex classification

m_{ijk}: is the number of persons in the group
n_{ijk}: is the number of persons in the group

To develop the proportion of the group migrating, a logistic transformation was transformed. The estimates of the parameters of the gravity model were obtained by using a weighted least-squares calculation:

$$w_{ijk} = n_{ijk}\, p_{ijk}\, m(1 - p_{ijk})$$

C. The Socioeconomic Modeling Process

The second part of the modeling process involved the use of a logistic response function regression process. It related to the occurrence or nonoccurrence of migration flows to a set of socioeconomic and other explanatory variables. One other variable was an impedance on distance function as developed in the gravity modeling process.

In order to develop the appropriate response function, a logistic transformation P_{ijk} was performed on the proportion p_{ijk}, as previously discussed in the gravity modeling section. The proportion was calculated as follows:

$$P'_{ijk} = b_0 + b_1 X_1 + b_2 X_2 + \ldots + b_{81} X_{81}$$
$$(y = P'_{ijk})$$

$X_i =$ socioeconomic, and demographic and other explanatory variables

$$i = 1, 2, \ldots, 81$$

As was mentioned in the previous discussion, a stepwise regression approach was used to estimate the parameters of the socioeconomic planning model.

IV. AN ANALYSIS OF AGGREGATED RESULTS

The models hypothesized in the methodology section were estimated using the explanatory variables listed in the prior section. As expected, the gravity models with distance (for the first stage of the model only) and population as the independent variables explained a major portion of the variation in the migration flows. The inclusion of additional variables enhanced the fit of the models. A detailed analysis of the results follows.

A. Interstate In-Migrants into Each New Jersey County from Other U.S. States—Final Model

The log of earnings through federal military sources was identified as the additional variable to be incorporated into the initial model. The log of earnings through federal military sources at the receiving county was highly positively correlated with the log of the proportion of in-migrants, with a Pearson correlation coefficient of 0.80.

The model used the log of the population and the log of earnings through federal military sources as the explanatory variables. The final model took the following form:

log (*Number of in-migrants into NJ*
    County/Total in-migrants into NJ state)

= −14.283 + 0.603 log(*population in receiving county*)
+ 0.222 log(*income, earnings, government*
federal military in receiving county)

Adj-R^2: 0.878

F-value: 72.8

Increase in federal military funding had a positive effect on the proportion of in-migrants into the county, with a coefficient of 0.22. That is, every 1% increase in earnings from this source attracted in-migrants into the county at the rate of 0.22%. The coefficient was significant with a t-value of 4.06. The population variable was also significant with a t-statistic of 6.41. The F-value of 72.8 indicated a good model fit. The R^2 increased from 0.78 in the initial model to 0.88 in this model.

Counties with higher federal military earnings appeared to attract more in-migrants than those without. Though this variable increased the explanatory power of the model substantially, caution must be taken. Possibly this variable is not stable over time, changing with the defense policies of the federal government. Currently, defense expenditures are being scaled back. Counties (or states) which had been heavily funded through defense projects and consequently attracted a large number of migrants may be losing that attraction at this time. Though interesting, this parameter may be unstable.

The proportion of actual and predicted in-migrants were unlogged and provided in original values, along with the difference between the actual and predicted values and the population of each New Jersey county. The prediction errors have reduced considerably in comparison to the initial model. The residual of Burlington County was reduced from 0.741 to 0.045, giving it a very good fit. Cumberland County and Passaic County continued to be the overestimated counties, but their residuals were smaller compared to the initial model.

B. Intrastate In-Migrants into Each New Jersey County from Other New Jersey Counties—Final Model

The log of household income of the county was identified as the additional variable to be incorporated into the initial model. The log of household income at the receiving county had a Pearson correlation coefficient of 0.37 with the log of in-migrants.

The final model took the following form:

$$\log(Number\ of\ intrastate\ in\text{-}migrants\ into\ New\ Jersey\ county)$$

$$= -11.383 + 1.138\ \log(population\ in\ receiving\ county)$$
$$+ 0.665\ \log(Average\ household\ income\ in\ receiving\ county)$$

Adj-R^2: 0.947

F-value: 178.3

Increase in household income had a positive effect on the number of in-migrants into the county, with a coefficient of 0.67. The coefficient was significant with a t-value of 2.15. The population variable was also significant with a t-statistic of 17.47. The F-value of 178.3 indicated a good fit of the model to the data. The R^2 increased from 0.94 in the initial model to 0.95 in this model. Counties with higher levels of household income attracted more in-migrants than those without.

The actual and predicted in-migrants were unlogged and provided in original values, along with the difference between the actual and pre-dicted values and the population of each New Jersey county. The predic-tion errors decreased for most of the counties, but they increased slightly for some counties. The residuals of Somerset County and Atlantic County decreased considerably but at the cost of increased prediction errors for Bergen County and Hudson County.

C. Summary

As expected, the gravity models with distance and population as the independent variables explained a major portion of the variation in the migration flows. There was a strong negative correlation between the number of in-migrants coming into New Jersey from other states and the distance between New Jersey and the sending state. This reflected the tendency that regions with high population density send more migrants to New Jersey.

These relationships were confirmed in the initial regression model. In evaluating the residuals, it was noted that four of the five under-predicted states were in the Sunbelt. This may be due to younger people moving to the Northeast in search of employment opportunities.

In the final model average income of the household in the sending state was the only variable added in the final model. The reason for this was possibly due to the interaction between high-tech states sending more white-collar workers to New Jersey.

When estimating migration from other states into New Jersey counties, counties with higher federal military earning appeared to attract more in-migration than those counties without such earnings.

When estimating migration from counties in New Jersey to counties in New Jersey, household income of the county was identified as having a positive effect on the number of in-migrants into the county. Stone (1971) and Miller (1966) reported a positive association for metropolitan areas in both the United States and Canada between income and geographic movement.

Thus, the significant effects of income and earnings on inter- and intrastate models of in-migration would support the hypothesis that social mobility is a motive for migration.

D. Interstate Out-migrants from New Jersey to Other U.S. States—Final Model

The additional variables included in the final model were log of earnings from military sources and the percentage change in employment from 1970 to 1980. The former was negatively correlated (−0.16), while the latter was positively correlated (0.59) with the log of the out-migrants from New Jersey. These variables were also, correlated with the distance and population variables, but the variance inflation factors were not high. The resulting model was:

log(*out-migrants into New Jersey*)

$$= -3.390 - 0.723 \log(\textit{distance})$$

$$+0.689 \log(\textit{population in receiving state})$$

+0.028 *percent change in employment from
1970 to 1980 in receiving state* +0.3015
log(*income, earnings, government
federal military in receiving state*)

Adj-R^2: 0.864

F-value: 78.9

A 1% increase in the earnings from military sources in the receiving state increased the out-migrants flow from New Jersey to that state by 0.30%. A 1% increase in percentage change in employment increased the flow of out-migrants from New Jersey to that state by 0.03%. The coefficients of distance and population were −0.72 and 0.68, respectively. All the variables were highly significant with low variance inflation factors.

A positive change in the general employment level in a given state encouraged more people to migrate to that state from New Jersey. States with a larger allocation of federal funds for the military sector were able to attract a greater number of New Jersey residents, reflecting the defense activity in New Jersey. The comments in the previous section concerning changing defense procurement trends were applicable here.

A comparison of these results with those of the initial regression model results illustrated the improvement achieved in the model by adding additional variables. The adjusted R-squared improved from 0.69 to 0.86. The F-statistic increased from 56.0 to 78.9.

A comparison showed that the magnitude of the residuals decreased for almost all states. The number of under- and overestimated were reduced by more than half as compared to the initial model. Florida and Hawaii continued to be the underestimated states. There was trading of places between some states, such as Vermont, but overall the prediction errors were reduced considerably.

Florida, Hawaii, and other Sunbelt states attracted more people than the final model estimates. The likely explanation of this phenomena was temperature. This variable, however, turned out to be insignificant when introduced into the model (in the form of minimum, maximum, and

average temperatures). Possibly a combination of factors, such as retirement preferences and job opportunities, among others, were responsible
for this unaccounted for out-migration flow. These states had ample job
opportunities and, therefore, attracted young and old alike. Berliner
(1990) noted that Arizona and Florida were receiving the wealthiest
elderly migrants, while needy and dependent migrants were moving to
California and Texas. A sensible procedure to capture this influence when
forecasting was to add these residuals, scaled up for population increases,
to the raw forecasts. In this manner, prediction accuracy would be
improved if it were assumed that the idiosyncrasies would remain
stationary. Implementing this procedure by age cohorts should improve
results.

E. Interstate Out-Migrants from Each New Jersey County to Other U.S. States—Final Model

The log of average household income in the sending New Jersey
county was positively correlated with the log of the proportion of
out-migrants leaving that county, with a Pearson correlation coefficient
of 0.42.

The final model for estimating the proportion of out-migrants from
New Jersey counties was:

$$\log(\textit{Number of out-migrants into New Jersey County/Total}$$
$$\textit{out-migrants into New Jersey State})$$

$$= -22.826 + 0.905 \log(\textit{population in sending county})$$
$$+ 0.784 \log(\textit{average household income in sending county})$$

$$\text{Adj-}R^2\text{: } 0.955$$

$$F\text{-value: } 213.4$$

Counties with higher average household incomes appeared to experience positive out-migrant flows, with the proportion of out-migrants
leaving the county increasing by 0.78% for every 1% increase in the
average household income. The effect of population was reduced slightly
compared to the initial model. A 1% increase in the county population
increased the proportion of out-migrants leaving the county by 0.91%.
Both the coefficients were significant with t-values of 18.68 and 3.40,
respectively.

The positive sign for the average household income variable reflected the fact that the wealthier counties had a higher proportion of white-collar workers who were more mobile. The white-collar workers in the high-tech industries were more likely to consider migrating to a state which offered them better opportunities than, for instance, blue-collar workers from a poorer county.

The *F*-value of 213.378 indicated a very good fit of the model to the data. A 96% (adjusted R^2) of the variation in the dependent variable was explained by the explanatory variables.

The proportion of actual and predicted out-migrants were unlogged and provided in the original values along with the difference between the actual and predicted values and the population of each New Jersey county.

The predicted errors were reduced considerably in comparison to the initial model, except for Burlington County. Average household income did not seem to account for the under-prediction of out-migration flow for this county.

F. Intrastate Out-migrants from Each New Jersey County to Other New Jersey Counties—Final Model

The log of persons 25 years or older, with one to three years of college education in each sending county, had a Pearson correlation coefficient of 0.86 with the log of out-migrants from those counties. This variable had a higher correlation with the log of outmigrants than the log of the county population. The log of the nonwhite population had a correlation of 0.39 with the log of out-migrants.

The final model took the following form:

log(*Number of intrastate out-migrants from the sending New Jersey county*)

= 1.702 +1.123 log(*persons 25 years or older with 1 to 3 years of college education in sending county*)

−0.290 log(*nonwhite population in sending county*)

Adj-R^2: 0.90

F-value: 90.67

The increase in the number of persons with one to three years of education had a positive impact on out-migration flow from the county.

As discussed earlier in the data description section, education was positively correlated with mobility. The coefficient of this variable was 1.12 with a highly significant t-value of 12.28. A 1% increase in the number of persons with one to three years of college education in a county resulted in a 1.12% increase in the number of out-migrants from that county.

The log of nonwhite population had a negative effect on the outmigrant flow from a county. The cohort of the nonwhite population was less mobile. This variable was correlated with the education variable at 0.75 level. The variance inflation factor was not significant, indicating that multicollinearity was not a problem. Clearly, both variables, although somewhat highly correlated, play a substantial role in explaining intrastate out-migration. The coefficient of the nonwhite population was 0.29, with a significant t-value of -5.701. A 1% increase in nonwhite population in a county decreased the out-migration flow by 0.29%. An adjusted R^2 of 0.90 and an F-value of 90.67 indicated a good fit of the model to the data.

The actual and predicted out-migrants were unlogged and provided in original values along with the difference between the actual and estimated values and the population of each New Jersey county. Except for Bergen and Ocean Counties, which are over- and underestimated by the model, the prediction errors seemed reasonable for the remaining counties.

G. Summary

As with the in-migration models, the gravity models with distance and population as the independent variables explained a major portion of the out-migration flows.

When the regression models were evaluated, a positive change in the general employment level in a given state encouraged more people to migrate to that state from New Jersey. States with a larger allocation of federal funds for the military sector were able to attract a greater number of New Jersey residents, reflecting the defense activity in New Jersey.

Florida, Hawaii, and other Sunbelt states attracted more people than the final model estimates. The likely explanation of this phenomena was temperature. However, this variable turned out to be insignificant when introduced into the model. Possibly a combination of factors, such as retirement preferences and job opportunities, were responsible.

In the analysis of out-migrants' leaving each New Jersey county, counties with higher average household incomes appeared to experience positive out-migration flows. Thus, wealthier counties had a higher proportion of white-collar workers. These white-collar workers were more likely to consider migrating to a state which offered them better opportunities than, for instance, blue-collar workers from a poorer county.

In the final model the magnitude of nonwhite population in the county and the number of persons 25 years or older with one to three years of college education appeared to best estimate the number of out-migrants moving out of a New Jersey county. Greenwood and Gormely (1971) reported that both white and nonwhite migrants tend to move to high-income states. Hamilton (1959) reported a bimodal distribution of migration, where both the lowly educated and highly educated are more mobile.

These results would support the hypothesis of social mobility as a motive for migration.

VII. AN ANALYSIS OF RESULTS BY AGE FOR INTRASTATE FLOWS

This analysis to investigate whether models developed for estimating intrastate in-migration and out-migration of New Jersey using the total population could be improved by partitioning the data by age cohort. The significance of the improvement was tested by using an indicator variable, x, to compare the two regression functions.

A. In-Migration

The in-migration model was developed to estimate the number of individuals coming to counties in New Jersey from other counties in New Jersey. The introduction of the indicator variable, x, and distinguishing the in-migrants by age cohort would hopefully improve the forecasting model. The regression used to test for improvement was run and indicated that only the slope indicator for the second age cohort was significant at the $\alpha = .04$ level. The variable with which the slope indicator was significant was the population of county i. The resulting model is as follows:

$$\ln(IM_i) = -14.321 + 1.179 \ln(NJP_i) - x_{a2} * .027 \ln(NJP_i) + .689 \ln(NJHI_i)$$

where

IM_i is the number of individuals in age cohorts 1–7 from NJ to i county.
NJP_i is the population of the i county of NJ.
$NJHI_i$ is the average household income in the i county of NJ.
The subscript of x_{a2} indicates that this is for age cohort 2 (ages 16–24).

It should be noted that the R^2 for this model was .695 although the original model showed an R^2 of .952. This difference came from disaggregating the data to capture the age cohorts, which naturally decreases the reported R^2. Even though the improved model had a lower R^2, estimates are superior to the original model.

This model indicated that while individuals tended to migrate to the more populated counties, this result was even stronger for the 16–24 years old age group, called the "first job" cohort. This makes sense since both the universities and job opportunities for first-time employment tend to be in the more populated areas.

B. Out-Migration

The out-migration model was developed to estimate the number of individuals leaving counties of New Jersey for other counties in New Jersey. Again, by using an indicator variable to distinguish age cohorts, one can determine whether partitioning the model by age can lead to an improved model:

$$\ln(OM_i) = 1.702 + 1.123 \ln(1TO3COL_i) - .290 \ln(NJPN_i)$$

where

OM_I is the number of male individuals in age cohorts
i state to NJ.

$1TO3COL_I$ is the number of individuals 25 years or older with 1 to 3 years of college education in the i county.

$NJPN_i$ is the nonwhite population of the i county. The results indicated that partitioning the data by age cohort did not improve this model.

C. Summary

These analyses were conducted to test the hypothesis to determine the usefulness of partitioning, by age cohort, the migration models previously developed using the aggregated population. These models attempted to estimate the interstate in- and out-migration of individuals between New Jersey and the other states. For the interstate in-migration model, individuals living in states far from New Jersey were less likely to move to New Jersey, which supports the gravity model. This effect was even stronger for individuals in the 65+ age group. Possibly this is since New Jersey is in a temperate climate and, therefore, not necessarily a population place to move for retirement.

For the interstate out-migration age model, individuals 16–24 years old tended to leave New Jersey in larger numbers than those of other age groups. Possibly this is because persons 16–24 years old is dominated by students going to college and graduates finding their first jobs.

For the intrastate analyses, two results were noted. For the in-migration study, persons 16–24 years old tended to migrate to the more populated counties. Again, possibly this is because they are either going to college or looking for their first jobs. The out-migration model was not improved by partitioning the data by age cohort. Other research supports these findings.

In the United States, migration rates are highest among people aged 20–24 (Mueller 1982; White and Woods 1980). Lee (1966) found migration differentials by age to be bimodal, with the first peak appearing at an early age and the second peak at retirement. Age 65 and over is probably the most agreed upon category in migrations analyses. Retirees migrate because of detachment from the labor force or to see goods and services catering to the elderly (Chevan and Fisher 1979; Longino 1982).

In summary, for the 65+ years old cohort, only the average household income variable was significant, thereby supporting the hypothesis. For the 16–24 years old, employment change between 1970–1980, income from federal government military and average household income also support the hypothesis.

VIII. CONCLUSIONS

A series of regression-based forecasting models have been completed which examine the relationship between social mobility and in-migration and out-migration between New Jersey and other states and between counties within New Jersey. The initial studies examined aggregated population flows.

A. Background

Predicting large-scale population movements is a difficult task even under conditions of reasonable political and economic stability. "Push" and "pull" factors are often operationalized in quite elaborate econometric models, but these are frequently distressingly disappointing when actually parameterized. Collinearity between variables assumed to be independent often reduces overall explanatory power, and visually simpler and more robust models of proven worth are more valuable when applied in concrete, empirical situations.

For example, simple "gravity model" formulations underlie a large number of spatial models ranging from interaction to diffusion studies. All gravity model formulations share the same basic form, strengths, and failings. It is gratifying, but not too surprising, that the simplest form, postulating migration as a spatial interaction, works remarkably well. That the logged form of $I = f(P,D)$, where P is the population of the receiving (or originating) region and D is the distance between the originating and the receiving regions, provides a remarkably good fit is encouraging. This is because the dependent variable P changes relatively slowly over time, while D, the simple distance is virtually invariable. This must be qualified if a more realistic surrogate measure of distance is used (say cost or time), although even these "more realistic" measures are unlikely to vary much over the next few decades.

The redistribution of economic opportunities (including the changing locations of industry), changes in the interstate highway system, and low-cost air transportation (which has decreased effective distance between places) have all played important roles in influencing the redistribution of the population. A spatial restructuring of America similar to the railways of the nineteenth, and the interstate highways of the twentieth centuries is not expected. Moreover, any technical change lowering or raising cost-distance, such as another oil crisis, would be felt equally throughout the system. In brief, the $I = f(P,D)$ model, when properly calibrated, is expected to be extraordinarily stable over most planning horizons.

In addition to these structural forces, there have been substantial changes in family composition, labor force participation, fertility patterns, and the increasing proportion of older people in the population. All these factors lead to changes in migration rates.

With this in mind, interstate migration was modeled in two phases. In the first phase flows between each state and New Jersey were modeled.

In the second phase the aggregate New Jersey flows were distributed to the counties within the state. This two-phased approach greatly simplified the modeling flows between each New Jersey county and each state. Intrastate migration was modeled between the counties.

Each of the above three models was completed in two stages. The first stage for the models for interstate migration between New Jersey and other states was completed with distance and population as the explanatory variables.

Distance was excluded as a factor in this study in the interstate New Jersey county models and the intrastate migration models since it is not a factor. The gravity approach may provide a good fit to a set of data, but the reliance on distance and population alone was not a complete explanation for the migration pattern. It said nothing about the causes of migrant behavior or about the many variables that go into the decision-making process that individuals use in their relocation behavior. Hence, in the second stage, residuals from the above regressions were examined with stepwise regression, correlation coefficients, and variance inflation factors to determine further explanatory variables including weather, demographic, and economic data.

B. In-Migration Factors

In-migration was modeled for the aggregate flows by sex and by age cohorts. For the aggregate population migration, distance and population (for the sending state or the receiving county) were the primary variables in accord with expectations. This supports the theory behind the gravity model. Population size at the origin is an acceptable index of people anxious to move and, at destination, of opportunities available. Also distance deters migration because of the difficulties and expense of traveling.

An additional push factor from the sending states was their mean household income. It appeared that more persons from wealthy states were migrating to New Jersey than the poorer persons. New Jersey, as an industrial state with high-tech industries and defense contracts, attracted residents of other states.

However, housing is typically the prime motive for local moves, and many workers are willing to make a job shift to another region but either cannot find a house to rent or buy at a price they are willing or able to pay or they are unable to sell their current home.

Reasons for movement vary significantly with distance. Within-area or local moves are mainly connected with housing adjustments to family and personal needs; and although inter-local authority motivations for migration are varied, the proportion of moves as a result of housing and marriage drop substantially. Transfer by firm and economic motives (to gain employment, and wage-earnings and redundancy motives) become important. Motivations and reasons for migration also tend to vary with the type of move being undertaken. Economic motives figure prominently in primary and secondary moves—to obtain a job or increase earnings—whereas personal and family motives often induce return migration.

In distributing the aggregate inflows into New Jersey to its various counties, Income from Federal Military Expenditures (a national income account category) provided further explanatory power. Employment by military contractors appeared to have been a significant factor, also supporting the hypothesis.

Disaggregating the models by sex added no explanatory power. Since the migration of singles and single parents could not be distinguished from that of couples. Due to data limitations, no significant differences by sex could be discerned. This result may indicate movement toward gender equality.

The sex segregation of occupations is becoming recognized as an integral feature of the occupational structure that must be understood in order to explain inequality between men and women (Reskin 1984). A number of studies have shown the striking stability of sex segregation over the course of the century. Other research has estimated the proportion of the gender gap in wages that is attributable to sex segregation (Treiman and Hartmann 1981). The call for equal pay for work of comparable value has brought the sex segregation of occupations to the attention of the public (Remick 1984).

Disaggregating the models by age cohorts did lead to interesting differences. At the interstate-NJ-from-other-states level, distance was a significantly greater push factor for age group 65+ years of age. This indicated that retired couples were less likely to move greater distances to migrate to New Jersey. At the interstate-NJ-to-counties level, ages 16–24 had a higher average in-migration rate than the other age migrating groups. For the intrastate in-migration model, population in the receiving county is a greater pull factor for ages 16–24 than for the rest of the migrating population.

This suggested that those leaving for their first job are more attracted to centers of population. Part of this data is updated in research in the *Chronicle of Higher Education* (1988). This research stated that some 85% of all first-time college students attend public or private institutions within home states. When the number of students who leave the State and the number who arrive was compared, New Jersey had the largest net loss, with 35,800 resident students leaving and 1,100 out-of-state students arriving. This supports the hypotheses related to education.

C. Out-Migration Factors

Again, note that distance and population were the most important variables, again supporting the theory of the gravity model. For migrants leaving New Jersey for other states, the percentage change in employment in the receiving state and Income from Federal Military Expenditures provided additional explanatory power as pull factors. The first factor suggested that recruiting in New Jersey had been an important migration factor, in keeping with the high mobility and high average income level within the state. Also, the importance of military contracting to the state was reflected in the second factor.

Interstate out-migration from New Jersey counties was not only affected by county size but by mean household income, supporting the hypothesis. This reflects the attractiveness of this group and their mobility to recruiters outside New Jersey. Intrastate out-migration found the population over 25 years of age with at least one to three years of college in the sending county as the most important push factor. This reflected students' leaving/graduating and moving to their first job, the only result supporting the theory. Non-white population in the sending county was a significant negative factor in out-migration, exhibiting the lack of mobility of this segment of the population. This finding supported research that the white population typically have higher mobility than the nonwhite population (Greenwood and Gormely 1971).

D. Applications

The models provided herein can provided a vehicle for forecasting both the magnitude and composition of migration into and out of the counties of New Jersey. From a sociological point of view, the output of those models provided a means of the level and nature of the forms and amounts of human services needed within the New Jersey counties (when combined with estimates of births and deaths in the counties).

Specifically, while some simple migration flow models provided estimates that are not explained in terms of various social, economic and other explanatory variables, these models provided a direct measure of the sensitivity of the level and composition of migration to a series of significant explanatory variables. The importance of this explanation is migration and its composition is directly and measurably related to such factors as government expenditures, seasonal income, education, and so on.

Thus, instead of presenting a static and fixed estimate of migration in-flow and out-flow, a dynamic estimation was presented, which is sensitive to changes in the environment. As the economy changed, its ability to attract/repel migrants directly impacts the labor source. Moreover, population increases/decreases in turn effect the demand level for government services.

REFERENCES

Anderson, T. 1955. "Intermetropolitan Migration: A Comparison of the Hypothesis of Zipf and Stouffer." *American Sociological Review* 20: 287–291.

Berliner, J.S. 1990. "Internal Migration: A Comparative Disciplinary View." Pp. 443–461 in *Social Mobility and Social Structure*, edited by R.L. Breiger. New York: Cambridge University Press.

Chevan, A., and L.R. Fischer. 1979. "Retirement and Interstate Migration." *Social Forces* 57: 1369–1380.

Greenwood, M.J., and P.J. Gormely. 1971. "A Comparison of the Determinants of White and Nonwhite Interstate Migration." *Demography* 8 (1): 141–155.

Hagerstrand, T. 1957. "Migration and Data: A Survey of a Sample of Swedish Migration Fields and Hypothetical Consideration in their Genesis." *Lund Studies in Geography* 13B: 127–158.

Hamilton, H.C. 1959. "Educational Selectivity of Net Migration from the South." *Social Forces* 38: 33–42.

Longino, C.F. 1982. "Changing Aged Nonmetropolitan Migration Patterns 1955–1960 and 1965 to 1970." *Journal of Gerontology* 37: 228–234.

Miller, A.R. 1966. "Migration Differentials in Labor Force Participations, U.S." *Demography* 3: 58–68.

Mueller, C.F. 1982. *The Economics of Labor Migration: A Behavioral Analysis.* New York: Academic Press.

Olson, G. 1966. "Distance and Human Interaction: A Migration Study." *Annals of Geography* 47B: 3–43.

Remick, H. (Ed.) 1984. *Comparable Worth and Wage Discriminations: Technical Possibility and Political Realities.* Philadelphia: Temple University.

Reskin, B. (Ed.) 1984. *Sex Segregation in the Workplace: Trends, Explanations, Remedies.* Washington, DC: National Academy of Sciences Press.

Stewart, C. 1970. "Migration as a Function of Population and Distance." *American Sociology Review* 25: 347–356.

Stone, L.O. 1971. "On the Correlation between Metropolitan In-migration and Out-migration by Occupation." *Journal of the American Statistical Association* 66: 693–701.

Stouffer, S. 1940. "Intervening Opportunities: A Theory Relating Mobility and Distance." *American Sociological Review* 5: 845–867.

Taylor, P.J. 1971. *Distance Decay in Spatial Interactions: Concepts and Techniques in Modern Geography.* Norwich, UK: Geo Books.

Treiman, D., and H. Hartmann (Ed.) 1981. *Women, Work and Wages: Equal Pay for Jobs of Equal Value.* Washington, DC: National Academy of Sciences Press.

White, P.E., and R.I. Woods. 1980. *The Geographical Impact of Migration.* London: Longman, Inc.

DETERMINISTIC AND STOCHASTIC FORECASTING OF HIGH-TECH MARKETPLACE COMPETITION

Eileen Bridges, Katherine B. Ensor, and
John A. Norton

ABSTRACT

Firm decisions to enter a dynamic, innovative marketplace depend in part on the competition anticipated at the planned introduction time. We develop, empirically test, and compare the performance of deterministic and stochastic versions of three models for forecasting growth in the number of products based on a new technological platform, as a function of time since the introduction of the technology. These models may be used in conjunction with demand growth models to assess efforts to commercialize new products, by helping managers predict the number of competing products a new entry will face.

Advances in Business and Management Forecasting, Volume 2, pages 219–234.

I. CONCEPTUAL DEVELOPMENT

In making a product entry decision, managers consider, among other things, (1) the anticipated demand in the category, and (2) the expected number of competitors, which partially define the market structure. Sales growth in innovative product categories may be predicted by diffusion models, which have been developed and tested in literally hundreds of studies. Mahajan, Muller, and Bass (1990) provide a comprehensive review of sales diffusion models; Bridges, Coughlan, and Kalish (1991) review literature focusing on firm and customer adoption decisions in innovative marketplaces. The degree of firm rivalry expected in the marketplace is a question considered by Gottinger (1987), Modis and Debecker (1988), Lambkin and Day (1989), and Reinganum (1989). However, in addition to forecasts of category sales and the number of competing firms, managers need estimates of how many products will compete in the category. It is one thing to enter a marketplace which includes eight firms and eight products, but another altogether to enter one with eight firms and 80 products. Forecasting the number of products competing in an innovative category is a topic which has been inadequately researched; we have found only three previous papers addressing this issue (Bridges, Ensor, and Norton 1993; Bridges, Ensor, and Thompson 1992; Modis and Debecker 1988).

To forecast the number of products based on a particular technological platform that will compete in a marketplace at a given time, we must select a model form which, first, describes the growth process, and second, provides a limit to growth. Epidemiological models meet these requirements, and may be used to describe the number of products competing in a high-tech product category. Such models are frequently used to describe sales diffusion (see Mahajan, Muller, and Bass 1990), and typically include two growth terms: one represents product adoptions due to "innovative" influences such as advertising and promotional activities, and the other represents adoptions due to "imitation" of previous purchasers. These two influences on growth may be similarly observed in new product introductions. Innovative influences are not related to the development of other similar products either within the firm or in competing firms; therefore, they are unaffected by the number of products already competing in the marketplace. Positive innovative influences include the "basic research" activities of a firm's R&D department, fit of the product category with the core competencies and strategic direction of the firm, and relative ease of educating customers in the use of the new product.

Imitative influences lead to development of a high-tech product in response to the success (or anticipated success) of a similar product, one which may be marketed by the same firm or by a competitor. Thus, the impact of imitative influences depends directly on the number of products already competing in the marketplace. Positive imitative influences include easily-copied technology, high barriers to market entry (such as the establishment of a de facto industry standard), and observable success of competing firms. Innovative and imitative influences are not mutually exclusive, and both may operate on any new product introduced into a high-tech product category.

If products may enter a high-tech marketplace, they may also leave; thus, a model for the number of competing products may better represent reality if exits are permitted (Bridges, Ensor, and Norton 1993; Bridges, Ensor, and Thompson 1992). Exit of a product from a high-tech marketplace may be viewed as similar to the case in social influence models when an information spreader becomes inactive (Kermack and McKendrick 1927). Thus, we assume that product exits occur in proportion to the number of products in the marketplace.

To estimate an epidemiological model such as ours, it is necessary to supply a theoretical limit, specifically, the maximum number of products which may compete in the marketplace. We note that this potential is externally determined and does not depend on the pattern of growth; thus, such estimation has been a source of uncertainty and difficulty (Heeler and Hustad 1980; Lawrence and Lawton 1981). One consideration that we make use of is that the maximum number of products which may be supported in a particular high-tech marketplace depends heavily on the availability of distribution facilities. While product proliferation may occur due to heterogeneity of the potential market, the number of products which can successfully compete is limited by the available channels. For a particular industry, these may include department stores, specialty stores, and catalogs, for example. Because of the wide variety of distribution facilities that may be available, the number of competing products may be very high, but it is not unlimited.

II. DETERMINISTIC AND STOCHASTIC MODELING

Previous researchers who have used epidemiological models to represent competitive intensity in innovative markets have typically suggested a single model form and assumed that growth was either deterministic or stochastic. We make an important contribution by estimating three model forms under first deterministic, and then stochastic, assumptions. Finally, we compare and contrast results obtained by the deterministic and stochastic versions of the most complete model.

Deterministic models are appealing because, in general, it is easy to obtain parameter estimates. However, these models require the restrictive assumption that error is additive. The first deterministic model we estimate has a precedent in Modis and Debecker (1988), who modeled growth in the number of products competing in a high-technology marketplace as an increasing function of the number of products previously introduced (in other words, growth was modeled as being due exclusively to imitation of existing products). We generalize this model by incorporating additional terms representing (1) new product entry due to innovation, and (2) product exit. The three deterministic model forms that we compare were previously tested by Bridges, Ensor, and Norton (1993), and we make use of results obtained in that research.

Our second approach uses stochastic modeling techniques similar to those used in the sales diffusion models of Monahan (1984) and Böker (1987), who develop pure birth process models for durable products, and Tapiero (1975), Deshmukh and Winston (1977), and Albright and Winston (1979), who develop birth-and-death process models. One of our stochastic models was discussed by Bridges, Ensor, and Thompson (1992). A stochastic model (which depends only on the previous number of products to predict the next value), reflects the probabilistic nature of the growth process, and adapts readily to changes in this process. Which approach is more useful in a particular situation depends in part upon the applications the resulting forecasts are intended to support.

Before proceeding with model development, we summarize our key observations. It is possible to model with considerable fidelity the growth in the number of products in a particular class using a relatively simple epidemiological model. Including in the growth model terms for both innovative and imitative influences on product entry improves the model technically and managerially, as does inclusion of a term for product exit. Because the maximum potential number of competing products is determined by factors outside our model, we estimate this potential externally.

For managerial purposes, use of a stochastic model adds complexity in comparison to a deterministic model, but it provides an alternative means of forecasting. Stochastic modeling (and the estimation procedure described herein) may have even greater value under other circumstances, particularly in cases where the appropriate deterministic growth model does not yield a closed form solution. In addition, use of stochastic models may become more prevalent as state-of-the-art software is developed, making stochastic models more accessible to managers. We believe the current research will be particularly relevant to managers when this choice is readily available.

A. The Deterministic Approach

If all high-tech product introductions were due strictly to imitation of the first product entry in the category (and each new entrant exhibited no innovative contribution to the marketplace) we could model product entry as

$$\frac{dn(t)}{dt} = \lambda_i \left[\frac{n(t)}{N} \right] [N - n(t)] \tag{1}$$

where $n(t)$ represents the number of such products on the market at time t, N is the maximum number of products based on the particular technological platform which may be supported in the marketplace, and λ_i is a coefficient of imitation. Model (1) was used by Modis and Debecker (1988) and Bridges, Ensor, and Norton (1993) to model the number of products competing in a high-tech marketplace. This model may be solved analytically to obtain

$$n(t) = \frac{N}{(N-1)e^{-\lambda_i t} + 1} \tag{2}$$

for the case where $n(0) = 1$; in other words, for all time periods after the first product based on the new technology has been introduced into the marketplace.

We extend model (1) to incorporate effects of innovative as well as imitative influences on product entry. To obtain this more complete representation of influences which potentially impact entry of additional products into a high-technology marketplace, we use an epidemiological model form comparable to the sales diffusion model of Bass (1969). This form, which was also tested by Bridges, Ensor, and Norton (1993), is:

$$\frac{dn(t)}{dt} = \left[\lambda_e + \lambda_i \left(\frac{n(t)}{N} \right) \right] [N - n(t)] \tag{3}$$

in which λ_e is a coefficient of innovation, and other variables are defined as in equation (1). Model (3) may be solved analytically to obtain

$$n(t) = \frac{-\lambda_e N^2 - \lambda_i N + \lambda_e N(N-1)e^{-(\lambda_i+\lambda_e)t}}{-\lambda_e N - \lambda_i - \lambda_i(N-1)e^{-(\lambda_i+\lambda_e)t}} \tag{4}$$

for the case where $n(0) = 1$.

Because we are interested in the number of products active in a marketplace rather than the number that have ever been introduced, our most complete model allows for product withdrawals. This model was the most complete form tested by Bridges, Ensor, and Norton (1993) and is given by:

$$\frac{dn(t)}{dt} = \left[\lambda_e + \lambda_i\left(\frac{n(t)}{N}\right)\right][N - n(t)] - \mu n(t) \tag{5}$$

where μ is the rate at which existing products are withdrawn from the marketplace, and other variables are defined as above. We assume, for tractability, that the number of products exiting the marketplace is a constant percentage of the number competing at any given time. Model (5) may be solved analytically; the solution is

$$n(t) = \frac{N[a(1 - ce^{tb}) - b(1 + ce^{tb})]}{2\lambda_i(1 - ce^{tb})} \tag{6}$$

where $a = (-\lambda_e + \lambda_i - \mu)$, $b = (4\lambda_e\lambda_i + a^2)^{1/2}$, $c = [N(a-b) - 2\lambda_i]/[N(a+b) - 2\lambda_i]$, and the initial conditions again specify $n(0) = 1$.

B. The Stochastic Approach

To permit comparison of the forecasts obtained by stochastic and deterministic models, we test stochastic process models corresponding to deterministic models (1), (3), and (5). For models comparable to (1) and (3), growth in number of products is represented in terms of stochastic birth processes; for model (5), which permits product exit from the marketplace, we use an analogous stochastic birth-and-death process.

The assumptions required for a stochastic birth process comparable to model (1) are:

A1. The probability of two or more entries (or exits) in $[t,t + \Delta t]$ approaches zero as Δt approaches zero.

A2. The probability a product enters the market in time $[t,t + \Delta t]$ is proportional to the imitative growth rate

$$\lambda_n = \left[\lambda_i \left(\frac{n(t)}{N} \right) (n - n(t)) \right] \Delta t \tag{7}$$

where λ_n is the rate of product entry.

Based on these two assumptions, the probability of one entry by time t is given by the distribution function

$$F_e(t) = 1 - \text{Pr(no entries in time } t)$$

$$= 1 - e^{-\lambda_n t}. \tag{8}$$

To obtain a stochastic birth process model comparable to model (3), we retain assumption A1, but replace assumption A2 by the following:

A2′. The probability a product enters the market in time $[t, t + \Delta t]$ is proportional to both the innovative and imitative entry rates, therefore

$$\lambda_n = \left[\lambda_e + \lambda_i \left(\frac{n(t)}{N} \right) \right] [N - n(t)] \, \Delta t. \tag{9}$$

The distribution function representing the probability of a product entry by time t is the same as that given in equation (8), except that λ_n is now defined by equation (9).

Finally, to obtain a stochastic birth-and-death process comparable to model (5), we incorporate a third assumption (in addition to A1 and A2′) which allows for product exit from the marketplace:

A3. The probability a product exits the market in time $[t, t + \Delta t]$ is proportional to the number of products currently on the market; therefore

$$\mu_n = \mu n \Delta t. \tag{10}$$

The distribution function for the probability of one entry by time t is the same as that for model (3), as defined in equations (8) and (9). Based on assumptions A1 and A3, the distribution function for probability of one product withdrawal from the marketplace by time t is given by

$$F_w(t) = 1 - \text{Pr(no exits in time } t)$$

$$= 1 - e^{-\mu_n t}. \tag{11}$$

As noted by Eliashberg and Chatterjee (1986, p. 163), a stochastic model incorporating an imitative birth process cannot be solved analytically. However, we can estimate the parameters of such a model using a simulation-based technique (Ensor, Bridges, and Lawera 1993). To do so, we simulate the birth (or birth-and-death) process which represents product entries into (and withdrawals from) the marketplace using the distribution function(s) defined for each of the three stochastic models. The simulated processes are compared to the actual data in order to estimate model parameters.

III. EMPIRICAL RESULTS

We empirically tested the applicability of our models to actual marketplace behavior, using data from the personal computer industry. This data set includes 749 personal computer products, described by brand and model number, and introduced by 190 firms during the period 1972 through 1988. During the time period of the study, 320 of the products were also withdrawn. The deterministic and stochastic forms of models (1), (3), and (5) were estimated using the complete data set, to permit comparison of fit among the three models and between the deterministic and stochastic forms. In addition, to allow comparison of forecasting ability of one model under deterministic versus stochastic assumptions, we estimated both forms of model (5) using successive updating as described by Armstrong (1978).

A. Deterministic Model Estimation

Estimations of deterministic model parameters were performed using nonlinear least squares (NLS), the preferred method for estimating parameter values in sales diffusion models (Mahajan, Mason, and Srinivasan 1986; Srinivasan and Mason 1986); we tested both quasi-Newton and simplex algorithms. To ensure stability, we fixed the maximum number of personal computer products (identified by brand and model number) which may be supported by the marketplace, N, at 500. This method is suggested by Heeler and Hustad (1980) and by Lawrence and Lawton (1981).

Estimation of model (1), which includes imitative effects only, for the entire data set (1972–1988) resulted in parameter value $\lambda_i = 0.5132$ (0.011). (Standard errors are given in parentheses.) Comparing the fitted and actual values, the mean squared error (MSE) was 1128.49.

Model (3) incorporates innovative effects on product entry as well as the imitative effects of model (1). Estimation of this model for the complete data set resulted in $\lambda_e = 0.005342$ (0.001) and $\lambda_i = 0.3305$ (0.013); MSE was 169.25.

Model (5) extends model (3) by including the effects of product withdrawal from the marketplace. The parameter estimates obtained for model (5) were $\lambda_e = 0.003027$ (0.000), $\lambda_i = 0.4787$ (0.039), and $\mu = 0.07032$ (0.023). Using these parameter values to estimate the number of personal computers on the market resulted in a MSE of 132.12.

As noted earlier, in further testing the ability of model (5) to forecast the number of products competing in the marketplace, we used a successive updating technique. We first estimated the parameters for the model in equation (6) based on the first 12 years of data (1972–1983). We then used these parameter values to project the number of personal computers on the market for the next five years (1984–1988). This procedure was repeated for the first 13 years of data, estimating for 1972–1984 and projecting for 1985–1989. This procedure was continued, using 14 years of data, 15 years of data, and so forth until all of the data (1972–1988) were used to estimate the parameter values and projections were made for 1989–1993. Comparing these estimates and forecasts to the actual data, the mean squared errors (MSEs) are reported in Table 1.

Table 1. Comparing Mean Squared Error for Short-
and Long-Term Forecasts

	Within Series	1 Step Ahead	2 Step Ahead	3 Step Ahead	4 Step Ahead	5 Step Ahead
Deterministic, series through:						
1983	3.8	355.4	3448.0	4425.0	1989.0	582.3
1984	7.3	831.5	502.1	144.5	1794.0	—
1985	23.0	53.9	2404.6	7157.1	—	—
1986	186.5	85.2	2.2	—	—	—
1987	76.2	2336.6	—	—	—	—
1988	132.1	—	—	—	—	—
Stochastic, series through:						
1983	6.6	819.2	6301.8	9130.2	6197.3	3714.8
1984	18.3	2901.5	5662.3	4099.5	2606.7	—
1985	94.1	19.5	291.8	1215.7	—	—
1986	118.2	703.5	2312.1	—	—	—
1987	151.2	337.8	—	—	—	—
1988	153.7	—	—	—	—	—

B. Stochastic Model Estimation

We obtained estimates of the parameter values in our stochastic models using the simulation-based estimation (SIMEST) technique of Thompson, Atkinson, and Brown (1987). This technique allows estimation of the stochastic model parameters directly from the assumptions defining the process, making it unnecessary to obtain a closed form solution to a stochastic differential equation. The SIMEST methodology consists of simulating the mean path for the model at a given set of parameter values and evaluating the proximity of the simulated mean path to the observed data. Estimates of the mean path are obtained by minimizing the mean squared error (MSE) over the parameter space. As the number of realizations averaged to obtain the mean path increases, this method is equivalent to NLS estimation of the model parameters when a closed form solution is available (Ensor, Bridges, and Lawera 1992). Standard errors of the parameter estimates are obtained by evaluating the MSE in a neighborhood of the optimal parameter estimates and computing the sample standard deviation of the values in the parameter space which yield a value of the MSE within the 95th percentile of the simulated distribution of the MSE at the parameter estimate. As in our estimation of the deterministic models, we fixed N, the maximum number of PCs which might compete in the marketplace, at 500.

Estimation of the stochastic form analogous to model (1) resulted in $\lambda_i = 0.517255$ (0.00214). Using this estimated parameter value to simulate the growth process resulted in mean estimates of the actual growth process having a MSE of 345.6.

The stochastic form comparable to model (3) obtained estimates of $\lambda_e = 0.003095$ (0.0000183) and $\lambda_i = 0.35398$ (0.00106). The mean path of the simulated growth process obtained using these parameter estimates resulted in fits with the actual growth process having a MSE of 164.4.

Estimation of the model (5) parameter values for the entire data set resulted in $\lambda_e = 0.002706$ (0.000023), $\lambda_i = 0.3802$ (0.002212), and $\mu = 0.03571$ (0.000228). Using these parameter values to fit estimates to the actual growth data, we obtained a MSE of 153.7.

To permit comparison of the forecasting abilities of the stochastic and deterministic versions of model (5), we used a successive updating technique to obtain stochastic model forecasts. The implementation of this technique was slightly different than that for the deterministic model. While the deterministic model (6) can be used to make one-, two-, three- four- and five-step ahead forecasts directly, the stochastic model requires an estimate for each step, to be used in projecting the next step. For example, a five-step-ahead forecast using the stochastic model requires model-based forecasts for the first through fourth steps for use in the estimation. (Note that providing this information to the deterministic model would not lead to any change in the forecast for the fifth step ahead, because including model-based forecasts for the first through fourth steps in the parameter value estimation does not significantly impact the deterministic model parameter values.) The resulting MSEs for the estimates and forecasts are presented in Table 1.

C. Comparison of Deterministic and Stochastic Model Results

Our parameter estimates and fit statistics for models (1), (3), and (5) are similar across the deterministic and stochastic versions of the models. Because model (5) provides significantly better fit than model (1) ($p <$ .01) or model (3) ($p < .1$), we use model (5) for further comparison of the deterministic and stochastic model forms. Successive updating permits estimates and forecasts for both types of models over a range of data periods as well as a range of forecast periods; we compare these results for both within-series fits and short- and long-term forecasts. The MSEs for both deterministic and stochastic forms of the model are provided in Table 1.

As mentioned earlier, the deterministic form of the model is easy to fit and assumes additive error. In fitting a sequence of data points, NLS estimation considers each point in the sequence equally and obtains the parameter values which minimize the sum of squared error. Consequently, in a short series of points, when the next data point is appended to the series (as is done in successive updating), it may have a large effect on the optimal parameter values. Therefore, it is possible for fit statistics to vary considerably as additional points are appended to the series. This occurrence is observed in the results shown in Table 1. Not coincidentally, a graph of the deterministic model estimates as each new data point is included in the series shows that the estimated mean path is heavily dependent on the number of data points included in the estimation (see Figure 1).

Stochastic model estimation (via SIMEST) considers each new data point as a starting point for the stochastic growth process. Therefore, a stochastic model form is able to adjust to changes in the ongoing growth process more readily than a deterministic form. Thus, the stochastic form will often have a MSE larger than the deterministic form, but the

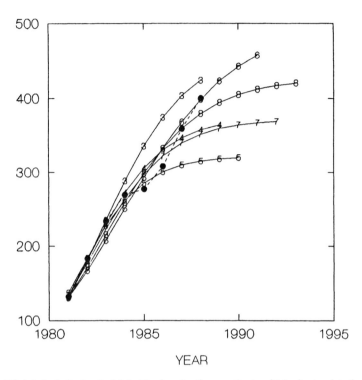

Note: Filled circles indicate actual data. Numbered paths are estimates obtained using data through
        year number indicated (e.g., the path obtained for 1972–1983 data is indicated by the numeral
        "3").

Figure 1. Estimates of Mean Paths Using Deterministic Model (5)

stochastic path estimates obtained as each successive data point is
appended to the series show markedly greater stability (see Figure 2).
Particularly where an anomaly is found in the data series (see 1985), the
stochastic model is able to adapt more readily than is the deterministic
model.

In summary, the deterministic form of the model is easy to estimate
and provides better fit statistics, in general, over the entire sequence of
data presented. The stochastic form, while more difficult to estimate,
provides stable forecasts as additional data points are included in the
parameter estimation. It also provides greater flexibility, because it can
be adopted for complex model forms which cannot be solved in closed
form for deterministic estimation.

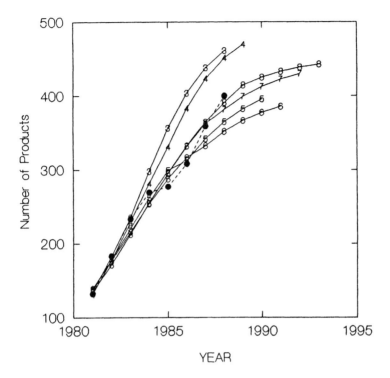

Figure 2. Estimate of Mean Paths Using Stochastic Model (5)

IV. CONCLUSIONS AND DIRECTIONS FOR FUTURE RESEARCH

Our results suggest that an epidemiological model form (common in
sales diffusion models) may be used to model and forecast the number
of products competing in a high-technology marketplace such as personal computers. Because we obtain significant estimates for the rate of
product exits from the marketplace, we recommend that product withdrawals be incorporated into forecasting models for the number of
competitors in dynamic, innovative marketplaces.

We obtain good within-series estimates and excellent predictive validity for one through five step-ahead forecasts using the deterministic
version of our complete model, which includes terms representing prod-

232   E. BRIDGES, K. B. ENSOR, and J. A. NORTON

uct innovation, imitation, and exit. However, the mean path of the estimates is heavily dependent on the number of data points included in the series for estimation. Using the stochastic version of our complete model, we obtain adequate fit statistics, and, importantly, mean path estimates which are much more robust to changes in the number of data points used for estimation.

The deterministic modeling approach is managerially useful because it is easy to estimate. However, the path of stochastic estimates more closely represents what actually occurs in the marketplace than does the deterministic path, because a stochastic model projects each value based on the immediately preceding value. Our results suggest that deterministic estimates offer a reasonable approximation to reality and to the stochastic estimates. However, many growth models cannot be solved in closed form; in these cases, a stochastic model may be estimated using the SIMEST procedure. Therefore, further model enhancements undertaken to improve the model for application in a particular industry or to solve a particular problem may make it necessary to use a stochastic model whose parameter values can be estimated without the need for a closed form solution.

Our projections in the personal computer marketplace suggest that the period of rapid category growth has already passed. Typically, in a high-tech category, decreases in growth in the number of competing products occur after product sales begin to slow; in fact, slowing in growth in number of products may potentially be useful as an (upper bound) estimate for slowing in sales. Mahajan and Muller (1989) find that the peak in number of products is one of two optimal introduction times for new products based on a particular technology; this is expressed in their "ASAP or at maturity" principle. The interrelationship between number of products and sales is worthy of further research.

The use of alternative and complementary models as well as multiple forecasters yields superior forecasting results to those obtained with a single method. We believe that modeling the number of firms, number of products, and level of sales in a particular marketplace leads to greater managerial insight by far than would the use of any of these estimates in isolation.

ACKNOWLEDGMENTS

The authors wish to express their appreciation to Scott Armstrong, Murali Mantrala, Charlotte Mason, Kalyan Raman, Edwin Tang, and Al Wildt for helpful comments; the second author also wishes to express her appreciation for computer hardware support provided by NSF grant #DMS 9005783. This work draws from a paper published by the authors in the *International Journal of Forecasting* (1993); they wish to acknowledge the copyright holder, Elsevier Science Publishers, Ltd., for permitting the use of portions of the work.

REFERENCES

Albright, S.C., and W. Winston. 1979. "A Birth-Death Model of Advertising and Pricing," *Advances in Applied Probability* 11: 134–152.

Armstrong, J.S. 1978. *Long-Range Forecasting*. New York: John Wiley and Sons.

Bass, F.M. 1969. "A New Product Growth Model for Consumer Durables." *Management Science* 15: 215–227.

Böker, F. 1987. "A Stochastic First Purchase Diffusion Model: A Counting Process Approach." *Journal of Marketing Research* 24: 64–73.

Bridges, E., A.T. Coughlan, and S. Kalish. 1991. "New Technology Adoption in an Innovative Marketplace: Micro- and Macro-Level Decision Making Models." *International Journal of Forecasting* 7 (3): 257–270.

Bridges, E., K.B. Ensor, and J.R. Thompson. 1992. "Marketplace Competition in the Personal Computer Industry." *Decision Sciences* 23 (2): 467–477.

Bridges, E., K.B. Ensor, and J.A. Norton. 1993. "Forecasting the Number of Competing Products in High-Technology Markets." *International Journal of Forecasting* 9 (3): 399–405.

Deshmukh, S.D., and W. Winston. 1977. "A Controlled Birth and Death Process Model of Optimal Product Pricing Under Stochastically Changing Demand." *Journal of Applied Probability* 14: 328–339.

Eliashberg, J., and R. Chatterjee. 1986. "Stochastic Issues in Innovation Diffusion Models." Pp. 151–199 in *Innovation Diffusion Models of New Product Acceptance*, edited by V. Mahajan and Y. Wind. Cambridge, MA: Ballinger Publishing Company.

Ensor, K.B., E. Bridges, and M. Lawera. 1993. "Simulation Based Estimation for Birth and Death Processes." *Proceedings of the Thirty-Eighth Conference on the Design of Experiment in Army Research, Development, and Testing*. U.S. Army Research Office Report Number 93-1, June: 343–352.

Gottinger, H.W. 1987. "Economic Choice and Technology Diffusion in New Product Markets." *Weltwirtschaftliches Archiv* 123: 93–120.

Heeler, R.M., and T.P. Hustad. 1980. "Problems in Predicting New Product Growth for Consumer Durables." *Management Science* 26 (October): 1007–1020.

Kermack, W.O., and A.G. McKendrick. 1927. "A Contribution to the Mathematical Theory of Epidemics." *Proceedings of the Royal Society of London, Series A* 115 (August): 700–721.

Lambkin, M., and G.S. Day. 1989. "Evolutionary Processes in Competitive Markets: Beyond the Product Life Cycle." *Journal of Marketing* 53 (3): 4–20.

Lawrence, K.D., and W.H. Lawton. 1981. "Applications of Diffusion Models: Some Empirical Results." Pp. 529–541 in *New-Product Forecasting*, edited by Y. Wind, V. Mahajan, and R.N. Cardozo. Lexington, MA: Lexington Books.

Mahajan, V., C.H. Mason, and V. Srinivasan. 1986. "An Evaluation of Estimation Procedures for New Product Diffusion Models." Pp. 203–232 in *Innovation Diffusion Models of New Product Acceptance*, edited by V. Mahajan and Y. Wind. Cambridge, MA: Ballinger Publishing Company.

Mahajan, V., and E. Muller. 1995. "Timing, Diffusion, and Substitution of Successive Generations of Technological Innovations: The IBM Mainframe Case." Working Paper, University of Texas, Austin, TX.

Mahajan, V., E. Muller, and F.M. Bass, 1990. "New Product Diffusion Models in Marketing: A Review and Directions for Research." *Journal of Marketing* 54 (1): 1–26.

Modis, T., and A. Debecker. 1988. "Innovation in the Computer Industry." *Technological Forecasting and Social Change* 33: 267–278.

Monahan, G.E. 1984. "A Pure Birth Model of Optimal Advertising with Word of Mouth." *Marketing Science* 3 (2): 169–178.

Reinganum, J.F. 1989. "The Timing of Innovation: Research, Development, and Diffusion." Pp. 849–908 in *Handbook of Industrial Organization*. New York: North-Holland.

Srinivasan, V., and C.H. Mason, 1986. "Nonlinear Least Squares Estimation of New Product Diffusion Models." *Marketing Science* 5 (2): 169–178.

Tapiero, C.S. 1975. "On-Line and Adaptive Optimum Advertising Control by a Diffusion Approximation." *Operations Research* 23 (5): 890–907.

Thompson, J.R., E.N. Atkinson, and B.W. Brown. 1987. "SIMEST: An Algorithm for Simulation-Based Estimation of Parameters Characterizing a Stochastic Process." Pp. 387–415 in *Cancer Modeling*, edited by J.R. Thompson and B.W. Brown. New York: Marcel Dekker.

A LOGIT MODELING APPROACH TO FORECASTING SALES USING SELF-REPORTED CONSUMER PURCHASE INTENTIONS

David B. Whitlark, Michael J. Swenson, and Michael D. Geurts

ABSTRACT

One commonly used method of forecasting a product's sales is to survey potential buyers regarding their likelihood of buying. Then, based on the proportion of respondents in each likelihood category, a forecast is created. Potential buyer intentions are often used for new products where there is not any sales history. The survey technique also lends itself to forecasting existing sales. The authors examine the percent of people who buy a product for each category of their self-reported predisposition to buy. A logit model is introduced which predicts probability of purchase based on purchase intention and mediating variables like product affordability, product familiarity, and forecasting time horizon. In most cases this logit forecasting model improved the accuracy of estimated purchase rates over those obtained from using purchase intentions alone.

Advances in Business and Management Forecasting, Volume 2, pages 235–253.
Copyright © 1998 by JAI Press Inc.
ISBN: 0-7623-0002-7

I. INTRODUCTION

For almost three decades now the marketing literature has shown interest in collecting, analyzing, and interpreting purchase intention survey data (Smith 1965; Axelrod 1968; Bass, Pessemier, and Lehmann 1972; Sewall 1978; Morrison 1979; Jamieson and Bass 1989). In particular, purchase intention applications in marketing research include evaluating automobile advertising effectiveness (Smith 1965), predicting actual purchase behavior (Axelrod 1968), assisting new product development (Silk and Urban 1978), and segmenting markets for new or redesigned products (Sewall 1978).

In spite of their frequent use, however, the predictive success of sales forecasts based on purchase intention survey data is unclear. In the United States the Bureau of the Census abandoned their Consumer Buyer Expectations Survey in the early 1970s because a "large number of data users and subject analysts representing universities, private firms, non-profit research organizations, and other government agencies" concluded upon review of survey results that the data were "only marginally useful" (U.S. Department of Commerce 1973, p. 5). In Canada the government-sponsored buying intentions survey has also provided mixed results. In describing the survey, Murray (1969, p. 60) states that "buying intentions, when used alone, have limited predictive ability for sales of (consumer) durable goods over time." Yet, in practice many firms still use purchase intention surveys to estimate future sales (Jamieson and Bass 1989). For new or somewhat new products consumer perception surveys or judgment may be the only methods of producing a forecast. Perhaps the forecasts can be made more accurate by using purchase intention adjectives that have low variance associated with them or by gathering additional information about the respondent.

In many instances self-reported consumer purchase intentions are not good predictors of purchase behavior on an aggregate or individual basis. For example, Jamieson and Bass report for one product in their study that more buyers came from the "definitely will not buy" than from the "definitely will buy" response category.

The problem addressed in this paper is that a widely used forecasting methodology seems to produce somewhat inaccurate results. The question then is: why use buyer intentions to forecast sales? The answer is that other methods produce even poorer results.

The objective of this paper is to report the results of an empirical study designed to improve the accuracy of sales forecasts based on purchase intentions that relate probability statements (purchase intentions) to actual purchasing behavior over a three-month and a six-month time horizon, and to develop a forecasting model that uses situational information together with purchase intentions to improve forecasting accuracy.

II. HYPOTHESIS DEVELOPMENT

A. Mediating Factors

In the previous section we report that, when used by themselves, self-reported purchase intentions may not be particularly good predictors of purchase probabilities. An extensive literature review published by O'Connor (1989) reports that an individual's level of calibration, that is, the level of agreement between an individual's prediction and actual outcome, will depend on their (1) familiarity with the topic of interest, (2) familiarity with making probability assessments, (3) availability of clear, repetitive, and unambiguous feedback, (4) level of task difficulty, and (5) motivation to provide accurate predictions. Jamieson and Bass (1989) identify perceived product affordability and availability as key situational factors. Mahajan (1992) reports that respondents' experience in making previous predictions and the feedback they receive on those predictions is an important issue.

B. Hypothesis I

Lawrence (1986) reports that student subjects make better predictions for familiar topics versus unfamiliar topics. Jamieson and Bass do not include product familiarity in their forecasting model. They report, however, that wider product availability leads to a smaller revision in purchase probability estimates than the revision due to narrower product availability. Because product availability and familiarity are highly correlated in their study ($r = 0.886$), we interpret this finding as greater familiarity leading to better predictive accuracy. The above research suggests the first hypothesis.

H1:   Product familiarity is correlated with the accuracy of purchase intentions. Higher product familiarity results in a closer match between purchase intentions and purchasing behavior.

C. Hypothesis II

Kalwani and Silk (1982) report for five data sets that the difference (error) between the mean of observed intention scale values and the observed actual purchase probabilities is much less for durable than nondurable goods. In the studies cited by Kalwani and Silk the durable goods are much less affordable (higher priced) than the nondurable branded goods, suggesting that increased affordability leads to decreased predictive accuracy. In their forecasting model Jamieson and Bass estimate that increasing affordability leads to increasingly large revisions in purchase intention scores. The above two studies report the surprising (to us) result that increased affordability reduces the accuracy of purchase intentions. Perhaps the reason for the above is that less affordable products induce more thought process (evaluation) than very affordable products. The additional evaluation may produce more reliable assessments of the purchase intention.

The second hypothesis we tested is:

H2:   Increasing product affordability leads to less accurate purchase intentions.

D. Hypothesis III

Jamieson and Bass did not find the relationship between the factor "need to consult with others" and predictive accuracy to be strong enough to warrant inclusion in their forecasting model. We assume the two variables were not strongly linked in their study. O'Connor (1989) reports that predictive accuracy decreases as the difficulty of the task increases. It seems reasonable, therefore, to assert that the predictive accuracy of purchase intentions will decrease as more sources of information are needed to make the purchase decision.

H3:   An increasing need to consult with others before making a purchase decision will result in less accurate purchase intentions.

E. Hypothesis IV

Confidence in prediction poses an interesting problem. O'Connor (1989) reports that easy tasks lead to underconfidence and difficult tasks lead to overconfidence, particularly when subjects are unfamiliar with probabilistics assessments. One can only speculate about the role of a respondent's confidence as a mediating factor in revising purchase intentions. It is uncertain, from a respondent's perspective, whether purchase intention surveys represent easy or difficult tasks, whether there exists adequate or inadequate feedback, or whether respondents are or are not motivated to provide accurate predictions. We therefore speculate on a fourth hypothesis:

H4: As confidence in predictive accuracy increases, the accuracy of purchase intentions also increases.

F. Hypothesis V

Choice of time horizon for use with purchase intention scales may be another important mediating factor (Kalwani and Silk 1982). Time horizon may be linked with the level of task difficulty. Longer time horizons for forecasting sales based on personal judgment have been shown to be less accurate than sales forecasts based on shorter time horizons (Armstrong 1983). This factor suggests an additional hypothesis:

H5: Accuracy of purchase intentions will increase when using a shorter time horizon with the purchase intention scale.

III. METHOD

The potential success for improving forecasting accuracy by revising purchase intentions based on product familiarity and affordability (Jamieson and Bass 1989; Kalwani and Silk 1982) suggested a two-by-two experimental design with independent variables of product familiarity and product affordability. The design was replicated across a three-month and six-month time horizon.

Through a series of pretests using undergraduate and graduate business students we selected two products to fit into each cell of the experimental design for each replication. Pizza, paperback novel, ticket to the discount movies, and a *Wall Street Journal* subscription were selected as having high affordability and familiarity. A business suit and new or used car were selected as products being very familiar but difficult to afford. Stayfresh milk and stayfresh microwave dinners, both of which are newer products that do not need refrigeration, were selected as having high affordability, but low familiarity. Finally, a mountain bike and laser printer were selected as products being unfamiliar (in 1989) and difficult to afford. We collected data from two different sources. Our first sample consisted of 99 graduate business students, of whom 82 completed surveys reporting their purchase intentions for a group of 10 products. Two products, telephone answering service and "wet" electric shaver, were used as a hold-out sample in order to validate the logit forecasting model. We followed up this initial survey in six months to determine actual purchase rates for these 10 products among these subjects. We also collected a second sample consisting of 280 undergraduate business students. From those 280 students we received 209 completed surveys reporting purchase intentions for 10 products. Again, two products, telephone answering service and "wet" electric shaver were used as a hold-out sample. We followed up this survey in three months to determine actual purchase rates.

A. Experimental Measures

We collected six experimental measures. After identifying the time horizon for the study (three months or six months), we asked the respondent how likely they were to buy each product. We used a five-point scale anchored by the words: definitely will, probably will, might/might not, probably will not, and definitely will not. We used this scale because it was successfully used by Jamieson and Bass, and was found by Johnson (1979) to be a commonly used purchase intention scale.

Following the purchase intention scale, we asked respondents how confident they felt about their predictive accuracy, how familiar they were in making predictions about purchasing that particular type of product, how likely they were to confer with other individuals or sources of information before making the purchase, and how familiar or knowledgeable they were about the product. These scales used four main points and were anchored with the words: very, somewhat, not very, and not at all. Finally, we asked about product affordability using a four-point scale anchored with the words: very easy, somewhat easy, somewhat difficult, and very difficult. Similar four-point scales are used by Jamieson and Bass.

In the follow-up study we asked the respondents whether they did or did not purchase the product during the preceding three (six) months. As mentioned earlier, time horizon differed by study. We used a six-month time horizon for the graduate students and a three-month time horizon for the undergraduate students.

We selected products for the two surveys that were available in locally operated stores. Consequently, we did not include product availability as an experimental measure.

IV. RESULTS

A. Manipulation Checks

Table 1 lists average scores for affordability and familiarity obtained from each survey. Scores are organized by experimental treatment and listed for each product. For both sets of survey data, products that were chosen as having low affordability have much lower affordability scores than products we selected as having high affordability. These differences are statistically significant ($p < .0001$). We observe a similar pattern with regard to product familiarity. Differences in low and high familiarity scores are statistically significant ($p < .0001$). We conclude that the manipulation achieved the desired effect.

B. Tests of Hypotheses

Comparing actual purchase rates with predictions made from purchase intention scales is somewhat problematic. In his survey of experienced users of intention scales, Johnson (1979) reports that six different weighting schemes are commonly used to translate purchase intentions into predictions of purchase rates. With our approach, each category percentage (from the five-point purchase intention scale) is multiplied by a certain percentage which reflects a belief about the actual purchase rate associated with each category. The products of the two sets of percentages are then summed across the five categories to obtain the overall prediction of purchase rate. If we denote the percentage of responses in each category as c_i and the probability of purchase associated with each category as p_i, then (assuming a five-point intention scale) the predicted purchase rate is:

$$Purchase\ Rate = \sum_{i=1}^{5} c_i p_i \qquad (1)$$

Table 2 lists the conditional probabilities of making a purchase associated with each purchase intention category for a three-month and

Table 1. Average Scores for Affordability and Familiarity Treatments by Product

Treatment	Graduate Student Survey			Undergraduate Student Survey		
	Product	Affordability	Familiarity	Product	Affordability	Familiarity
Low Affordability, Low Familiarity	Laser Printer	1.09	2.67	Laser Printer	1.24	2.59
	Mountain Bike	1.77	2.67	Mountain Bike	1.83	2.78
High Affordability, Low Familiarity	Stayfresh Milk	3.81	2.07	Stayfresh Milk	3.57	1.96
	Microwave Dinner	3.57	2.36	Microwave Dinner	3.60	2.34
Low Affordability, High Familiarity	Business Suit	2.02	3.23	Business Suit	2.05	3.21
	New or Used Car	1.23	3.38	New or Used Car	1.34	3.34
High Affordability, High Familiarity	Novel	3.84	3.32	Novel	3.97	3.84
	Pizza	3.70	3.80	Pizza	2.87	3.26

Note: Scores range from 1 to 4, where 4 denotes very easy to afford and very familiar with product.

Table 2. Probability of Purchase Intent: Mean (Standard Deviation)

Time Horizon	Purchase Intent				
	Definitely Will Not Buy	Probably Will Not Buy	Might/Might Not Buy	Probably Will Buy	Definitely Will Buy
Three Month	.0111 (.0024)	.0212 (.0016)	.0495 (.0062)	.2274 (.0426)	.6405 (.0833)
Six Month	.0428 (.0069)	.0899 (.0148)	.2076 (.0104)	.5284 (.0330)	.7530 (.0435)
Ad Hoc[1]	.0367 (.0734)	.0483 (.0876)	.0750 (.1283)	.2250 (.1914)	.7483 (.2354)

Note: [1]Means and standard deviations from the six weighting schemes reported by Johnson (1979).

six-month time horizon. The conditional probabilities are estimated using a jackknife procedure (Fenwick 1979). With this technique, each product is omitted in turn from the data set while the conditional probabilities are repeatedly measured. The method is believed to yield less biased estimates as compared to other approaches like computing simple or weighted averages.

For purposes of comparison, we include means and standard deviations from the six weighting schemes reported by Johnson (1979). The values in this "ad hoc" weighting scheme appear to be a mixture of the conditional probabilities we observed in the three-month and six-month survey data. Jamieson and Bass report that none of the six weighting schemes reported by Johnson was clearly better than the others when comparing predicted and actual purchase rates.

In the paper we use the conditional probabilities estimated from the three-month and six-month survey data. We obtain predicted purchase rates by using equation (1). We refer to this procedure as the purchase intention model. We compare the predicted purchase rates from this model to the actual purchase rates to test our hypotheses.

Familiarity, Affordability, and Time Horizon

We report the mean absolute percent error (MAPE) between predicted and actual purchase rates in Table 3. The statistics are organized by experimental treatments (affordability and familiarity) and time horizon.

Overall, predicted purchase rates are more accurate for the three-month versus the six-month time horizon. We found a MAPE of 3.2% for the shorter time horizon and 6.1% for the longer time horizon. The difference in the error rates is statistically significant ($p < .10$). This finding supports hypothesis five; accuracy of purchase intentions increases with shorter time horizons. The implication in using consumer intention survey research to forecast sales is to use the shorter time horizon when practical.

Our hypotheses regarding familiarity and affordability are not fully supported by our survey data. First, we hypothesized that increasing product familiarity should result in improved accuracy of purchase intentions. This is clearly not always the case. One may argue that in the case of highly affordable items increased product familiarity actually decreases predictive accuracy.

We also hypothesized that increasing product affordability will lead to decreased forecasting accuracy. The hypothesis is supported for prod-

Table 3. Mean Absolute Percent Error by Affordability and Familiarity
(Purchase Intention Model)

A. Graduate Student Survey (Six-Month Time Horizon)

Affordability	Familiarity		
	Low	*High*	*Overall*
Low	4.9%	4.3%	4.6%
High	4.2	11.2	7.7
Overall	4.5	7.7	6.1

B. Undergraduate Student Survey (Three-Month Time Horizon)

Affordability	Familiarity		
	Low	*High*	*Overall*
Low	1.5%	0.6%	1.0%
High	1.8	8.9	5.4
Overall	1.6	4.7	3.2

ucts judged as being highly familiar. The strong interaction between high familiarity and high affordability in decreasing forecasting accuracy agrees with results reported by Kalwani and Silk (1982). Their paper indicates that sales for consumer packaged goods (in established product categories) appear to be much less predictable than sales for consumer durables. In the case of our survey data, the purchase rates for these types of products (highly familiar, highly affordable) are substantially under-forecast for three of the four products. That is, products in this category are much more likely to be purchased than indicated by the purchase intention scores. We may observe this result because purchases in this category are much more responsive to impulse buying and marketing inducements than products in other product categories.

Consulting with Others

To test our hypothesis regarding "consulting with others," we organized the percentage of responses in each purchase intention category: the categories very likely, somewhat likely, not very likely, and not likely at all to consult with others. We were then able to estimate a purchase rate for each product for each category of the "consulting with others" variable. The MAPE for each category is listed in Table 4.

Because individuals in this study were more likely to consult other sources of information for less affordable products ($r = 0.42$), we expect that Table 4 reflects some of the effect due to high affordability, high

Table 4.   Mean Absolute Percent Error by Likelihood of Consulting
with Others Before Purchase (Purchase Intention Model)

	Time Horizon of Survey	
Consult with Others	*Six Months*	*Three Months*
Very Likely	5.2%	2.9%
Somewhat Likely	7.4	3.3
Not Very Likely	5.1	3.8
Not Likely At All	6.5	5.0

familiarity products reported in Table 3, and therefore conflicts with our hypothesis. That is, we may find that forecasts for individuals who are very likely to consult with others are more accurate than forecasts for individuals who are not at all likely to consult with others. This is, in fact, what we observe. The differences in error rates, however, are not statistically significant for either time horizon. Consequently, these data do not provide any clear findings on this hypothesis.

Confidence in Prediction

The variable "confidence in prediction" has four response categories. It is interesting to note that only a handful of individuals marked the bottom two categories of not very and not at all confident about their prediction. Most individuals responded that they were either somewhat or very confident in their prediction. This result may reflect the general overconfidence shown by decision makers often described in the behavioral decision theory literature (e.g., Solomon, Ariyo, and Tomassini 1985). Because of the small number of responses in the bottom two response categories, we did not attempt to estimate the error in forecasting actual purchase rates for these categories. Error rates for the top two response categories are listed in Table 5. To obtain these values, we computed a forecast of purchase probability using the purchase intention model for each product for respondents that were very confident about their prediction and for respondents that were somewhat confident about their prediction. These forecasts were then compared to actual purchase rates to compute the MAPE statistics listed in Table 5.

We hypothesized that greater confidence in prediction should be accompanied by greater accuracy of purchase intentions. Results from our data do not support this hypothesis for the six-month and the three-month surveys. Even though the MAPE for those somewhat con-

Table 5. Mean Absolute Percent Error by Confidence in Purchase
Prediction
(Purchase Intention Model)

Confidence about Prediction	Time Horizon	
	Six Months	*Three Months*
Very	6.3%	3.0%
Somewhat	9.8	6.2
Not Very	N/A	N/A
Not At All	N/A	N/A

fident in their prediction is higher than that for those very confident in their prediction for both surveys, the variance of the error rates is too high for sampling error to be ruled out as the cause of the differences.

V. DISCUSSION

These results indicate that several situational factors in addition to purchase scores may help researchers obtain better estimates of actual purchase rates. Information about time horizon of the survey, and respondent judgments about product affordability and product familiarity all should help improve forecast accuracy. Shorter time horizons improve predictive accuracy. Also, increased product affordability coupled with increased product familiarity typically led to underforecasted purchase rates. We also note that most other product purchase rates were overforecasted. These properties of purchase intention forecasts are shown in Table 6.

Based on these findings, we believe a model that integrates purchase intention scores together with information about time horizon and respondent judgments about product affordability and product familiarity will lead to better estimates of actual purchase rates than would be obtained from using purchase intentions alone. As a first step, we can adjust the numerical value of purchase intention categories for a three-month and six-month time horizon. For example, we are asserting that the purchase probability for individuals responding that they "probably will buy" is different for three-month versus a six-month time horizon. These probabilities are, in fact, 22.74 and 52.84%, respectively. Probabilities of purchase conditioned by purchase intention category and time horizon are shown in Table 2. As a second step for improving forecasting

Table 6. Forecast Error by Product (Purchase Intention Model)

A. Graduate Student Survey (Six-Month Time Horizon)

Product	Affordability Score	Familiarity Score	Forecast Error
Novel	3.84	3.32	−12.7%
Pizza	3.70	3.80	−9.6
Business Suit	2.02	3.23	+6.0
New or Used Car	1.23	3.38	−2.5
Stay Fresh Milk	3.81	2.07	+7.8
Microwave Dinner	3.57	2.36	+0.5
Laser Printer	1.09	2.67	+4.0
Mountain Bike	1.77	2.67	+5.8

B. Undergraduate Student Survey (Three-Month Time Horizon)

Product	Affordability Score	Familiarity Score	Forecast Error
Discount Movie	3.97	3.84	−14.3%
Wall Street Journal	2.87	3.26	+3.5
Business Suit	2.05	3.21	+0.7
New or Used Car	1.34	3.34	+0.4
Stay Fresh Milk	3.57	1.96	+1.5
Microwave Dinner	3.60	2.34	+2.1
Laser Printer	1.24	2.59	+1.4
Mountain Bike	1.83	2.78	+1.5

accuracy we can develop a logit model that integrates the two other powerful situational variables, product affordability and product familiarity.

A. Model Development

To adjust our initial forecast of a product's actual purchase rate based on respondent perceptions about product affordability and product familiarity we propose a logit model that predicts purchase probability based on product affordability and familiarity scores and our initial estimate of purchase probability. The logit model (Theil 1966; Malhotra 1984) is useful for determining the probability that a particular event will occur, because it produces probability estimates that range from 0 to 1 and can be used when the dependent variable itself is expressed as a probability. Like the approaches based on linear regression, the logit model makes use of the informational value of the interval-scale data from the affordability and familiarity scores. The linear regression approach, however, can easily produce probability estimates that are less than 0 or exceed 1. Another advantage of the logit model is that it naturally captures any interactions among variables that may exist. In logarithmic form the model is:

$$\log \frac{p}{1-p} = \alpha + \beta_1 \log A + \beta_2 \log F + \beta_3 \log \frac{\hat{p}}{1-\hat{p}}. \qquad (2)$$

In this formulation, p denotes the actual purchase rate, A and F denote product affordability and familiarity scores, and $\hat{p}$ denotes our initial estimate of the purchase probability. If we denote the righthand side of equation (2) with the letter L, our revised forecast of the purchase probability (p^*) can be computed as:

$$p^* = \frac{e^L}{1 + e^L} \qquad (3)$$

When using the 16 products from the two surveys to estimate the parameters of this model we obtained the results shown in Table 7. There is an extremely good fit between the data and the model (which we call the logit model). The regression goodness of fit (r^2) is 95% and the MAPE is reduced for the six-month survey from 6.1 to 5.0%, and for the three-month survey from 3.2 to 1.0%. The biggest gains in accuracy are for high availability, higher familiarity products.

As an example of how to use the logit forecasting model consider a survey asking consumers how likely they are to purchase a particular new product sometime in the next three months. The forecaster also collects consumer perceptions regarding product availability and familiarity. Imagine that 10% of the respondents say they definitely will buy, and 15, 25, 40, and 10% say that they would probably buy, might/might not buy, probably would not buy, and definitely will not buy, respectively. Our initial estimate of the product's purchase rate is about 12% ($.10 \times .6405 + .15 \times .2274 + .25 \times .0495 + .40 \times .0212 + .10 \times .0111$). In addition, the

Table 7. Coefficient Estimates for Logit Forecasting Model

Model Variable	Coefficient Estimate	Coefficient T-Value
Constant (α)	−2.5251	−6.33
Affordability (β_1)	0.4077	1.40
Familiarity (β_2)	1.8646	2.53
Initial Forecast (β_3)	1.0410	1.06

Table 8. Forecast of Purchase Probabilities and Error Rates for
Hold-out Sample

A. Graduate Student Survey (Six-Month Time Horizon)

Product	Actual Purchase Rate	Purchase Intention Model		Logit Model	
		Forecast	Error	Forecast	Error
Telephone Answering Service	11.1%	15.6%	4.5%	13.0%	1.9%
"Wet" Electric Shaver	16.3	16.7	0.4	14.6	1.7
MAPE			2.5		1.8

B. Undergraduate Student Survey (Three-Month Time Horizon)

Product	Actual Purchase Rate	Purchase Intention Model		Logit Model	
		Forecast	Error	Forecast	Error
Telephone Answering Service	2.4%	2.9%	0.5%	1.8%	0.6%
"Wet" Electric Shaver	1.9	2.5	0.6	1.8	0.1
MAPE			0.5		0.4

average affordability and familiarity scores are 3.8 and 2.1, respectively. Then using equations (2) and (3), our revised forecast of the product's purchase rate is about 6.5% L = −2.5251 + .4077 × log 3.8 + 1.8646 × log 2.1 + 1.0410 × log (.12/(1 − .12)).

VI. MODEL VALIDATION

To test the comparative usefulness of the purchase intention model and the logit model we forecast purchase probabilities using a hold-out sample of two products from the three-month survey and two products from the six-month survey. These products were not used to estimate the conditional probabilities for the purchase intention model or to estimate the parameters of the logit forecasting model.

The first product, telephone answering service, has product affordability and familiarity scores that do not fit cleanly into high or low affordability and familiarity categories (three-month survey 2.36, 2.67; six-month survey 2.85, 2.85). The same is true for the second product, "wet" electric shaver (three-month survey 2.71, 2.80; six-month survey 3.11, 2.87). In each case the affordability and familiarity scores are too low to fit into the high category and too high to fit into the low category. Consequently, a priori, we do not expect the logit model to greatly improve upon our initial estimates or purchase rates for these products because the biggest improvement in forecasting accuracy from the logit model will be for high affordability, high familiarity products.

This is, in fact, what we observe in Table 8. The MAPE for the three-month survey is reduced from 0.5 to 0.4%, a 20% improvement in accuracy, and for the six-month survey from 2.5 to 1.8%, a 28% improvement in accuracy. We expect that the logit model will be even more effective for other product types.

We are encouraged by the accuracy of the forecasts for the products in our hold-out sample.

VII. CONCLUSION

For many product types and situations it appears as though purchase intention survey data can lead to good forecasts of actual purchase probabilities. In this study we explored the effect of product familiarity, affordability, need to consult with others, confidence, and length of time horizon on the accuracy of purchase intentions. From this list of possible mediating factors we found that length of time horizon and product affordability and familiarity had the biggest effects. Shorter time horizons yield better predictive accuracy of purchase intentions. The purchase probabilities for highly affordable and familiar products are more difficult to forecast than those for other types of products.

Based on our findings we proposed an alternative forecasting model to those typically used for forecasting actual purchase rates from purchase intention scores. To make forecasts of purchase probabilities, the percentage of responses in each purchase intention category is usually weighted by one of several ad hoc weighting schemes (Johnson 1979) or by values (numerical probabilities) the respondent associates with each probability phrase (Jamieson and Bass 1989). With our first forecasting model (purchase intention model), we weight the percentage of responses in each purchase intention category by the conditional probability of an individual actually making a purchase given a particular predisposition to buy. For this model, we estimated a separate set of conditional probabilities for a three-month and six-month time horizon. Six-month conditional purchase probabilities tend to be larger than those for a three-month time horizon. We find that over a three-month time horizon, only individuals stating that they definitely will buy have a high probability of actually making a purchase.

In a second model we build on the systematic bias in purchase probability forecasts introduced by differences in product affordability and familiarity. In this forecasting model we use logit regression to produce adjusted estimates of purchase probabilities based on respondent perceptions about product affordability and familiarity as well as on our initial forecast of the product's purchase rate. When testing these models using a hold-out sample of two products across a three-month and six-month time horizon we achieved a MAPE of 1.5% for the purchase intention model and a MAPE of 1.1% for the logit model. The forecasting accuracy of these two models is very encouraging. We are quick to point out, however, that a good forecast of the purchase probability is only one element of making an accurate forecast of unit sales.

REFERENCES

Adams, F.G., and F.T. Juster. 1974. "Commentaries on McNeil." *Journal of Consumer Research* (December): 1–15.

Armstrong, J.S. 1983. "Relative Accuracy of Judgmental and Extrapolative Methods in Forecasting Annual Earnings." *Journal of Forecasting* 2: 437–447.

Axelrod, J.N. 1968. "Attitude Measures that Predict Purchase." *Journal of Advertising Research* 8 (March): 3–18.

Bass, F.M., E.A. Pessemier, and D.R. Lehmann. 1972. "An Experimental Study of the Relationship Between Attitudes, Brand Preferences and Choice." *Behavioral Science* 17 (November): 532–541.

Fenwick, I. 1979. "Techniques on Market Measurement: The Jackknife." *Journal of Marketing Research* 16 (August): 410–414.

Jamieson, L.F., and F.M. Bass. 1989. "Adjusted Stated Intention Measures to Predict Trial Purchase of New Products: A Comparison of Models and Methods." *Journal of Marketing Research* 26 (August): 336–345.

Johnson, J.S. 1979. "A Study of the Accuracy and Validity of Purchase Intention Scales." Phoenix, Arizona: Armour-Dial Co., privately circulated working paper.

Kalwani, M.U., and A.J. Silk. 1982. "On the Reliability and Predictive Validity of Purchase Intention Measures." *Marketing Science* 1 (Summer): 243–286.

Lawrence, M.J. 1986. "Individual Bias in Judgmental Confidence Estimation." Paper presented at International Forecasting Symposium, Paris.

Mahajan, J. 1992. "The Overconfidence Effect in Marketing Management Predictions." *Journal of Marketing Research* (August): 329–342.

Malhotra, N.K. 1984. "The Use of Linear Logit Models in Marketing Research." *Journal of Marketing Research* 21 (February): 20–31.

McNeil, J. 1974. "Federal Programs to Measure Consumer Purchase Expectations, 1946–1973: A Post-Mortem."

Morrison, D.G. 1979. "Purchase Intentions and Purchase Behavior." *Journal of Marketing* 43 (Spring): 65–74.

Murray, J. 1969. "Canadian Consumer Expectation Data: An Evaluation." *Journal of Marketing Research* (February): 60.

O'Connor, M. 1989. "Models of Human Behavior and Confidence in Judgment: A Review." *International Journal of Forecasting* 5: 159–169.

Sewall, M.A. 1978. "Market Segmentation Based on Consumer Ratings of Proposed Product Designs." *Journal of Marketing Research* 15 (November): 557–564.

Silk, A.J., and G.L. Urban. 1978. "Pre-Test Market Evaluation of New Packaged Goods: A Model and Measurement Methodology." *Journal of Marketing Research* 15 (May): 171–191.

Smith, G. 1965. "How GM Measures Ad Effectiveness." *Printer's Ink* (May 14): 19–29.

Solomon, I., A. Ariyo, and L.A. Tomassini. 1985. "Contextual Effects on the Calibration of Probabilistics Judgments." *Journal of Applied Psychology* 70: 528–532.

Theil, H. 1966. *Economics and Information Theory*, Volume 7 in the series, *Studies in Mathematical and Managerial Economics.* Chicago: Rand McNally.

U.S. Department of Commerce. 1973. "Consumer Buying Indicators." Current Population Reports, Series P-65 (April) (46): 5.

CPSIA information can be obtained at www.ICGtesting.com
Printed in the USA
LVOW070240061112

305990LV00004B/216/P